T3-BUK-573

DISCARD

Ingrained

Ingrained

The Making of a Craftsman

CALLUM ROBINSON

An Imprint of HarperCollins*Publishers*

This is a work of nonfiction based on the life, experiences, and recollection of the author. However, in some cases names of people, places, dates, sequences, and the detail of events have been changed, amalgamated, or blended to reflect the author's experiences while protecting the privacy of others. The author and publishers disclaim as far as the law allows any liability arising directly or indirectly from the use or misuse of any information contained in this book. The author has stated to the publishers that, except in such minor respects not affecting the substantial accuracy of the work, the contents of this book are true.

INGRAINED. Copyright © 2024 by Callum Robinson. All rights reserved. Printed in the United States of America. No part of this book may be used or reproduced in any manner whatsoever without written permission except in the case of brief quotations embodied in critical articles and reviews. For information, address HarperCollins Publishers, 195 Broadway, New York, NY 10007.

HarperCollins books may be purchased for educational, business, or sales promotional use. For information, please email the Special Markets Department at SPsales@harpercollins.com.

Ecco® and HarperCollins® are trademarks of HarperCollins Publishers.

Originally published in Great Britain in 2024 by Doubleday, an imprint of Transworld Publishers.

Woodcuts © 2024 by David Robinson
Endpaper image by Graeme Hunter

FIRST U.S. EDITION

Library of Congress Cataloging-in-Publication Data has been applied for.

ISBN 978-0-06-335083-0

24 25 26 27 28 LBC 5 4 3 2 1

For Marisa, and for my father

Contents

Part 1
Raw Materials

A small compromise leads to another small compromise, and finally we wind up doing something that we do not really love. It's a sneaky thing.

—*James Krenov,*
A CABINETMAKER'S NOTEBOOK

I

Picture the biggest tree you've ever seen, laid on its side and sliced lengthways into boards no thicker than expensive steaks. Every difficult year, every drought and every flood, all the minerals and pigments leached up from the particular spot in which it took root, the rippling shadows of a woodworm's pinhole excavations, the relentless tension required to hold up those mighty limbs, and the torturous scarred stains from a barbed wire choker oh-so-gradually absorbed. It's all there, folded into the heartwood. Centuries of character, as individual as a fingerprint, written in the figure of the grain and revealed by the teeth of the saw. Now, imagine there are hundreds of trees like this. Literally thousands of years of life and history, stacked together hugger-mugger. That they are all around you.

Climbing out of the Land Rover, the air is heavy with the scent of damp leaves and woodsmoke, the loud metallic *tick-tick-ticking* of the engine in the early morning mist. Pale birch trees, rhododendron scrub, and walls of crumbling stone fringe the glade, and towering above them, a pair of hulking Scots pines lurk in their own long shadows, guarding the entrance to this hidden place. We stretch off the long hours on the road, stamping the life back into our feet, then without a word we assemble our kit. We rummage for thick blue marking crayons, clipboards and runic timber lists, we slip tape measures onto our belts. My father pulls on a battered felt hat, tucks a pencil behind his ear, and squelches off into the yard.

Dominating the yard is a ramshackle cluster of post-and-beam sheds; these are the drying sheds, and to reach them we must skirt around several mighty logs. Ash, oak, sycamore, and smooth gray elephantine beech are strewn haphazardly about, each awaiting their turn at the saw. They have such presence, these woodland behemoths. Such irrefutable dinosaur-haunch heft. The fresh ones—those still close to half-filled with water—weigh several tons. I watch as my father runs a hand along the fissured bark of a huge ash log, as another man might caress a dog's flank. As if to say: *Good log.*

Beneath their sagging tin roofs, the drying sheds' walls are clad with slim spruce logs, roughly sawn into planks and spaced a handsbreadth apart. This is to encourage air circulation, critical to the wood's curing process. Allowed to move freely around the freshly milled timber like this, the relentless Scottish wind will slowly wick away the moisture, a year for every inch of thickness, plus another for luck. In places the walls have been left entirely open to the elements—gaps just wide enough for a tractor's forks, or a father and son, to enter. So, together, we duck into the gloom.

Inside it is silent and still, and a lingering musky perfume begins to invade our nostrils: earthy, mossy, and barky. The soil underfoot is dry and fine as talcum powder, tamped down flat by countless tiny scurrying feet. This must be how it feels to creep into a fox's earth or a rabbit's warren. As we move further into the shed, the smell gets stronger, until it is more than a smell; it is an overpowering presence. As if the forest itself has grabbed me by the lapels and is exhaling deeply into my face. This is because we are surrounded, almost comically outnumbered, by *trees*.

These days, of course, it is entirely possible to order your timber from some distant faceless sawmill or builders' merchant. To have it delivered in neat, square-edged packs of uniform planks, sight unseen. Elegant, clean-limbed hardwoods from Europe, prodigious giants from the Pacific Northwest, iron-hard exotics from South America and Africa, and close-grained, slow-growing birch from the fringes of the Arctic Circle. From aspen to zebrawood, purpleheart to ponderosa pine, and a hundred species in between. With a modern crane-armed truck, a skilled delivery driver can actually lift the stuff directly into your workshop. This is far more convenient, simpler, and faster than selecting in person. And because the timber from big suppliers is commercially logged, kiln-dried, treated, and graded, there's considerably less risk that hidden rot or unexpected color may be lurking inside as well. But just because it's easier, cheaper, and less chancy . . . doesn't necessarily mean it's better.

Ask any chef worth their salt: Would they rather get that expert nose stuck right in at the fish market before the sun's even glanced up from the pillow, or unpack the goods from an insulated box?

Forage for chanterelles in rain-sodden glades, or peel away the cellophane behind closed doors? There are exceptions, naturally, but they'll tell you: when it comes to sourcing the finest ingredients, perfect in ways that can't be defined or categorized, with qualities that must be perceived rather than picked from a catalog, there are times when it pays to get your hands dirty. And Ben's timberyard, in the far upper reaches of northern Scotland, is a place to get your hands very dirty indeed.

This yard has no sign, no digital footprint, it doesn't even have a phone. Secreted away at the end of an unmarked track, five winding miles from the nearest village of any size, its name and whereabouts have spread quietly, organically. Whispered on the lips of tree surgeons, furniture makers, wide-eyed woodturners, and canny farmers. For all intents and purposes, it might as well be invisible. And for those of us who do know of it, there's a very good reason to try and keep it that way. Much of Ben's stock comes from old-growth hardwoods, some that were many hundreds of years old when they fell. Trees like this are uncommon, protected, not the sort of things that come down every day. But because the turnover here is slow and the sheds are small, this wood, when it comes, has a habit of piling up—the old being gradually buried beneath the new. Storm-blown, wizened and gnarled, and often very large indeed, these are trees that found root in an unforgiving environment and somehow scratched out a living. Trees, that is to say, of distinctive character. And while they certainly aren't to everyone's tastes, as the world grows ever more manicured, to some this individuality is a rare and precious thing.

All around me, in all shapes and sizes and every conceivable cranny, hundreds of the straight, branchless lower trunks of trees are piled twice my height. Where there is no space left to put them, they hang precariously from heavy canvas slings. Each has been sliced lengthways and then carefully reconstructed into stacks of planks that resemble the full log in the round. In this way the even pressure of the boards, spaced with dozens of slim wooden sticks—imaginatively named "stickers"—and tightly lashed together, helps to keep them flat as they slowly air-dry. These are plain, through-and-through or slash-sawn logs. But bound back together again like this, they are known to many as *boules*.

Boules are monstrous, magnetic objects, and yet there is something fantastically cartoonish about those neatly splayed slices—so like a log in the first moments of an explosion you can almost imagine Wile E. Coyote himself slamming home the detonator's plunger. But it isn't simply their appearance that's enchanting . . . it's what might be locked away inside.

What did the world look like when these trees first broke through the soil? How many hard years and epic storms might they have weathered? Who might have climbed in their branches, sheltered beneath their canopies, carved a lover's name into their living flesh? And how many lives depended on them over the years? For a native oak—part of the weft and weave of the British Isles' landscape for millennia—this number is all but incalculable. Mammals, birds and bats, butterflies, moths, insects and plants; thousands of species are supported, and over three hundred depend upon the oak for their survival. As Robert Macfarlane has written, weighing an acorn in his palm, "I hold in my hand not a single tree, but a community-to-be, a world-in-waiting." Think of that.

From outside, we hear the reluctant stutter-grumble of a chain saw being coaxed into life, drawing us back to the task at hand. Following our ears, we pick our way through the narrow alleys that cut canyonlike between the towering stacks until we are back out in the light.

With its perpetually smoldering bonfire, antique machinery, and strutting half-wild chickens, Ben's yard feels unchanged or (more likely) unnoticed by time. There are tall brimming firewood pens—timber-framed and wire mesh–sided so the split logs can air-dry—great rusting blades, billhooks, and sickles dangling from rafters, dented enamel mugs and beer cans from another age sprouting like brightly colored puffballs after rain. I wouldn't be at all surprised to uncover a moonshine still bubbling away behind a sheet of corrugated iron, or to find myself propositioned by a poacher, his pockets bulging with rabbits fresh from the snare. It's the sort of place that Jack London might have conjured, Butch Cassidy or Huck Finn holed up in. The sort of place I could lose my father in for a month.

Between the carcasses of two ancient Land Rovers that are slowly being reclaimed by the earth, timber in process is loosely stacked. Fat chunks of pine, fir, spruce, and oak, for fencing, construction, and green-oak building. The ragged ends of fresh-cut timber peek out from under a grubby canvas tarp, coarsely textured and pinkish-yellow, oozing resin as only coniferous wood does. Pulling back the covers, I crouch and run the soft meat of my thumb over a board's blade-riffled surface. The sawdust is granular and damp to the touch, like coffee grounds between my fingers. It is Douglas fir—the "Oregon pine"—a North American emigrant and a vigorous one at that. Ripped into planks for cladding and fencing by the teeth of the yard's mean old saw. Like its neighbor from the Pacific Northwest, the Sitka spruce, these trees are capable of growing almost twice as fast as anything native to the UK—in the right conditions, close to a meter and a half per year. Small wonder, then, that after just two hundred years, the pair already accounts for more than half our commercial forestry.

When we come upon him, Ben is working a twenty-inch blade through a log held fast in a sawhorse, knee-deep in a pile of freshly chopped firewood. Pine shrapnel and blue smoke belch from the machine with a noise like a million angry wasps. The sweet smell of sap mingling with the petrol's heady fumes. His aging Alaskan Mill—the mobile system of cables, wedges, and metal braces that operates the far larger, slab-milling chain saw—sits idle beside him for now.

Like his yard, the man is remarkable to survey. Rail-thin, sinewy, somewhere, I would estimate, between sixty and three hundred years old. Today he's sporting chunky logger's boots, armored safety trousers suspended by heavy braces, and a threadbare flannel shirt so permeated with oil, grime, and sawdust it could probably stand up on its own. From under his hard hat, errant wisps of yellow hair escape like smoke. A Quentin Blake illustration with a chain saw.

As we wander over, he kills the engine, kicks his way clear of the log pile, and lifts his visor. His voice, when he speaks, is surprisingly high and soporific, its foxy intonation suggesting I may just have found my poacher. "Aye . . ." he says, softly. "And what can I do for you lads today?"

My father gets immediately down to business, checking off his list, cocking the occasional eyebrow at Ben, his pencil dancing like a conductor's baton. The sawyer considers each item thoughtfully, saying little, leaning on his sawhorse. Until, that is, my father reaches the bottom of his clipboard, the main event, and the real reason we are here. "I need something big," he says. "Something . . . that feels like *water*." Ben's eyes narrow a little at this, the very act seeming to conjure a wry smile. "Come wi' me."

A skinny yard dog tracks us warily, flitting like a wraith, materializing between rusting oil drums and high banks of creosote-soaked railway sleepers. Its eyes never leave us. Ben moves with a feline ease, padding down a narrow passageway between the backs of two sheds. We pass the rotting hollow trunk of an oak, broad as a water butt, and a rack that lists with hoarded burrs, hunkered down like fat warty toads overwintering. Ben pauses, then dodges right and drags open a huge door built into the shed's cladding. Inside, pulling off a leather glove and patting his chest for tobacco, his weathered features are half-hidden, bathed in shadow. But catching his eye, we follow his nod toward a high stack of timber. And a-treasure hunting we go.

You never quite know what you'll find in a place like this. Just as Ben didn't know what he'd find when he first dragged his saw through the newly felled tree. And that's the thrill of it. The same gambler's frisson that once drew countless gold-fevered prospectors over lethal mountain passes, kept them bent-double down brutal Klondike shafts and panning over freezing Yukon rivers. The terrible, irresistible allure of *what if.*

Squeezing down a treacherous corridor, I position myself at the far end, and together my father and I begin to work our way through the uppermost elm boule. In the confined space it's awkward and unwieldy, a thoroughly back-threatening business. But it's not our first time. We move quickly, smoothly and collaboratively, glancing at each board in turn before placing it gingerly down. Knowing from bitter experience the terrible clubbing that fingers will cop if both ends are not dropped simultaneously. Anything with even a hint of potential we lay to one side. But the wood's surfaces are rough and dry, thickly coated with years of caked-on sawdust and grime, making them difficult to read. It is almost as if they are bound in waxed butcher's paper. So often it is instinct, a feeling, as much as anything else, that alerts us to a contender or condemns a reject.

With a practiced flick of his thumb, and an oily *snick*, my father unclasps his lock-knife. I watch as he scrapes down to the clean flesh of the topmost board. But even in the shed's gloom we can see the wood is far too pale. So pale, in fact, that I'm not even entirely sure it is elm. With wild wood like this, it's not always easy to tell. What we are looking for is dark, brooding, virulently swirling grain. Rich color that will only deepen when the wood's pores are saturated with oil, suggesting dense timber that will work finely and take a finish well. It may be that this tree came down at the wrong time of year, when the sap was high, discoloring the timber. The ground in which it found root might not have been sufficiently nutritious. Or it could just be sickly, the insidious scourge of Dutch elm disease creeping in. But to me it lacks weight, too. Something my father can't fail to have noticed. We want heavy timber, the heavier the better—presuming it's dry, perhaps the best portent of density there is. Ben will undoubtedly know more; his knowledge of the stock is encyclopedic. But looking up I can see that he is off pottering around well out of earshot. So, leaving my father to his scraping, I haul myself up onto higher ground and begin to scramble through the sheds alone.

Years of slipshod restacking have left traps and hidden deadfalls everywhere. With the toes of my boots groping for purchase on the teetering piles of boards, I skirt along minute ledges, twist around splintery uprights, kneel and crawl and high-step over shadowy crevices. All too aware that, at any moment, several tons of timber might come crashing down, crushing my bones like twigs. My eyes, though, are busily scanning—not just for likely timber but for stray nails, precariously hanging logs, and savage, rusting blades—so it is my hands and feet that must probe for disaster. Feeling around for that one loose board, the badly balanced or the poorly secured, that might initiate an avalanche.

Huddled in this close, I am struck again by the smells. They are markedly different from the open yard. Gone are the high lush resinous notes of freshly sawn softwood, damp grass, and petrol. Replaced by a dry, earthy, fungal miasma. In some corners I catch the sharp tang of ammonia, where rot and woodland creatures have crept in and found a hiding place, and in others, pockets of cedar's spicy sweetness. It is an ensemble piece, and the aroma somehow of great age. And there's so much of the bloody stuff that it's difficult to focus on. Soon though, as light shafts in through the many gaps in the shed's rough walls and my eyes become accustomed to the gloom, the silhouettes sharpen into forms I recognize.

And all I can see is possibility.

There is rich, golden oak, dense and heavy as bullion, skillfully wrought by carpenters for three thousand years. So implacably hard that its mighty structures endure for centuries—from the latticework roof of Notre Dame's doomed twelfth-century cathedral, so intricate and comprising so many individual oaks its carpenters nicknamed it *the Forest*, to Nelson's flagship and Westminster Hall's mighty seven-hundred-ton hammer-beam ceiling. There is ghostly, almost luminescent sycamore. Fecund and prolific, a rampant tree. One that, according to tradition, must be cut in the light of the full moon. There is vivid-orange yew, ancient, supple and immensely strong. Before the introduction of composites, the bowmaker's timber of choice. In the right hands, a wood that was capable of propelling an armor-piercing arrow the length of three football pitches, making it the stuff of battlefield nightmares and tipping the scales of fate for England's armies for two hundred years. There is hard maple, sweet chestnut, black walnut, and great wide immovable slabs of flesh-colored beech. There is tense, fretful, crimson cherry. Beautiful, but so shot through with splits and flaws that it's next to useless. And then there is elm, the tenacious swaggering dandy of the forest. Decimated by disease, with some *sixty million* trees gone in the UK alone since the 1960s. But resilient. Surviving, like a forty-a-day whiskey-sipping octogenarian Highlander, for reasons that science still cannot entirely explain.

Flipping a narrow elm board from the nearest stack, I carefully brush away the dirt from the surface with my palm. Waiting— half wincing—for the hidden splinter's bite that mercifully does not come. The board is far too small for my father's purposes, but it is still rather beautiful. Honeyed browns and swirling reds, slashed through with greens and purples. Colors and features that are just faintly visible beneath its dust-caked surfaces. Pressing my thumbnail into the wood's flesh, I scrape and drag but it leaves no mark. Even elm so young as this is incredibly tough. Its high tensile strength demanding the very sharpest of tools to work. So durable, in fact, that it was once used to make dock pilings and cartwheel hubs, and even bored out to serve as water pipes in major cities. Elm was the coffin tree too. And the hanging tree.

Several of the board's companions bear the chalk-scrawled hieroglyphics of earlier treasure seekers. *6 LEGS, DRAWER FRONTS, NO!!* For a moment I scan for initials I recognize, or my father's distinctive architectural block capitals. And as I do, my eye falls on some wider stock, a little way off to the side. This will be more to the old man's liking. Half-heartedly, I try to lift one of the giant slabs, but it doesn't even budge. They are all far too heavy, interlocked and awkwardly positioned to risk moving alone. And in any case, it is probably still on the small side. The kind of things my father is really after are giants up to five feet across. Boards that will each weigh close to a hundred kilos—two hundred if fresh-sawn.

I catch sight of his distinctive shape farther down the shed, moving in the shadows, and watch for a moment. He disappears from view, reappearing again seconds later, high up and stooped beneath the beams. Quick-drawing his tape measure, flicking open his knife in single fluid motions. *Willing* the wood to be what he needs. Utterly absorbed.

Magical as it is to clamber recklessly among all this history, for me there is a melancholy about it too. It's been a long time since I worked with this kind of wild wood. Since I, or any of my team, had the chance to cut a gem from this much rough. Coming from such a small independent sawmill, and being air-dried, it lacks the certification it needs to be exported, pretty well essential for a business like mine. At a yard like this, the only paperwork you're likely to see will be carefully rolled around a pinch of tobacco, or a grubby envelope stuffed with cash. To Ben and those like him, trust and a handshake mean far more than fine print, and I'm okay with that. But without some cast-iron documentation to prove the wood's provenance, that it's been treated and kiln-dried (slow-cooked at a low temperature, to draw out the last of the moisture and kill any lurking beasties) and that its characteristics are predictable, it is unlikely ever to leave these shores.

Like unpasteurized cheese, raw shellfish, or beef on the bone, it's simply got too much individuality. Too much risk.

Support staff, that's all I am today. Here to hunt and haul. And though my eye is undoubtedly keener than most, it isn't roaming with anything like the same skill or care as my father's. True, we're both looking for pretty, dense, dry and rot-free timber. Wood that won't buckle and contort the moment a blade cuts into it, unleashing the tension that may be hidden within. If it has been dried too quickly, or improperly stacked, or if it has spent its life stooped against strong prevailing winds and developed thick muscular tension-wood to compensate, a sawcut might begin to close almost immediately around a powerfully spinning blade. And *that* you do not want. But my father's is an artist's eye as much as a craftsman's, and it can see other things too—things that mine cannot. With his hands and face almost intimately close to the boards, he's trying to divine the ebb and flow of the grain. To see, and to see past, the flaws. To intuit beneath the shrouds of grime the traces of a scene, a movement, or simply an energy. Something he can coax out and bring to life with his carving chisels.

It's not new, this carving; he's always dabbled. A scuttling dormouse here, an ear of wheat or an initial there. The Gaelic or Latin in-joke, like a street artist's tag on a finely crafted kitchen, whether the client realized it was coming or not. Lately, though, things have progressed far beyond mere embellishment. Beyond what even he probably thought was possible. He loves all this, always has, but the carving work has ignited something new, something . . . incendiary. And if he thinks he's found what he's looking for, his reaction will be that of a child discovering a yearned-for Christmas present under the tree: a mix of pure excitement tinged with wide-eyed disbelief. It's something I haven't been able to feel for a long time. If I ever could.

With this thought jangling in my head, I venture farther out toward the fringes than usual, beyond the big main stacks, into the ancient and the rarely sifted outliers. I shimmy down a gap that's narrow even by Ben's standards, shins and thighs grazed and bruised by the bristling ends of forgotten stickers. Picking my way carefully over the loose and jumbled boards, my eye barely registers it. But something, glimpsed just for a moment, is out of place. I shuffle back, and there it is again. Silhouetted by the light slanting in through the walls. The perfect waney edge of a fully strapped boule. A boule that should not really be here.

Sheets of corrugated iron are piled against the timber, all but concealing it. It is obscured too by sawn and stacked softwood logs, old fence posts and bearers, broken stickers, weathered tarpaulins, and heavy straps that have been dumped on top. It feels as if it has not been touched for years, perhaps even decades. Clearing away the mess takes time, but soon I am dragging off the last of the sharp-edged metal panels, revealing the neatly spaced sides of the boards. Brushing away the dirt and getting in close, I can see that it's not elm, but oak.

And *what* oak.

Without really knowing why, I shout my father over, and despite his protestations, we try to dig out the first slab. The board is at least two inches thick and *seriously* heavy. "Couldn't find anything a bit more difficult to get at?" he wheezes, twisting and gurning—but grinning. I just grit my teeth and try to remember to lift with my knees. Together we grumble and tangle, swear and snarl, but eventually manage to hoist the great thing up and over the shed's tangled chaos until we have it safely out into the light of the yard.

"Tough old life that fella had," Ben says, having softly appeared. His tongue slides along a cigarette paper and his fingers twist. "Hundred, hundred and fifty years old I'd say. And not an easy one among 'em." There is a crunch, a spark, a sweet plume of Virginian tobacco. "Aye," he says, "a tree of considerable character."

"*Character!?*" With sickening speed my father's knife is out again as he erupts, the wicked point digging into one of the board's many shakes—the deeply riven fault lines, like cracks in the skin of old hands—that streak across the wood's surface. His experienced fingers probe for flaws that may run through half the log, lingering on the weeping blue-black stains where fencing wire and horseshoe nails have reacted with the tannins and bled into the grain. Grumbling wordlessly to himself, he pokes at fissures and ragged holes and the dark bruises of knots as big as fists, where limbs have broken off leaving scars that are brittle and useless as cracked ceramic. And all the while those bushy eyebrows of his dance with contempt. Silently communicating what he's too polite to say out loud in front of Ben.

The eyebrows are right of course. Peppered with the scrapes and bruises, dents and half-healed wounds of what has clearly been a hard fighting life, the oak has the face of an aging football hooligan. Aesthetically, there isn't much to love. There is something else, though . . . a sensation I can't quite articulate. But running my hands over the board, caressing the tiny ridges riven by the saw, feeling the shape and the texture, the live edges—and the attitude—I do know one thing: I know that it makes me smile.

Down on my knees in the damp grass, I lift the great slab up onto one edge, getting an eye along the length of it. Even for oak—the heaviest of our native timbers—the weight is striking. But it feels dry, so density is likely the reason. It must just have grown very slowly. Battled, as Ben suggests, for every last inch. There's not much twist or bend, though, and what little there is can easily be accounted for in the board's thickness. Even if I must lose a good deal of it in the process, I know I should be able to safely flatten it out. Dropping it down again with a mighty thud, I inspect its swirling grain more closely, seeing only now that it is dappled with tiny brown catspaw markings. As if a mob of muddy kittens has been playing on its surface. Beauty is difficult to define . . . but there's certainly no denying this tree has character to spare.

Twenty minutes later, strained and sweating, we've got all six of the boards dragged out. Each is at least two inches thick, a little over two-and-a-half meters long, and as broad as I am. The color is pale gold, and flecked as they are with dark brown, they have the look of chocolate chip shortbread. Much to my father's amusement, Ben even tries his luck with the outermost boards: the final pair, where the tree's concave surfaces are still covered with bark and the thin slivers of solid timber are virtually useless. "Surely," he says, over my father's wild hooting, "you'll be wanting the whole family?" But I am barely listening. With the boards all standing now, leaning against the immovable deadweight of a stricken tractor, there is just the glimmer of something, something I haven't felt in years. It's right there, sizzling on my fingertips. I can almost feel it.

2

The bathrooms at Gleneagles Hotel aren't quite as luxurious as the Dorchester's. They don't have the old-world checkerboard romance of Claridge's. Or the mints, colognes, and palatial marble urinals of the Savoy. But the water from the taps is just as cold, the towels just as extravagantly fluffy. And the red-rimmed eyes staring back from the mirror tell a familiar story. That last dram with the old man was a mistake. The last three, if you want to know the truth.

The slabs of elm he finally settled on were genuine monsters, with flared butt-ends close to six feet across. Dense and rich with turbulent grain the color of treacle toffee, and each as heavy as a full-grown man. Handing over the cash to a twinkle-eyed Ben, he'd known there wasn't the slightest chance of fitting them into his car, parked back at my house where he'd left it. But I'd had to admit that getting my hands dirty had been a nice change of pace. That despite my aching back and splintered hands (and the reams of paperwork waiting for me back in my office) I was dangerously close to aglow. So being the dutiful son (with no real enthusiasm for his paperwork) I climbed back behind the wheel to make the long trip out to my childhood home—a quarter of a ton of elm jammed in the back of the Land Rover and my own wild oak strapped to the roof.

My parents live in a rambling eighteenth-century farmhouse, the ruins of which my father has been gradually restoring since before I was born. In the manner of all penniless self-builders, over the years he has squirreled away anything and everything that might conceivably one day come in handy. And though not quite as treacherous as Ben's arboreal assault course, actually finding somewhere to put the slabs in among half a lifetime's detritus took almost as long as hunting them down in the first place. There was the usual assortment to navigate: rusting anchors, worm-eaten propellers, crumbling snowshoes, great iron cartwheels, bunched headless pheasants, pulleys, grommets, nuts and bolts, and the bulging racks of cardboard and curling sheet material—all of it, presumably, vital for something. But there were other things too, things I hadn't seen before. Sketches of animals, fish, crustaceans, and sea birds, oddments of bone and feather. The delicate skull of an otter, most of a rabbit's skeleton, wings and shells and claws. Evidence, I realized on closer inspection, of his carving research. By the time we'd cleared a suitable space, doused each slab with preservative (rot and woodworm are always a risk with air-dried timber), and wrestled them into position, late afternoon had drifted irretrievably into evening, and I'd needed little encouragement to share a cold beer or two.

Two beers quickly became three, and, sitting together at the big elm table in the kitchen, putting the world to rights a glass at a time, the nagging feeling that I was forgetting something soon began to melt away—dissolving entirely when the whiskey came out. It was late when I finally staggered up to the spare room. There to stare at the hot crimson backs of my eyelids for what seemed no time at all before dragging myself back downstairs at six a.m. to make the long, bouncing drive home. And it was only here, snapping paracetamol from the pack and thumbing blearily through my phone, that I made the unwelcome discovery: I was due to be thirty miles away, in beautiful Auchterarder, in less than an hour.

Out in the light-drenched breakfast room the presentations have already begun. The speaker is carefully scrubbed and buffed, with the clear-eyed vitality of a man with the good sense to get a shower and a proper night's sleep before venturing out in public. Finding a place toward the back, I squirm in a plushly upholstered dining chair, feeling the timberyard's exertions and the long hours on the road in the small of my back. And as the coffee goes down like bitter medicine, and beads of poisonous perspiration muster on my temples, I do my best to pay attention.

I learn of the *electrifying increase* in retail sales in the capital, and the *unmitigated success* of countless-thousand new camper vans steaming along the Highlands' fragile roads. I watch as swooping Scottish vistas and slow-motion raindrops soar and splash on the big screen, and I am tempted by *exciting, not-to-be-missed* opportunities for coachloads of deep-pocketed tourists to descend upon quaint little workshops just like mine. And as the morning wears on, the dull ache creeps further and further up my spine, curling over the top of my head to perch, throbbing, just above my eyes. What was it Jim Harrison said? "Hangovers have all the charm of a rattlesnake cracking its jaws as it swallows a toad." Yes, that about covers it.

With the gentle patter of applause still hanging in the air, I lever myself up, bypassing the cucumber water and the glistening pastries and heading instead for another dose of caffeine. As the waiter pours the coffee from a silver pot, all around me, tartan money is talking. "Heritage" "Ambassador" "Campaign" "*Daar*ling!" Most of it is coming from directors. I am just surrounded by directors. Marketing directors, managing directors, financial directors, brand directors . . . their little badges tell me so.

With my cup trembling in its saucer, I circle the room, keeping my back to the wall. One room feeds into another, then another. All are immaculate. Country house traditional meets contemporary style, oozing with glossy-mag chic. Trying to muster some enthusiasm but, as ever, finding the environment far easier to engage with than the people, I examine my surroundings with a bloodshot eye. Doors and cabinets are tall and slim, elegantly paneled with knife-sharp joinery, in rich, warm, expensive tones. There are grand candelabra and gilded picture frames, crystal vases of fresh-cut flowers, yards of starched white cotton, and thick drapes that spill like caramel from the ceiling's flawless plasterwork. It's altogether too perfect, and I can't escape the feeling that the only thing out of place in here is me.

Trying to make conversation, I press deeply embossed business cards into soft hands whose owners I shall probably never hear from again, doing what I must to keep my name in rotation. I smile and trot out my lines, showing pictures on my phone, struggling, even after all these years, to sum up precisely what it is that we do. "Well . . . anything, really . . . presuming it's made of wood." (And complex and expensive, of course.) All the while trying to ignore the surges of high school discomfort rippling out from my past. The knotted little cliques I must sidle up beside, the false grins and the earnest nodding. The desperate wordless pleading to be let in.

It wasn't always like this.

Back when it was just Marisa and me—long before we were married, and when I'd never even been inside a five-star hotel much less been an invited guest—all we really needed to keep the wolf from the door was a couple of half-decent jobs a year. They didn't even need to be half-decent. Word of mouth was advertising enough, and rent is always cheap in the windowless industrial units that no one else wants. Our romance was a couple of years old by then, a pull that had been magnetic from the first night-club glance. But the drive to collaborate, to go into business and create something special, that had taken longer to grow. Nourished, without our really realizing it, by shared tastes and values and childhoods shaped by spirited creative parents. Finding our way back to Scotland, after traveling the world together, it just seemed obvious: Why would we want to spend our working lives apart? We dreamed and we schemed, and we fought like cats and dogs. The disillusioned architectural designer and the untrained woodworker debating endlessly about the things they would build, the places it would take them, the name they would make for themselves. It was exciting and creative and challenging. And it was ours.

Being a trained professional, Marisa was years ahead of me, but little by little my skills began to catch up with hers—and with our ambition. Until eventually, so too did the size and prestige of our clients. And then came London, where the streets, for a time, felt paved with glamorous opportunity. Mayfair, Pimlico, Design Week, and the King's Road. The place so thick with potential we could almost smell it in the air. It was daunting and intoxicating, and new; you didn't smell it much where we came from. With the boldness reserved for the hopelessly naïve, we were game for whatever was on offer. The suite of complex leatherbound trunks for the motor show ("Perhaps you'd consider flying to Paris to fit them?"), the finely carved treasure chest for the million-dollar watch ("The Royal Ballet's performing at the unveiling—you simply *must* come"), the challenges and the stakes, the brand names and the bright lights. The chances to prove our mettle. Money never had a thing to do with it. And it wasn't love or even passion, really. From the first it was infatuation, pure and simple. Limping home, burnt down to the filter, I knew beyond doubt that I could never stay in a big city for long. But creating remarkable things for the people who do? Why would I ever want to do anything else?

Prestigious clients lack patience, though, and this we soon discovered. And making things by hand takes a very long time. So to keep up, we did what all new businesses are strongly encouraged to do, ready or not: *we grew.* The workshops got bigger, the tools got better, and before long we'd hired our first maker, then our second and third. With all the insurances, accountants, safety equipment, sick pay, tool sharpening, tea and bastard bloody biscuits that come along with them. And while that might not sound like a particularly large enterprise, paying for it all still meant finding, securing, and developing a hell of a lot more work than we were used to every month. Work I genuinely expected the team to do with the same scruffy tool-bag-full of jury-rigged techniques, and the strange and often indescribable detailing that had accidentally become my hallmark. The jobs took longer, and the profits got smaller, and the tension grew and grew. And the better we got, the shorter the list of clients who could afford us became. Month by month, job by job, there was less and less room for me, my double-sided tape, and my temper in the benchroom.

Where once my tools were drills and saws, chisels and screwdrivers, gradually I began to spend my days wielding a laptop, a telephone and, from time to time, even a champagne flute, as slowly, insidiously, I migrated to the office. To managing projects and inventing solutions, sitting behind a desk instead of standing at a workbench. But we were making special things, meaningful things, things that *needed* to be made, so for the chance to progress, to keep on improving and to pay the bills every month, I did what I needed to do. The punchline is that I'm probably better at this than I ever was at that. But even after all these years, there's one thing I never could figure out how to make: small talk.

At eleven o'clock, a kilted doorman with a brogue as thick as Islay malt whisks me outside. Freedom smells like fresh-cut grass. With every crunching step I feel lighter, cleaner. And down in the visitor's carpark I feel better still. As the day's first truly authentic grin spreads across my face, it is with the sure and certain knowledge that, of the many, *many* Land Rovers on show, mine is not just the oldest, and the dirtiest . . . but the only one with half an oak tree strapped to its roof.

Woodsmoke curls from the chimney as I turn off the road; even through the windscreen's plate glass I can smell it. Is there a more primeval smell? Pulling up to the gate, three sets of eyes wander to the roof rack, taking in the timber with professional interest. The boys are drinking coffee in the yard, sprawled out in the weak sunshine, looking for warmth and some phone reception in the forest's impenetrable air. Behind them, beneath a wall of towering spruce trees swaying gently in the breeze, the workshop dominates the clearing. Like a child's drawing of a log cabin, painted vibrant blue.

It was the dog that found this place. Dragging us up the hill beyond the loch. Scrambling over tree roots and snuffling through bracken and thorny bramble scrub, following her nose and doubtless scenting trouble. All of a sudden, the foliage opened out and there it was. Its rough timber cladding smothered in an ugly scout-hut-chocolate-brown, tufts of grass and the seedlings of young trees sprouting from its gutters, shuttered and silent on the edge of the treeline. Knowing in my bones that a farmer would emerge at any moment, all red-faced wrath and dog and shotgun, I fretted from a safe distance. But Marisa—whose particular mix of mountain Tuscan and East End Glaswegian makes her garrulous and gregarious, and entirely immune to fear—ventured up to peer through its dusty windows. The tips of her fingers gripping the sills and her toes straining for purchase on the crumbling, lichen-slick walls below. Minutes passed and the farmer never came, so eventually I peered in too.

As it turned out, the building was a sawmill, or at least it had been. And it *was* occupied, just not by farmers. Its tenants were mice and rats and fat gray squirrels, swallows and sparrows and tiny darting wrens, and the enormous old machines that half-filled the place. We would soon discover that it had no running water, toilet, electrical outlets, insulation, heating, or usable wiring, and that its damp concrete floor would need to be replaced—or built over with something dry and flat and stable. But we looked past all that, because we both knew the instant we saw it. I think you always know.

Perching on the side of the desk in our little office, I tuck the phone's handset into the crook of my neck, punching in the number from memory. I hear the receptionist's chirpy answer after a single ring and ask to be put through to Chris, the lead designer. Strange to think that these almost daily calls might soon be a thing of the past. For months we've been developing this project, but we are now just days away from getting started.

Wings flutter in my chest just thinking about it. The standard of joinery and the quality of finish, the prestige of the client and the sheer *volume* of units . . . frankly, it's daunting. But it's nearly half a year's worth of work—nearly half a year's worth of consistent income—and the deposit alone will lift us all the way out of the overdraft, covering wages until Christmas. There might even be something left over for new machines, maybe even a little bonus.

As the hold Muzak tinkles away, I try with my free hand to riddle the ashes through the little potbellied stove, readying it for a new fire. Scrunching bills and steepling the finest kiln-dried kindling money can buy. Outside the window, Robin is strutting about on the roof rack, slipping the canvas belts through their heavy steel ratchets, deftly unstrapping the oak boards. Having hired him on with this job in mind, we're still getting to know each other, but already he's proving himself an invaluable member of the team. The boys like him too, and so does the dog. His energy is different, but it's complementary, vital in a small workshop like this—a team this close-knit. He looks just as at home up there as he does under a bonnet, or inside virtually any machine come to that. At his very happiest when the tunes are blaring and he's up to his elbows in something mechanical. I watch as he extravagantly doffs his flat cap, pouts and postures. Halfway between a young Mick Jagger and an oil-stained Victorian puffer boat engineer.

Laughing and shouting up at him, dressed today in immaculate Air Jordans, Carhartt, and priceless Supreme, Tommy appears. Taking the hard gig as usual, walking backward, glancing down now and then at the wood's wild grain. He's in his early twenties now, but in some ways he'll always be eighteen to me. He certainly looks no older than he did on his first day, fresh-faced and straight out of college, all those years ago. A good deal wiser and stronger perhaps, and with a sharper set of skills, but still without an ounce of fat on his graceful, long-limbed boxer's frame. Still wearing the same tireless grin. That just leaves Andrew. And Andrew must be on the board's other end because, although I can't see the dark-haired Shetlander, even through the window, I *can* hear him. To my certain knowledge, and definitely not in the time he's been with us—which must be what, coming up for two years now?—Andrew has *never* been fully silent. He probably whistles in his sleep, or yodels, or hums. Or all three. I can't say he didn't warn us . . . but if someone tells you in their interview they were once fired for singing too much, you don't actually believe them, do you?

The blowtorch is already roaring, the paper twisting in the grate, when Chris comes on the line. After months of development, I've come to think of Chris as more than just another client. In my head I'm already composing the setup and punchline: how best to tease out my morning's misadventures, to make the most of my terrible last-minute moment of realization? His voice, though, is unusually somber, and he gets right to it. "I'm really sorry to tell you this, mate . . . we've just found out ourselves. There's, ahh, there's been some changes of management and, well . . . the client has decided to go another way. It's not happening. The job's dead."

I've heard it said that miners working deep underground prefer wooden pit props to modern materials like iron or steel.

Timber lacks metal's strength, but it creaks and moans if the load becomes too great. Wood warns you when it's about to break, giving you a fighting chance to escape. The others simply crumple and your world caves in. I hear no warning, only a *click*, a dial tone, and the hammer-thudding of my own heartbeat. And as the terrible weight of the situation begins to crash down around me, the darkness and dread threatening to overwhelm, in my mind I retreat to an entirely different forest. And all of a sudden, I am twelve years old again.

My father, gray and cadaverous after months without rest, eased open the door to the little croft. The low winter sun, as much a stranger as we were to the windowless porch, followed us meekly inside. As the dogs drove in around our legs and the damp chill crept out to meet us, the light played over the whitewashed stone walls, glittering on the trails of long-departed slugs and snails. "Need to take a tree down this trip," dad said, with me close on his heels, nodding toward the dwindling stack of firewood.

Drawn as always to the array of weaponry dangling from the door, I hung back. Reaching out with chubby fingers to test their edges, feel their danger. My father had always carried a knife, the handle carved from fruitwood, the folding blade honed like a razor. His was no letter-opener, no fangled multi-tool, but the sort of bloodstained bulky custom job that airport security takes very seriously if you forget you're carrying—as he frequently did.

But the axes, machetes, log-splitters, and bow saws that clanked together on their iron hooks, they were something else entirely.

My father's voice wrenched me away, and in the croft's main room I found him fiddling with an oil lamp. I watched, intrigued, as he pumped the handle, struck a match, held it to the thick cotton wick, and settled the fragile glass shroud, filling the air with thin black smoke, pungent with sulfur and burning paraffin. As he adjusted the dial, the sputtering flame relaxed, the smoke paled, and the room was suffused with a buttery glow. The lamplight, though, did nothing to soften its chilly austerity.

We'd been visiting the croft for years by then, and the place was just as I remembered. A pair of moldering wingback chairs—high and stiff and straight-backed—sitting rigidly to attention before the fire's cold grate. An antique cabinet of dark wood, its shellac puckered and white at the edges like the corners of an old man's mouth. Shelves of yellowing paperbacks, and here and there the nubs of candles grotesquely fused to empty wine bottles. And, above it all, an ornate brass chandelier throwing eerie shapes onto the ceiling.

I followed as my father hefted the lamp and made his way farther into the croft, the two of us casting our own skulking shadows on the rough stone walls. He peered into corners, sniffed at bottles and jars, knocked thoughtfully on pipes, and threw open shutters. Looking for signs of break-ins, water ingress, rot, or vermin. I watched and listened. Our feet echoed like gunshots on the bare concrete floor. Together we investigated the bathroom just off the porch, with its peat-stained clawfoot tub, meat-locker chill, and single tiny window, the half-finished blockwork kitchen with its dangling bare bulb, and the damp bedroom where I knew my brother and I would sleep. Vivid blue pellets of rat poison sat in trays on the sill beneath the big arched window, its glass seeming almost to move with lazily buzzing flies.

Nodding to himself as if to say that all was as well as could be expected, my father ushered me back toward the front door. With my little sister draped sleepily over one shoulder, my mother smiled warmly at me as we passed. From the porch's little arsenal dad selected a chipped steel T-bar—thick as a man's thumb, about five feet long and a foot wide at the top, with a toothed end—and a parang: a short, curved, heavy machete. My eyes widened as he handed them both to me, saying nothing but subtly tilting his head toward the woods. There was no mistaking the implication.

"Frozen water takes up more room than unfrozen water," he'd explained to me once. "So full water pipes will swell if they freeze, and the joints will crack. And when the weather relents and the frozen water melts, it'll flood—could be in dozens of inaccessible places. And see if you can guess who'll have to fix it?!" He would know, he'd installed the croft's plumbing, just as he'd installed, built, or rebuilt just about everything in the little stone building. From the floors to the windows to the frigid wooden toilet seat. To prevent winter flooding, then, the system must be locked off and drained whenever visitors departed. Meaning that with each new visitor it had to be turned back on manually. The remote stopcock was buried a quarter-mile up the hill, spurring off the main water line. Over the boundary fence and deep into the heart of the forest.

I'd been up there with my father before, my short rubber boots laboring over the steep trail as I struggled to keep pace with his mighty strides. But I'd never even considered venturing into that dark mass of trees without him. They were too huge for me to comprehend; wet and slimy underfoot, riddled with fairy-tale red blobs of fly agaric fungi. For years my brother and I had kept to the narrow grass forestry tracks, or the stone ford straddling the burn, just as we'd been told. We *never* went into the woods alone.

But I knew my father had his own jobs to do. Firewood must be chopped, the fires laid and lit, the car emptied, and the stove coaxed into life. The diesel generator out in the barn must be checked and fueled, heaved into action before the daylight gave out. And if the water system, or any one of a dozen other things, *had* developed any issues over the empty months, he'd need to deal with them too before nightfall. Before he could finally stop and rest. So, reluctantly, but with a little pride swelling too, I clutched the long T-bar and slung the parang's leather strap around my wrist, and whistling up the dogs, I struck out up the hill.

Trees bullied at the fence line, their closely packed ranks palpably greedy for this last scrap of unclaimed territory. The forest's strongest, most storm-resistant front line, standing shoulder to shoulder around the croft's little clearing. It all looked the same to me, but the dogs knew where they were going, and glad at least of their company, I scrambled over and followed closely behind.

I made heavy work of it in the beginning, stumbling over hidden roots in ground that rose and fell like a tidal swell. My boots quickly sinking into the black mulch of decaying needles, as I stooped, crab-walking, to avoid being whipped about the face by low branches. But it was more than just the physical obstacles I was battling. Sitka spruce, for that is what surrounded me, has found its ideal environment in Scotland. Peaty acidic soil, high rainfall, almost laughably mild winters after the hardships of its North American homeland. And planted so close together, those monstrous, thick-necked giants had powered up through the ground until their limbs mashed together into one great scrum—all but blotting out the light. The weight of the shadows, the ominous silence, the trees' physicality, it all seemed to grow heavier with every step, pressing down from above, making me paranoid and twitchy. There was no greenery, no wildflowers, grasses, or ferns, not a hint of life other than those immense trees. It was spooky and forbidding. Clutching the weight of the steel in my fists until the knuckles showed white, I tried not to listen to the fear whispering in my ear.

A little farther on the canopy thinned, and my world began to brighten. The going became muddier and rockier as the trees opened out. But though the footing was tricky at times, I found I was able to stand almost upright, moving more easily over the ground. Undergrowth thickened, and here and there a rotting wooden post marked the way. Then there came the sound of trickling water up ahead. The burn wasn't particularly wide or deep here, but its rust-colored banks were glutinous, and some civic-minded soul (probably my father) had positioned a log between them. The log was dark and sodden, its bark long since rotted away. I stepped onto it, and I remember thinking—as I skidded violently sideways, crumpling hard into the burn—that very few things are as slippery as old wet wood. That I *knew* that . . . and I really should have known better.

Trickling brown water, peat-stained dark as tea, tinkled beside my ear. I took stock. I was soaked from the waist down, muddy, and sore. But by some miracle the ugly blade slung around my wrist hadn't got its teeth into me, and the T-bar hadn't skewered me like a kebab. My injuries amounted to little more than numbed shock in my knees, hands, elbows . . . and pride. Undoubtedly, though, the first darkening clouds of a black mood were closing in. Irritated, wet, and bruised, I hauled myself up and continued on.

I squelched over mud and rubble, as the trail all but vanished. There were smaller trees too, now that the spruce was thinner. Seedlings carried by birds or animals or on the wind—making their homes in firebreaks and on the banks of the burn. The spindly elms, rowans, and willows made the going difficult, and the ankle-hungry snares of hawthorn and gorse raked at my skin and clothes. From under my breath the muttering grew louder as I began to curse it all: the log, the fall, the trees, my father most of all. I slashed at anything I could find with the parang, kicking at loose stones to banish them into the undergrowth. I worked myself up into a fine little tantrum.

Then some atavistic instinct stopped me in my tracks. It was just the merest flicker of a movement teasing at the corner of my eye, but it made my blood run cold. It wasn't the dogs. After hours in the boot of the car, they were off somewhere burning through a day's cooped-up energy. And I had neither seen nor heard a rabbit or even a bird since I'd dropped over the fence. But although I couldn't see anything, I could feel it. The forest had opened its eyes, and something was out there. Something was watching me.

My mind *shrieked*.

Slowly, I turned. Both fists gripping my weapons. Electrified. Blood rushing in my ears.

The deer's limpid black eyes took me in, but it did not move. I must have come upon it from downwind and was near enough to reach out and touch it. Grayish about the muzzle, the rest of its svelte body was a rich russet brown like a fox. I could make out the individual hairs on its coat. For a long, heavy moment, we just sized each other up. Neither of us blinked. I had never been so close to a wild animal that large before. I could feel its vitality. Moments later, the dogs came crashing through the branches and in three graceful bounds the deer was gone. But I was galvanized by the meeting and pushed on full of resolve. I found the stopcock a little farther up the hill, the decaying remnants of a fencepost marking the spot.

Grubbing at the slippery orange cap, inch by inch I unscrewed it to reveal the pipe buried a few feet below. It was hard to see clearly, but somewhere down in the shadows I knew the stubby rectangular valve was hiding. I could just make it out, at right angles to the pipe, locking off the main supply. Aligning the mud-clogged key of the T-bar's end over the valve took forever. But when they were finally locked together, I planted my feet, bent at the waist, and twisted.

Nothing.

I tried again, bunching my shoulders, neck, and back, teeth gritted and knuckles white on the pitted steel.

Not. One. Millimeter.

After five futile minutes I gave up. Blundering back down the trail, pissed off, feeling the cold leaching into my bones, I barely even bothered to slash at the branches. Deflated, and more than a little ashamed, I ran over scenarios. How best to break it to my father? He shouldn't have sent me, surely? Should have come himself. I'd tried, hadn't I? Jammed? Rusted? Not my fault! But as I stooped and stumbled toward the fence line, the *putt-putt-putting* of the diesel generator growing louder with every step, I could feel the hot spiders of doubt crawling their way up my spine.

The dogs surged past me like a tidal race. The porch still smelled musty, but there was a hint of something else now too. In the main room, the air was veiled with the acrid lacy smoke of a new fire in a cold grate. It was no warmer. Crouched on the floor, a pair of ancient leather bellows in his fists, my father was fighting a losing battle with damp newspaper and a chimney full of refrigerated air. "That it on then?" he said. Then: "Oh come on, you *BASTARD*!" This last to the smoldering newspaper.

I made my excuses, avoided his eye, heard myself whine. Pumping the bellows, he didn't even look up. "The stopcock's not frozen, just stiff. Lots to do, need that water on." I opened my mouth to argue, but he raised a warning eye, and it was enough. Shutting my trap with an audible snap, I slouched back out the way I had come, glowering and muttering fit to grind my teeth to powder. The dogs, scarcely able to believe their luck, left their empty food bowls spinning on the concrete floor.

That second time up the hill I was really cooking, and the higher I climbed the angrier I became. The forest itself seemed to revel in my souring humor: mud was deeper, branches were lower, spikier and even more vindictive, and the rain that had begun to fall found its way down the back of my neck with extraordinary precision. I virtually ran over the pine-needle hillocks, so very nearly slipping again on the wet log that I almost had to grin. I smashed through the gorse and bulldozed my way through the brambles, the prospect of any more magical wildlife encounters wasted on me, and by the time I reached the stopcock again I was sweaty, grumpy, grazed, soaked, and utterly fed up.

"Right, you bastard . . ." I cursed through gritted teeth, feeling the keyed end of the T-bar bite onto the valve with an audible *bink*. Scrunching my eyes, I put everything I had into the twist. All my indignant fury, the hot shame of fear, the withering look on my father's face. The impotent humiliation of failure.

Nothing.

I tried again. Twisting suddenly, aggressively. Hoping that the element of surprise might help. But it still would not budge. I howled into the trees. Then I begged. Neither made the slightest difference.

Smoke was drifting from the chimney by the time I returned. A thin skein of white against the sullen sky. Music drifted softly under the door as I lingered outside, standing for a long time with my thumb on the iron latch—rusted thin and scooped like a cat's tongue. My brother Bobby looked up from the floor when I finally walked in. He can't have been more than nine or ten at the time. The fire was crackling now, and he was sitting in front of it, clutching a book in gloved hands. He looked at me, raised his little eyebrows wryly, then looked back down at his book.

I found my father in the kitchen, lying on his back like a mechanic, with his great beard poking out of the cold stove. His hands were black with soot, the floor about him littered with tools and grizzled firebrick. He heard me come in, wriggled free of the stove and sat up, his shadow stretching across the concrete. He'd looked tired before, but now he looked completely done in: the grayish pallor of well-done liver, unimproved by the harsh glare of the single bare bulb. "Any trouble?" he grunted, in a tone of voice I recognized as dangerously close to the edge . . .

The stubborn metal yielded slowly at first. Seized brass breaking grudgingly free. The torch clutched under my arm clattered into the mud as the stumbling surprise of moving water singing up through the T-bar drew the breath from my chest. I don't know how long I'd been up there that third time—alone in the gathering darkness. Just how many more times or how many different ways I'd tried before the valve reluctantly creaked open.

Twenty-five years later, placing the phone back in its cradle, with woodsmoke and desolation spicing the air once more, I am back there in those woods so vividly I can almost feel the steel in my hands. Assailed again by fear and doubt, unsure which way to turn, hemmed in on all sides by looming shadows and the nightmarish specter of the unknown.

Beyond the window I can still see the boys laughing and joking in the yard, blissfully unaware that, without any warning, all our livelihoods have just been snuffed out. That there is now no money to pay wages, rent, or the stacks of unpaid bills, no savings or line of credit to fall back on. And even as the thought whispers insidiously into my ear—that as much as I might want to, need to, I *can't* fix this—my father's words echo down through the years.

"Nevertheless . . . it must be done."

3

For a long time I just stare, unblinking, at the flames dancing in the stove. Everything and nothing flickering in front of my eyes. Listening to the *plink-plink-plink* of the black iron swelling in the heat. And the dog, gnawing at her backside on the hearth, enviably absorbed in simpler matters.

Three doors away, one of the big plant machines thrums into life. Its tone changes slightly, downshifts. Too much fibrous wood meeting cutthroat steel. The motor's labored bass note makes me wince. I know the bite it's trying to take is destructively thick, just as I know we have nothing else in the order book: with a chilling, bone-deep certainty. I know this because it is entirely by design. The project in hand was simply too big and too complex to allow anything else into our headspace, let alone our workspace. And so, blinded by the intoxicating prospect of climbing out of the overdraft once and for all, of breaking free from all that seemingly insurmountable debt in one gigantic leap, we have cleared the decks with smiles on our faces and cheery whistles on our lips. For weeks we've talked of little else, thought of little else, as every last scrap of open work has been completed, the money mentally spent and the workshop readied for the onslaught to come. There are no eager clients waiting in the wings, no plans or drawings or half-finished projects ready to go. Nothing. Cold dusty nothing.

Despite the gravity of the situation, the irony of our horribly urgent need for work is not lost on me. Ironic, because no one really *needs* the things we make. Not urgently, anyway. The handcrafted whiskey cabinet, the elegant picnic trunk for the supercar's boot, the elaborately carved credenza for the flat-screen TV, there's no denying that these are all luxuries. And luxuries are, almost by definition, things that people can get along very happily without. Indeed, there have been instances where new projects have taken several *years* to gestate. Commercial clients (like ours) only make matters worse, because of the sheer volume of design and bureaucracy that must be managed before you can even think about getting paid. Fickle and risky as it undoubtedly is, our tiny, exacting, globally spread market can be navigated— if a little precariously—assuming you have a financial cushion (which we don't), a good-sized project already in the works (which we've just lost), or some other revenue stream to keep things afloat (which we've been too blinkered to organize). And so here we are, unhappily floundering in the hottest of water. That it was foolish to end up making *only* these sorts of things might seem obvious. But it was a gradual process, driven by heart rather than head. And like the proverbial frog in the saucepan, all I can really say in our defense is that the water felt safe enough when we climbed in.

Something dry and resinous in the stove catches with a report like musketry and, despite her size, the dog materializes in my lap, burrowing in under my arm. I know how she feels. How capricious the world can be. How nice it would be to hide away from it for a while. The wood flares brightly, intensely, and is quickly reduced to smoldering ash.

Driving home I stop in for supplies. Hurling the bags onto the passenger seat, I can hear the bottles tinkling together. Their music comes again with every crunching gear change, as the transmission strains and we head up the hill toward the edge of town. Outlying houses soon dwindle away, giving way to a smattering of farms and rust-red agricultural sheds, then only the gently rolling fields and the long, lonely sweep of the road. And as they do, in spite of the day that's behind me and the storm that's brewing up ahead, I can't help but feel my mood lift, just a fraction.

You do not so much drive a Land Rover as launch one—an Alaskan bush pilot cajoling a cranky old floatplane into the sky. Climbing into the cramped cockpit, slamming the tinny door behind you, tapping dials and throwing the sequence of toggle switches just so, turning the huge key and waiting for that muscular diesel to shudder into life. There is the reassuring throaty growl, the exaggerated cabin wobble as you taxi out of the carpark and pick up speed, the almost comically restricted view through the plate glass window, the turbulence . . . and the *noise*.

Turning up our street, I catch fleeting glimpses of the water, froth-capped and cobalt-blue between the single row of fudge-harled buildings. Beyond it, bright daubs of color—herculean cranes in the dockyards of Rosyth—are strewn along the water's edge like titanic children's toys. The curtains of our little ground-floor flat are still tightly drawn. They are always drawn of course. I never could get used to peering out at people, or seeing them peer back in, so it is really only the dog who uses this particular vantage point. On the nose-smeared side of the glass, the flat is dark, cold, and silent. Marisa isn't home. Momentary disappointment is tinged with a glimmer of relief. For a little while longer at least, wherever she is, she is still unburdened with this weight. And even just a little more time to think about how best to break the news, to rack my brains for a solution—and cudgel them with a dram or two—feels like a blessing. How I wish I didn't have to tell her at all. She has worked so very hard to get us here.

Two days a week she's inside a classroom, combining her rare cask-strength enthusiasm for design with the kind of people skills that can really only be hewn by years in hospitality. Doing what she does in front of hundreds of students fills me with dread. But she loves it, she always has. More than that, I know she makes a difference. Helping teenagers, in one of Scotland's most deprived areas, to realize their potential. With the talented or the really dedicated ones earning university places, and then with luck a creative career. And doubtless all of them feeling supported and becoming better designers.

For a long time she worked the other three days too, at a small architectural practice, leaving only the evenings and weekends free to work closely together with me. Burning the midnight oil in our windowless little workshop, wearing every layer she owned, a phone glued to her ear, sketching away in the electrical cupboard that doubled as our office. With me screwing and hammering, battling with battered tools and secondhand machinery on the other side of the cupboard door. It was working seven days a week like this that meant we could pursue our dream. Her jobs provided the means and the breathing space to start the business, to hone our style and craft, to put a roof over our heads and food on the table in those early days. Plenty of times she covered the rent and overheads on the workshop as well. Month after month, year after year, she never complained, she just knuckled down and did it all.

Leaving the Land Rover ticking on the curb, I release the dog, sending her into near-nuclear frenzy by reaching for the ball-thrower and heading toward the park. Through the gate at the end of our street, out beyond the strip of woodland that tumbles down to the shore, I can see the bridges arcing out over the water. And as the dog flattens her ears and sprints away, low and fast and urgent, even though I have seen them a thousand times before, I cannot help but stare. Farthest away, seeming almost to crawl out of the sea like some great leviathan dragging itself inland, the thickly stanchioned Victorian rail bridge. Closer in, its decaying cables pinging and snapping quietly as they abrade away in the coarse salt air, the old, decommissioned road bridge. And nearer still, like a pale web of spider's silk slung across the wind-scoured channel, the sparkling new Queensferry Crossing.

Ours is an unlikely hamlet, and something of a hidden gem. Not so very far from the outskirts of Edinburgh—picturesque, coastal, and eminently commutable—but *just* remote enough to be affordable, even for the likes of us. Its craggy shores jut out over the low grubby sweep of the Forth Estuary as it cleaves its way into Scotland's flank, with the faint blue knuckles of the Ochil Hills hunkering down on the horizon. Just a scattering of homes, a tiny harbor, a pub, and a castle (all Scotland's basic essentials) nestled between the old industrial powerhouse of Bo'ness to the west and the sailing clubs, teashops, and hard rock candy of Port Edgar and Queensferry to the east, a mile across the water from the bustling dockyards of Fife.

It's low tide, and the sludgy gray flats are dotted with stranded boats lurching over on their keels. Gulls scavenge and scream. Wire rigging plinks out an agitated rhythm against forgotten masts. Somewhere out there to my right is the open sea. An unobstructed view, if I could see so far, all the way to Denmark and the foot of Norway. Away to my left, remnants of our industrial past blot the skyline. Beyond the soot-blackened chimneys lie Stirling, the Trossachs, Argyll, and the wonderful west coast. What I would give to be hidden away in one of those far-flung places right now.

Before the light begins to falter, much to the dog's chagrin, we head back to the flat. As soon as the door is open she barges past, leaving me on the porch fingering peeling paint and chipped plaster that's badly in need of my attention. Moments later, I hear the distinctive *whap-pang!* of her food bowl being brazenly battered like a dinner bell. But first things first. Breaking the seal on the Bushmills as I walk into the kitchen, glugging three fingers into a mug, I take a deep slug. Only after the honey-sweet burn of the whiskey has bloomed in the emptiness of my stomach do I hunt down her biscuits. Then to the sounds of frantic chewing, I retreat to the shadows of the curtained sitting room, taking the bottle with me.

"Wait . . . are you *quite* sure you've got this right?" Marisa says, rather accusingly. I'm caught off guard because she has been swearing for some considerable time, and the air around her still crackles with exclamation marks. "Sounded pretty unequivocal to me," I reply, as definitively as one can after three rapidly consumed double-measures of Irish whiskey. She sighs—a long pursed-lip blow—and rubs aggressively at her face. As if she is trying to scrub away the news with an invisible washcloth. For a long moment she is silent, then, seeming to accept the news, she motions for me to pour her a drink. A whiskey chaser to go with that familiar cocktail of adrenaline and despair. I find a glass and, huddling in closer to me on the couch, she takes a sip. And together we start trying to figure a way out of this.

Early the following morning, my head feels as if it is packed with rusting steel wool. But pushing again through the little gate at the end of our street, slipping and skidding over the dew-sodden grass, the inescapable grimness of it matches my mood. The dog is out front, hauling me on a long waist harness, rigidly on alert for the deer that make their home in the hinterland of beech, oak, ash, honeysuckle, and elder that curls around the lip of the coast like a bristling mustache. Marisa keeps pace beside me as we jog slowly toward the trees. She is uncharacteristically quiet now. All talked out. For years this strip of woodland is where we have come in search of answers, and after a long night where none was forthcoming, I only hope we can find some here today.

Pale sunlight flickers between the branches, bleaching out the color, giving everything the feel of an old movie. The hard black outline of the castle juts out toward the muddy tidal plain like a ship run aground. Half a mile passes, then a mile. Crunching and squelching, leaving fresh tracks in the rust-brown shale, we disturb a heavy winged raptor. It lifts ponderously from its perch, and I can feel the eyes on me, scanning us from above. This early, we're the only people around, but the woodland creatures have been up for hours.

"Any great brainwaves in the night?" Marisa says, her breathing steady and even. "I know you didn't get much sleep." I have had neither sleep nor brainwaves, and communicate as much with my look and the rings beneath my eyes. "I know I've said this before," I say, my own breathing ragged, "but we could try . . . sacrificing the dog?" As if hearing me, she zigzags wildly, setting a trip wire with her lead, then stops suddenly, threatening to take us all down in a tangled mess of paws and legs and mud and teeth. Marisa sidesteps her madly sniffing form, and when she pulls up, bending at the waist, she is smiling weakly. She tickles the dog's face, with the little collie squirming, eyes blazing, just desperate to *GO*.

"I'd say we've got about a month. After that . . ." she trails off, unable to finish. But by my rough, bleary three a.m. calculations, I'd say she's right on the money. The clock began ticking the moment Chris hung up the phone. The question is, can we find, secure, develop, design, and critically get paid for a new project before our time runs out? We look at each other for a long moment, neither of us willing to say it out loud; to think it, even. After ten years of hard graft, of taking little or no wage, of plowing *everything* we've made back into the business, of living and breathing design and woodwork and craftsmanship, relentlessly promoting and networking, watching friendships and hobbies wither away from neglect . . . is this really how it ends? One phone call? A single overplayed hand?

We speak little after that. There is nothing left to say. Climbing up and away from the water's edge and turning for home, our feet crunching rhythmically on the track and each alone with our own private demons, we savor these last quiet moments before we reach the workshop, and reality.

4

Five deflating minutes on the phone is all it takes to confirm the worst. Marisa quietly hangs up, closes her eyes, and drops her face into her hands. It feels like a long time until she speaks again. Swearing, I can handle, swearing, I'm used to. All this silence is far more worrying.

Taking a deep breath and composing herself, she lifts her head and finally starts talking. There is, Chris thinks, just the glimmer of a chance of clawing back some design fees from the client, but it might take months to come through, if at all. He's sympathetic, and apologetic, they've lost work unexpectedly too. But though there is some small measure of comfort in the knowledge that no one saw this coming, two things are made painfully clear: the job really is dead in the water, and we really are on our own.

"It probably goes without saying, but I think we keep this just between us for now?" I say, quietly. "Of course. But pretty soon we're going to have to tell them *something* . . ." Marisa leaves the word hanging in the air, and together we watch it drift and shiver until it fades into nothing. And then without another word, we do the only thing we can do. We become archaeologists.

Battling Wi-Fi that is almost nonexistent out here in the trees, we begin to comb painstakingly back through the inbox. Hunting for old clients, poring over phone contacts, text messages, even social media comments. Teasing out every kind word and cold lead we can find. We upend shoe boxes filled with hundreds of dog-eared business cards, compliments slips, and scrawled handwritten notes from trade shows and exhibitions years in the past. Searching for something, *anything*, that might contain the slightest scrap of potential. Always brushing the dust and dirt away delicately, lest these fossils crumble away to nothing.

Time crawls past, and with it thousands of emails. But when, at eleven, a pair of steaming mugs appears with a knock at the window, I for one still have little to show for my morning's efforts. Out in the yard there is cake to go with the coffee. I've not much in the way of appetite, but it's one of Andrew's delicious creations, and I can't very well say no. Marisa and I try to talk low without sounding suspicious. "Is the bank really a no-go?" I ask, through a mouthful of crumbs. The shaky start making me broach extending our already frightening line of credit for perhaps the fifth time in twelve hours. I know the overdraft we already have will take years to pay back, if it's even possible, and the idea of piling on even more debt is frankly hard to contemplate. But it would buy us some time to think. Marisa's wan smile says it all. She's ahead of me as usual, and she lays it out in no uncertain terms. "We're maxed out. *Beyond* maxed out. Right now, the bank is far more likely to call in its markers than to offer us any more cash." Short of taking on high-interest credit cards, the business has borrowed its last penny.

"Have you called your dad yet?" she asks softly. I haven't, but it has been playing on my mind. Truthfully, I would like to talk this over with my father—he's one hell of a problem-solver. But even the thought of that conversation makes my innards tighten like a fist. He helped build this place, the previous workshop, and the one before that. Marshaling a team half his age, leading from the front as he always does. The long grueling winter days and late nights bonded him to these walls, and to these boys, just as surely as they scarred his body. He's helped us out of more jams and disasters and last-second deadlines than anyone else, is as much a part of the team as any of us, and he'll take it hard if this really is the end. More than that, he'll take it personally. And what if he blames me? Not so very deep down I know how reckless he thinks I am. That I always did sail too close to the wind, never paid enough attention to what I was spending, or to where the next paycheck was coming from. He's right, of course, which only makes it worse. But any trace of that, of disappointment even subtly in his voice . . . it's just not something I'm ready to hear.

For the next three days we scarcely look up from our screens. We call, we email, we cajole, wheedle, and beg. Chasing down anything and everything we can find. It's demoralizing work, reaching back through the years, and to all four corners of the globe. And hour by hour, our hopes of a client-in-shining-armor diminish. Our thinly veiled entreaties, suggesting some variation on the themes that we "just happen to have a window in our schedule," that lucky clients might "act fast and be fitted in straight away," falling on deaf or disinterested ears.

We do scrape together one or two potential fill-in jobs. Fiddly, small, risky bits and pieces. Projects and clients we've always kept at arm's length in the past because we knew, at best, that the most we could expect was to break even—and then only if we were lucky. Nothing substantial enough to make a real dent. Quietly, we both know that even if we can find someone willing to commit to a good-sized new project, or to blow the cobwebs off something antique, battling payment terms that might be as long as ninety days it will probably be too late. Marisa, as ever, tries to be optimistic. But by the end of the third day, when a short, upbeat *"Maybe later in the year"* email snuffs out our last serious prospect, even she begins to look hopeless.

Out in the workshop, the atmosphere could not be more different. With the bombshell yet to drop, and Marisa and me so distracted, the team's mood is ebullient. Music blasts from speakers bolted to the beams at ear-bleed volume. The boys' voices are loud and playful, full of irreverent humor. Spring has been unseasonably cold and, even for Scotland, relentlessly wet. After a long winter of burst pipes, thermal underwear, gloves and hats and fingers they could scarcely feel, the sun is shining at last. As far as Tommy, Robin, and Andrew know, we're about to climb a mountain together. To begin something new and exciting and challenging. Hell, they might even be getting a bonus. With nothing substantial to get their teeth into, and having already spent a week or two twiddling their thumbs, make-work has slipped into a new and previously unseen gear. Hidden crevices have been vacuumed, tools, windows, and surfaces buffed until they gleam showroom bright. Machines have been waxed, sharpened, fettled, and tuned like musical instruments. Even the yard has taken on the clipped and manicured appearance of a country estate.

On my brief sorties for caffeine and paracetamol, I've tried to keep my chin up, unclench my jaw and make conversation. I know they are only doing what they can to keep themselves busy; but knowing that and smiling about it are not the same thing. Was that hardwood windowsill always behind the toilet? Those soft-close tool drawers in the benchroom? And when did the species and dimensions get neatly chalked onto all the boards in the racks? *Ash, tapering, 1200. Elm, shaky, 850.* From every corner of the workshop, wherever I look, the stark evidence of their underemployment leers back at me.

Bespoke work is always up and down—with last-minute changes and races to the finish, grand client ideas that never quite get off the ground—but lately we've had a few more downs than ups. It's never been *quite* this bad before, but they have all seen this sort of thing too many times not to be alert to the signs. The job will take just a little too long to materialize, the workshop will get just a fraction too tidy, or my own mood will spike from frazzled to fuming—just for a moment—and the atmosphere will change. Before long, they'll know there's a problem, and their trust and confidence will not be easily won back. We can solve this; I know we can. All we need is some time and space to find a solution. But for that, I need to keep them occupied.

Keeping three skilled and energetic craftsmen just the right amount of busy is a tall order, and I know that planning even the most basic jobs will require more bandwidth than we can spare. Whatever we give them to do can't be too small, or it will be over almost before it's begun, but it can't be too large either, or it will take too long to organize and will almost certainly involve buying materials and supplies we can ill afford. Striding around the workshop, my desperate eye falls first on the bulging timber racks. Doubtless because of the tidying effort, every last scrap of wood that's been loitering in forgotten corners for months—buried under reams of old drawings, camouflaged by science-project coffee cups, or stacked five-deep against any available inch of wall space—has been rounded up. They're crammed now into deep ranks of heavy-duty shelving, thrust down into the cavities behind the sliding pull-saw, or hauled up into the rafters. Some of them are even arranged along the window frames as a sort of hidden-in-plain-sight decoration. The stuff is *everywhere*, and the more I look the more I see. And it gives me an idea, albeit a desperate one.

In any workshop there is always the conundrum, the heartbreak, of the offcuts. No matter how careful you are, you are essentially always dealing with very old slices of dried plants. Tempting as it is to believe otherwise, timber is not, as R. Bruce Hoadley has wryly noted, "a material designed to satisfy the needs of woodworkers." Almost every piece of wood you handle will be just a little too long, too short, too wide, too damaged, too misshapen, or too discolored to be used in its entirety. The grain, often obscured until the surfaces are machined—peeled away like the skins of muddy vegetables—will deceive you; your cutting list will call for awkward divisions of the board's usable length; or the wood will contort wildly the moment the blade cuts into it, rendering some of it all but useless. So, even with the best intentions, the best wood, and the best eye in the world, there will always be leftovers. Woodworkers themselves only worsen the problem, because they are all inveterate hoarders, possessing a near pathological inability to throw even the smallest or most unsalvageable pieces away. They know only too well how long it takes to make things, and just how often, when they do throw something away, it turns out to be exactly what they need the following week. Those beautiful, chunky foot-long oak butt ends with the deeply riven splits. The *almost* useful inch-wide elm strips. The tiny, but perfectly uniform, sections of rich pink American cherry. Those elegant ash pyramids somehow engineered by the chance convergence of sawcuts that would be oh-so-impossible if you were actually *trying* to make them. All are stashed away for a rainy day that will probably never come. Until eventually the workshop is so choked with the stuff that there's no room left for anything else.

Some offcuts do eventually find their way into details, and if they are large enough even whole small-scale projects. But for fine woodworking you're always trying to use timber from the same tree for all the components, if at all possible. It's not just the color and character that wants to be a good match throughout the whole piece, it's about stability too. That the wood will twist and shrink and warp the very instant you move it from a chilly workshop into somewhere warm and dry is utterly inevitable. But by using wood from the same tree—with the same moisture content, tension, and density—there is at least a chance that this movement, and the color change over time, might be reasonably uniform. Over the years we've tried selling and donating these leftovers too, and the boys would probably be more than happy to spend their time doing it. Anything to see them going to a good home. But realistically, even hefty chunks of the most exotic timbers will only fetch a few pounds each. Nothing like enough to cover their time, or the workshop overheads, to sort them, grade them, mark them up, advertise, and sell them. The numbers simply don't add up. And besides, it does have one other use. Firewood.

Kiln-dried hardwood is valuable and rare, and up until now we've really only ever burned the smallest, least useful scraps. Using them for kindling but never really as a serious fuel source. But at least this way I might save a few quid on logs for the stoves.

The first piece to hit the floor is a length of brown oak; short, broad and thick, tiger-striped and jaundiced by the "beefsteak" fungus that gives it its distinctive color. The rest of this timber went into a cabinet that tested me to my limits as a maker. A cabinet that, despite being made with just a handful of secondhand tools, was something Marisa and I stood proudly beside in the Royal Academy. Next, I drag out a gnarled and heavy block of elm. A piece I've carried with me through two workshops and ten long years. A piece I rescued from my father's stove. Then a tall stack of moisture-curled beech slabs. Canapés were served from these at our very first exhibition, before we were married, and the first time anyone really saw what Marisa and I could do. There are fine lengths of ash, square section, from the first travel trunk I ever tried to make: the first thing I built with my hands that I saw between the pages of a book, and our first real international job. There are even chunks of redwood from the construction of this workshop, and the one that came before. All of it, every last piece, connects me back to something. The memories coming thick and fast as the pile grows around my feet. But seeing the team standing idle, hearing the laughter, and knowing we just need a *little* more time, it galvanizes me—and I keep on hunting, ripping through the racks with ruthless resolve. As clouds of acrid sawdust balloon out from forgotten corners, making my sinuses burn and my eyes itch and stream, the rubbish, the useful, and the downright beautiful are tossed onto the floor. The more of this stuff I can drag out, the more time we have to find a solution. The dust cloud gets thicker, and the mound grows larger. And as it does, the boys gather softly around. They're not laughing anymore. Heartsick at the destruction, at the waste, they're eyeing the condemned with distaste.

I stomp back into the office and the middle of a conversation. Marisa puts a finger to her lips. "No, no, I totally understand, thank you . . . please do keep us in mind," she says sweetly, as I slump into my chair. Then the phone goes down with a dreadful finality and I watch as she draws a line through another name. "Well that about does it. And unless you've got any better ideas, I'm going to start calling all the makers we know, see if anyone needs a few extra pairs of hands." I feel my blood begin to boil. Pride, and yes, probably ego, scream at me not to consider it. Go cap in hand to our peers, admit to the very people whose respect we've been trying to earn for all these years that we've got *nothing*? I can't. I *won't*. But short of starting to sell off the machines, what else is there to do?

Our options all but played out, and almost sick with worry, by the end of the afternoon I am ready to give in. When out of the blue, as if cast before it on the wind, the seed of an unlikely idea flutters down before us. An idea that, despite the infertile times, threatens to take root. It appears, as all our best ideas do, in the woods.

We are scrambling up behind the workshop, dragged by the dog over twisted spruce roots on the trail of phantom deer. Brainstorming, in the Italian fashion (raised voices, suspicion, ugly vendetta threats), when Marisa reminds me that, although it has been a while, we always did pretty well out of dining tables. "A couple of good-sized dining tables would be bloody welcome right about now—tide us over, temporarily at least."

"Dining tables?" I hiss, days of bottled-up frustration just dripping from every syllable. "And where exactly do you propose we find buyers for these *dining tables*?" Realizing, even as I say it, that it's actually been several years since we've made furniture for people's homes—and stranger still, that this is the first time either of us has seriously suggested it as a possible solution. "Local galleries, trade shows, exhibitions, magazines, social media, flyers in the supermarket, wherever," Marisa says, raising those Mediterranean eyebrows but refusing to rise to the bait. And as we continue up the track, I have to admit—to myself at least—that it is an interesting thought.

Financially, the hole we've dug for ourselves is simply too deep to climb out of with bespoke one-offs—the distinctive watch-cases and elegant compact cabinets we've become known for and may be able to scrape together fast. Development will take too long, and the margins will be too slim. (These razor-thin margins, of course, are a large part of the reason we're already in so deep.) And though neither of us wants to admit it, it's unlikely we've got the time to put together the sort of batch-produced commercial project that might save us, even if we could conjure one up. But if we could somehow find a private buyer, and quickly, a good-sized dining table commission does have the potential to bring in a useful sum of money. And without the kind of excessive development that complex niche works require, it could happen relatively fast. Materials would be a big outlay. Even in its raw form, enough good-quality hardwood for an eight-seater dining table might cost anywhere up to a thousand pounds before we've even got it into the workshop. But of all the things we could make, a big table would have about the best chance to turn an honest profit.

Not enough to cover payroll by itself, but a decent start. More than one table of the same design, then we'd really be moving up in the world. By no means breathing the rarefied air of financial security, but definitely still breathing.

Why tables, and not some other piece of furniture? Well . . . not all furniture is created equal.

Chests of drawers, cabinets, and wardrobes are now so inexpensive to buy from chain stores that, even for a woodworker, it's hard to make a case for bespoke in any but the most unusually shaped space. Generally, these pieces are hidden away in bedrooms anyway, so for the most part they are constructed from engineered sheet material like medium-density fiberboard (MDF), pine, or plywood. Materials with far less character and longevity than hardwood, but materials that are quietly excused in the name of function and economy. Which is sensible and practical, even if it isn't terribly sustainable.

Hardwood coffee and side tables can find a market, but design will still take time, and the income from such small pieces wouldn't keep us going for long. Big dining tables, on the other hand, are often the focal point of a busy room, and because of their size they feel, entirely reasonably, like an investment. Their size also means the joints and components are larger, so they are often more straightforward to make. And because there generally aren't many moving parts, the construction can be relatively simple. It's not that complicated is bad—complicated is unfortunately rather my thing—but complicated takes time, and time is something we simply do not have. Perhaps better than anything else we could design fairly quickly, a good-sized table might buy us two or three weeks of solid, well-paid work for a maker.

The chairs to go with it are another matter.

A Brief Note On: Chairs

Think for a moment about the last time you leaned back deeply in a wooden chair, tilting it up onto two legs perhaps, in a manner that would induce a teacher to shout at you. Just *imagine* the forces that were at work on the wood and the joints. Tables of any variety need really only withstand their own weight, and that of the dinner service, but chairs must be built to withstand the forces of a fully grown adult lounging in them, day after day, year after year, stressing the connections and flexing the timber. To give their construction strength, then, chairs will often need to have as many, if not quite a few more, components and joints than the tables they gather around. And that's in addition to being comfortable, ergonomic, lightweight, and elegant. (Chunky chairs are not at all the thing.)

Making chairs is as much an exercise in engineering as furniture design. But no matter how fiendishly tricky they are to create, how many more parts and joints and extra costs, such as upholstery, may be involved in their manufacture, they must be economical too. Because, thanks to their scale and ubiquity, the sheer number of alternatives on the market, and the volume that often need to be bought all at once, the price of a chair is always expected to be a fraction of a good-quality table. All this is to say that although there is almost nothing a furniture maker will ever be called upon to make with the capacity to look quite so beautiful . . . it pays to be very, *very* wary of chairs.

"Well, galleries are out," I say firmly, provoking a penetrating look from Marisa. A look that says: "This is a *discussion*." But she knows as well as I do that with a gallery's markup—which could be as much as fifty percent—we'd be lucky to break even. Exhibitions and trade shows usually take a smaller percentage, and some have no commission on sales at all, but generally they don't begin until late summer, still some months away. Participation would be expensive, too, and to reach a really big audience would probably mean traveling to London. Delays and costs we can ill afford. Conscious of the power that getting our work physically in front of people has, for a few uncomfortable minutes we even consider showcasing tables in our office. Clearing out all the junk and setting up our own pop-up exhibition. But as we have neither the insurance, the parking facilities, nor the footfall, this notion is quickly relegated to the offcut pile.

Back at the workshop, offcuts are something of a theme. A dozen bulging sacks of firewood are lined up just inside the open shutter door. If they've grudgingly dispatched the last of these, I know it means there is almost nothing left for them to do. With bags gripped in either fist, I load up the back of the Land Rover with a few for the stove at home, smarting again as I think about selling it. Unlike most secondhand vehicles, old Defenders hold their value well. But we don't really own this, the bank does. With luck, we'll be able to get rid of the monthly payments, but that's about the best we can hope for.

Passing the timber racks, I can't help but notice that much of the wood I furiously dragged out seems to have been discreetly slipped back into position: one more storm weathered. A short wide length catches my eye and I haul it out. A lustrous platinum blond, blushing to apple pink with lacy fiddleback figure that almost shimmers. It's sycamore and, if not for the enormous oblong knot slashed across its middle, twisting it cruelly like a puckered scar, a very handsome piece. Like Douglas fir and Sitka spruce, sycamore is a relative newcomer to our shores—though it has been here ten times as long. Taking hold quickly and rapaciously, providing good, dense broadleaf cover in places where almost nothing else will grow; the Romans carried its seedlings with them wherever they went. It must be two years or more since a blade has touched these surfaces, and yet they are still as smooth and fine as silk. What's to become of you, I wonder, as I slide the board back beside the others. And then I wonder, with another pang of regret: what's to become of them all?

Linlithgow is an old market town, a royal burgh with a single main street, far too narrow for the volume of traffic that thunders along it every day. Parking is scarce but wardens are few, so despairing local drivers often double- or even triple-park when running errands. Their high-risk/high-reward audacity borders at times on virtuosic, and at five p.m. the madness is reaching its zenith. Cyclists and camouflaged pedestrians weave between cars. Mud-splattered four-wheel-drives, hurtling vans, lumbering lorries, and the occasional monstrous tractor vie for supremacy. And batter-crazed gourmands lurch, zombielike, into moving traffic, enticed by the aroma of fish and chips wafting across the street, abandoning vehicles half-parked on the pavement. Generally, I try to avoid it, choosing instead to make my way down the steep hill on the eastern edge of town, rolling through quiet crop fields and over the Union Canal. But finding the backroad closed for repairs, I reluctantly join the jostling ranks.

Piloting the boxy old Land Rover along the busy high street is a mixed bag, and part of the reason I love it. Heart-stopping blind-spot near misses one moment, children's flashing smiles the next. Bouncing, creaking, and roaring, and all of it conducted at a genuinely exciting fifteen miles an hour. There is little point in trying to shout over the noise of the engine. We've talked ourselves in circles in the woods anyway. So instead we just take it all in. As we inch forward, I find myself aware of hot, meaty breath dampening my cheek. Wedged in with the firewood, the dog's head is resting between the seats. She keeps a keen eye out too, ready to warn me at the slightest provocation, her barking gear positioned just millimeters from my ear.

Down a narrow alley where two men hunch over their cigarettes, past hanging baskets of bright flowers and high walls of chunky red stone, for just a moment I catch the briefest glimpse of the loch. With the big supermarkets positioned at either end of the high street, and traffic so thick, I so rarely come this way that at times I almost forget it's down there. A pretty place, Linlithgow. Business feels quiet though. Shopfront after empty shopfront slides by. Half the street seems to be packing up and moving out. The place still bustles far more than many Scottish town centers, but much of the trade has been gradually strangled, as changing shopping habits choke out one independent business after another.

The lights turn red, and I pull up, the big engine throbbing and the cab rocking from side to side. To our left and right there are more vacant properties, and virtually above us, one particularly enormous sign thrusts out, bombastically proclaiming *TO LET* in letters two feet high.

The cab rocks gently and the engine grumbles. The sign hangs in the air.

And slowly, we turn to each other with the Clint Eastwood eyes . . .

I know what you're thinking.

Part 2

Back to the Drawing Board

You can't *invent* a design. You recognize it, in
the fourth dimension. That is, with your blood
and your bones, as well as with your eyes.

—*D. H. Lawrence*

5

When my brother and I were small, and my father's colossal reserves of pent-up creative energy were still some years from a sufficiently refined outlet, we used to make detailed (and frankly dangerous) wooden weaponry together every Christmas. Naturally my father did most of the construction, but he made sure we were never idle. One way or another, our dusty little fingerprints were always on there somewhere.

It all started with a catapult, cobbled together from chunky blocks of pine and tensioned baling twine. This wasn't a Y-shaped wrist rocket, but the sort of thing that medieval armies might have rolled up to besieged city walls. Presumably we were inspired by some primary school project, or a bronzed Kirk Douglas lobbing boulders in vivid Technicolor. *Our* catapult hurled balled-up paper, or walnuts and conkers if we were left unsupervised, launching them from its tiny woven basket with thrilling velocity.

And that might have been that. Had it not been for his sons' shrieking enthusiasm, or indeed his own delight at any fresh excuse to conjure something from nothing, my father might have returned his attentions to the drains or the rats under the floor, or any one of the hundred other jobs that were forever churning around in his head. But buoyed by our reaction (and much to my mother's dismay), instead he got serious, applying the same studious care and consideration to our festive arsenal as he would to any other design problem. As my mother must have known it would, the project quickly got out of hand, ranging wide and heedless of history, scale, and child safety, and crafted from whatever leftover materials happened to be lying around. As the big day approached, my brother and I would troop out to his glacial workshop, swaddled like polar explorers and our breath like gun smoke. And with the Pogues whooping and howling on the stereo, together we'd get to work making trouble.

There were long hydraulic rams made from closely fitted sections of plastic drainpipe that, forced down hard onto the ground, launched potatoes straight *UP* with a satisfying *pffhunk*; plumber's-copper-tubing blowpipes, propelling cotton wool–flighted darts; slim-bladed redwood Arthurian swords; A-Team machine guns; squadrons of long-range folded-paper fighter planes; clothes-peg paratroopers; and a fiendish wooden crossbow that fired bolts of tightly rolled newspaper. There was even a particularly lethal longbow fashioned from a flexible length of old ash ski. Close to six feet from tip to tip, with a cherrywood grip and arrows fletched with real feathers, the longbow represented a significant step-change in quality. Unfortunately, it also represented a step-change in violence, and after it was discovered just what it could do to a straw boss at twenty paces—let alone a child's precious eyeballs—it was hastily removed and unstrung before one of us was mortally wounded.

We employed these "toys" in gleeful bombardment of the tattered paper angel that sat atop the Christmas tree. A campaign that required power as well as accuracy, because my father always came home with something monstrous, and suspiciously fresh, sagging from the roof of the car. Squeezing the branches through the back door, as damp needles shed onto the carpet in their millions and the fresh clean scent of the forest filled the air, my brother and I would survey it carefully, figuring trajectories and range.

But it wasn't just the merry devilment we looked forward to. That time of year always meant a lot to my brother and me because, for much of the rest of it, we saw our father only fleetingly. And when we did it invariably meant that forced labor wasn't far behind. It wasn't that he was absent or inattentive, he was always just tremendously busy. It was not at all unusual for him to be up and dressed well before dawn, already elbow-deep in some project or another in his workshop. Dragging the nails from salvaged timber, scraping ancient varnish from reclaimed pieces of parquet flooring, forming up leadwork for the roof, or chipping the mortar from truckloads of secondhand bricks. Cramming in a couple of hours of work before the sizzle of butcher's bacon drew him back into the kitchen. Breakfast wolfed, he'd disappear to his day job as a landscape architect, leaving for "the office" before we were even off to school. In the evenings his paperwork usually followed him home. And though dinner

was always a family affair, and we never went without our bed-
time stories—delivered in a rich, tobacco-soaked baritone that
made his villains leap menacingly from the page—he spent every
other waking moment progressing something he called "the war
effort." Well into the wee hours, his clipboard would be resting
on his knee, a sweet haze of Bergerac smoke coloring the air as
he worked problems into submission with his trusty blue pencils.
Or else he'd be back out in the workshop, fixing or improving
or building or whittling. Hammering away until I really don't
know when. But Christmas was different. At Christmas *everything* stopped, and for a brief tinsel-gilded moment we had his
attention. And I mention all this because it was at Christmas that
it happened.

My father had just turned forty, the same age that I am now.
The decorations were about to go up and the weaponry wheeled
out, the good potatoes hidden away by my mother. When
abruptly he wasn't going into the office anymore. Redundant is
never a pleasant word. No matter the time of year, the tongue
spits it out with the same clucking distaste. The vagaries of running a small business seldom make allowances for the calendar
though, and the firm my father worked for simply ran out of
work. The timing was bad, that was all. But the financial implications for my parents were dire.

"We were so *poor*!" as my father often likes to exclaim. And I
can believe it. After my sister was born and there were three of us
to wrangle, my mother had largely stepped back from full-time
teaching work, leaving a family of five, two ravening collies, and

the never-ending costs of the house renovation almost entirely reliant on the income from his job. Using salvaged materials, and working singlehandedly, would have helped keep costs to a bare minimum, but even so, more than a decade spent restoring such a ruinous farmhouse must have drained away every spare penny. And plenty of it was still only half-finished, or else hacked together with whatever could be begged, borrowed, or convinced to make do. The roof leaked in a dozen places, the stove was on its last legs, and the car ran on prayers. With sheaves of bills bursting from every drawer and never enough hours in the day to fix the next broken thing, theirs was a precariously hand-to-mouth existence, achingly familiar to most self-builders.

We weren't sat down and told; I don't think it was even mentioned to the children. At the time, that sort of thing went considerably beyond our pay grade. And even if my father had seemed a trifle more frazzled or detached than we'd come to expect over the holidays, we were all so inured to him looking strained and overworked that it would barely have registered. They never raised their voices though. In fact, unless there was a car and a roadmap involved, I don't remember hearing my parents argue once throughout my childhood. The two of them had been walking a financial knife-edge for a long time, they were old hands and bore their anxiety better than most. But with no savings to fall back on, the costs of a family Christmas biting hard, and now without a steady income, behind closed doors there can't have been much in the way of holiday cheer.

The need to earn was urgent, so in the short term at least, there simply wasn't time for my father to go out looking for another professional job. But what he did know, what he had been doing on the side for years, was making things with his hands. He could do *that* straight away. So after what was doubtless a frantic, fraught, and whiskey-fueled few days, with the bank account close to empty and a family of five to support, he made a decision. Little knowing that it would go on to change and forever entwine both our lives. On New Year's Day 1995, he hurried out to his workshop, hunted around for scrap timber, and set about building his first serious piece of wooden furniture, hoping he might be able to sell it. Because he could. And because he had to do something.

Miracles aside, it's simple math. Another month, two at the absolute outside, and we're finished. The last of the overdraft will fritter away to nothing, distant alarm bells will sound, and the bank will come looking for its money. I can't even bear to *think* the word. Bankruptcy means the boys will lose their jobs, it means the workshop and everything we've worked for over a decade to build will be stripped for parts and auctioned off, it means that Marisa and I will still have our little flat to skulk back to and lick our wounds, but it means we will have failed. And failure, as my father so often likes to remind me, is not an option.

Just suppose, then, that we really did make a few big tables. Tried to sell them directly, to local customers. For the time being, we still have a workshop, tools, and a team of skilled makers standing idle. If we could move fast enough, and produce work that was desirable enough, to rustle up some quick sales, we might just be able to keep our heads above water. At least until something more substantial could be developed with a serious commercial client. It would be a big gamble, and we're under no illusions that it will be easy. This is a world we left behind a long time ago for a lot of very good reasons. At the premium end of the market there is plenty of competition from more established makers and manufacturers, and at the more affordable end there are almost countless alternatives. And we've been hidden away for years. Trying to find new customers fast and, more to the point, getting them to part with the sort of money that finely crafted furniture demands, would require more than hard work; it would require an enormous slice of luck. But making furniture speculatively would put us back in charge of our fates, and there is an attractive simplicity, even a certain swashbuckling romance, to the idea of going down swinging.

There is the glaring problem of seed money to consider, of course. Even if we could design something quickly, track down a few new customers, somehow make and sell enough mystery tables to keep us afloat, we couldn't do it instantly. Months of wages and workshop rent would still need to be paid, on top of expensive materials and perhaps even some basic marketing. And if we actually wanted to try and get this work physically *in front* of people, we'd need to scrape together enough for a trade show or the first few months of rent on a retail premises as well. The business is tapped out, which really only leaves one option.

Marisa and I have some savings put by. It's not much, but it's everything we have. And if we're careful, it might just be enough to get us started. We're all too aware we could just be throwing good money after bad, but factoring in the perilous depths of our debt, the urgent need for work, and the particular skill set of our team—not to mention the prickly matter of our pride—it's the best we can come up with. A bad plan is better than no plan at all. *Anything* is better than waiting for the phone to ring.

"Are you even listening to me?" Marisa says, putting a hand tenderly on my arm, giving it a squeeze. "When you speak to people, you have to *try* to say something nice. People like that."

Her tone is light and humorous, but it is carefully modulated, and there is genuine anxiety behind it. It's the way she talks to the dog when the dog is about to eat something dreadful. I can feel my hackles rising, but before I can bark back, she's blown me a kiss and slid from the cab. "Forty minutes, along at the cross," she shouts over her shoulder, smiling, disappearing toward the high street. Through the passenger window I watch her go. That unmistakable, bouncing, long-legged stride that, like her sense of adventure, is so very reminiscent of her father's.

Locking up, I catch sight of my reflection in the mirror, and for a fleeting moment it is my own father looking back. He lurks in the lines and shadows, the furrow of the brow, the rigid set of the jaw. With effort, I try to engineer a smile. Something nice . . . I'm sure I can manage that.

The first property is close, near the supermarket, so I suppose there would be plenty of foot traffic. My own feet soon carry me there and, trying not to look too conspicuous, I peer inside. Beyond the dusty plate glass, it's a smallish open-plan space. A single room that has clearly been long empty, and by the looks of it hastily vacated, but with plenty of natural light. Off to my left, every few seconds I can hear the swishing of a vehicle. The main road is not particularly big or fast, but it is busy, and so close by that anything on display in the window would be seen by hundreds of passing drivers every day. Tired though. Picking at peeling paint, wondering at drainpipes that appear to go nowhere, fingering decaying woodwork that my father would already have prison-shanked with the point of his knife, I try to shut out the world around me. I try to focus. I try to see it.

A hand-painted sign swings gently above the door, its neat gold lettering neither traditional nor contemporary, but timeless. The walls are a pale cream, no . . . a rich card-room green, complementing the finely made hardwood joinery details. The space is tastefully, warmly lit. Aspirational, but comfortable. Erudite, design-savvy customers are crowded around a big, beautifully crafted wooden table, beneath framed prints of the furniture being handmade. Wadded fistfuls of cash are being thrust wildly in my direction, but I am playing it cool. Sipping the tiniest of coffees, with classical piano wafting from hidden speakers, I am addressing the baying horde from the safety of the counter. "Stay calm," I'm saying, over the rim of my tiny cup. "There's plenty for everyone." Flashbulbs pop and the till rings violently. And as a dozen excited voices clamor for my attention . . .

A car door slams, and the visions are snatched away, and instantly the property is empty and unloved once more. Brushing the paint flakes from my hands, I take one last look and hurry off, following the road toward the high street.

They say location is everything, but we ruled out Scotland's most famous city in just a few minutes. Edinburgh is large and wealthy, and undeniably handsome—not to mention a tourist mecca. But there are really only a few areas that would attract the right sort of regular walk-in trade, and on closer inspection they are all well beyond our means. (And how many tourists are realistically going to ship an eight-foot dining table all the way home?) Besides which, even if the rents hadn't been too high, and the charming historical properties rather too small, the time and money involved in traveling regularly to the capital would kill us. Do you have any idea what it costs to park in Stockbridge, Newington, or Bruntsfield, for even an hour?

What did get our attention, though—what has us out here at seven o'clock in the morning peering speculatively through windows—was the surprising discovery that rental costs in a decent-sized property in Linlithgow might just be within our reach. In fact a full *year* in the sorts of empty properties that seem to abound here on the high street would cost us about the same as three days withering under striplights at a design trade show in London or Glasgow. Linlithgow is a prosperous place, and Edinburgh is only twenty minutes away by train. Renting something here would mean no extra travel, no long months of covering wages or nail-biting delays and, on the high street at least, no competition.

Which brings us to the proposition.

What if we could take something small and manageable on our doorstep, roll up our sleeves, and turn it into the sort of high-end furniture store you might find in London, Milan, or Copenhagen? What if we could create the sort of iconic, handcrafted wooden furniture that a steady stream of excited local customers would be simply unable to resist? That would draw people in from Edinburgh and Glasgow—from all over Scotland—and *fast*. Tables to start with, but desks, cabinets, and wooden accessories too. Create a destination. Fill the coffers. Save the day.

Most of the buildings on the high street are two-story affairs, soot-blackened or pastel-painted stone, with flats above and businesses below. Creams and pinks, greens and baby blues, under roofs of pitched gray slate. I take in a pretty bookshop, a barber, a big chain chemist, an optician, and a baker. At this hour, only the barbers seem to be stirring. Their candy-striped poles revolve optimistically as they vie for tidbits of early scissor work. Every fifty yards or so, something else lies vacant: the ghostly remains of a fishmonger, a newsagent, a butcher, a bank. Standing out among the living like dead teeth. Once upon a time I suppose someone else's hopes and dreams lived inside those walls. But not anymore.

Outside an estate agent's window, I pause. Always curious to see what a quarter-million buys you in this neck of the woods these days. Not much in the way of individuality, that's for sure. Does everyone *really* want to live in the same ugly identikit building as everyone else, or is there just no choice? They're still designing them and throwing them up in their thousands all over the country, so there must be a reason. Perhaps there is something about being packed in close, surrounded by shops and traffic, the irresistible allure of amenities that I'm missing? Linlithgow is one of the most expensive places to buy in Scotland, so none of the properties is cheap, but to my eye at least, not one has even a scrap of character. Marisa is probably right: the only way we will ever find, and certainly afford, something out of the ordinary will be to build it ourselves.

Up ahead, I spot a big, squarish, good-looking man lolling on a windowsill. Revolving pole, empty chairs, geometrically razored hair . . . this might be my chance to strike up a conversation. To inquire about life and trade on the high street. To ask about the things he wishes he'd known when it was *his* pen poised above the lease. To pan for nuggets of advice. Perhaps even to say something nice.

Sensing me approach, the big man glances up from his phone, but when I open my mouth to speak, nothing comes out. My voice just cowers in my throat. How long has it actually been since I talked to someone outside work? Since I struck up and held a conversation about anything other than the finer points of luxury woodwork?

This sort of thing is so easy for Marisa. Enjoyable, even. It's not just looking through windows and accosting strangers (what she would probably call "making friends"), it's nerve. From the moment we met, I've marveled at it. She's one of those rare people who doesn't just talk about things, she actually gets on and does them. Formulate a plan, act on it. No fucking around. She was born to it of course; the branches of her family tree fairly bristle with garrulous entrepreneurs. Whenever there's something challenging to be done, I can almost hear Luigi and Bobby and Marco whispering in her ear as her soul froths into action like a bottle of podium champagne.

When the moment finally grinds past, and the big man has looked back down at his phone, I shuffle on with my head down. And the echoing of my bootheels on the flagstones sounds a lot like failure.

The second property on my list is smaller than the first, but it is certainly much more interesting. Its poky mullioned windows are grilled with stout iron bars, set deeply into walls of coarse blocky stone, giving it the look and feel of a castle keep. It must be tremendously old, and in stark contrast to the homes in the estate agent's window it virtually drips with character. But though it isn't *completely* subterranean, the heavily studded door is so low to the ground that I'd have to stoop to get through it. Furniture would either have to be made in miniature, or else very cleverly designed for us even to get it inside. So, hastily, I move on.

All around me, the world is slowly waking up. Commuters trudge glumly toward trains, yawning workmen ready their traffic cones, neon joggers huff and puff. Quickening my steps, I find the next place less than a hundred yards farther up, positioned squarely in front of the pedestrian crossing, almost directly opposite the hidden entrance to the railway station. It takes me a beat to realize where I am, but the chirping of the crossing tips me off. Forty-eight hours ago, we were sitting together at these very traffic lights as an improbable escape plan was beginning to take shape.

Despite its gaudy electric blue exterior, there is plenty to like about the building. It's a good size, up at ground level, and it feels more modern than medieval. Beneath the years of thickly slathered masonry paint and exhaust fume grime, the stonework looks carefully cut and dressed. There is a traditional wooden signboard above the door, framed with a timber molding, stretching the full width of the property. And in part because of the crossing, the pavement outside is far broader than much of the rest of the street. Plenty of space to linger beside the expansive glass frontage. Checking that I am not being watched, I cup my hands against the glass and squint into the gloom.

The floorboards are grained to look like timber, but their flat gray tone and uniform vinyl sheen is altogether too perfect to be natural. Remarkable, that even just a photograph of wood, no matter the substrate, can do so much to elevate a humble plastic floor. Fitting those laminate boards will have been an afternoon's easy work for somebody, where a real hardwood floor—left to season in the space for a couple of weeks, cut and wedged tight to the next board's grooves, nailed and punched through the tongues to hide the fixings and finished with oil or varnish— might have taken a skilled joiner the better part of a week to lay neatly. The plasterwork too looks crisp, seams and skirting caulked and precise. All freshly painted in a blinding mint-imperial white. Dad's favorite.

The space itself is deeper than it is wide. Doglegged around a boxy radiator on the left but straight-walled on the right, with a single door to the rear. A door I know from the particulars leads on to a washroom, and likely a back entrance. Without keys and my tape measure I can't be certain, but I'm confident we'd fit a big table along that right-hand wall, with plenty of room left over for smaller pieces. There's an alcove with some shelves, and a deep windowsill just beneath my nose—more of a window seat really—where even quite substantial objects could be displayed for all to see. Once again, I muster the forces of my imagination: *the salivating, design-savvy customers, the finely crafted hardwoods, the softly tinkling classical piano* . . . the jolting shock of the hand that claps me on the shoulder is so surprising that it not only snaps me out of my reverie but sends my flinching forehead bouncing off the glass.

Reverberations still hang dully in the air as I turn, the hot flush of embarrassment coloring my cheeks, expecting to find my wife doubled over, wearing an expression far closer to glee than sympathy. Her childlike delight tempered only very slightly by concern for my well-being. Except it's not my cackling wife. Far from it. Instead, I find myself face to face with the man from the windowsill, the big man I took for a barber. He looks jumpy, and *his* face (which is anything but amused) is close enough to smell his aftershave. Pointing first at the empty property, then at me, he slowly shakes his perfectly manicured head and pleads bleakly: "*Please* . . . not another barber."

"Amazing!" Marisa says, taking in the smudged imprint of my forehead still clearly visible in the thickly rimed dust, barely keeping it together. Tracing the outline with the tip of an elegant finger, and pulling out her phone to capture the moment, she dissolves completely into hysterics as I drag her away.

For the past half an hour I have been hustling up one side of the high street and back down the other, studiously avoiding any further eye contact and very much on my guard. Thirty minutes isn't long, but with little more than half a mile of real estate cutting an almost dead straight line through the middle of town, it's been more than enough for some first impressions. I've been struck by just how different the town feels on foot. Noticing tiny details, things you never really see from the road. The care and personality that's obvious in some of the businesses, with friendly handwritten signs and vibrant, thoughtful displays. The sun-bleached goods and flyblown neglect that's all too clear in others. It can't be easy for any of them. After two days crunching numbers, I've got a fair idea of the rental fees they will all need to find. Electricity, water, insurance, taxes, wages—those rarely stray too far from my mind. Month after month, some of these places are keeping the doors open and the lights on, and they're doing it a cup of coffee at a time. More than that though, perhaps more than anything, I've noticed the growing, slightly shameful, sense of being a stranger in the town one thinks of as home.

Hurrying back toward the cross with an eye on the clock, even after seeing half a dozen more potential properties, there was really only one place standing out in my mind. Nothing else I'd seen had come close. Small enough to be affordable, but roomy enough for one or two pieces of large-scale furniture.

Freshly decorated and flooded with natural light, and conveniently positioned for foot traffic coming off the train. It comes as no surprise that Marisa has also recognized its potential. Long before my forehead left its smudged imprint on the glass, in fact. And even if her eyes are now filled with what look suspiciously like tears of laughter, she can see it . . . just as clearly as I can.

"Come on, you," I say, threading my arm through hers and leading her away from the empty property, crossing the road toward the station to put her on a train to Glasgow. Across the street, for a moment we look back, and I know we are both thinking about the same things. The stone walls, the wooden signboard, the grand window, and the light-filled interior. In our heads we are already designing it all, imagining the kind of environment we could create—the objects we could fill it with. The potential. Marisa squeezes my hand, and for the first time in days I feel a tingle of hope.

And even a little hope goes a long way.

6

The workshop is unusually quiet when I arrive. For the next hour at least, it's just me and the dog. I can hear her out in the yard. The curiously affronted tone of bark that can only mean she's chasing horntails again—the huge, striped, wood-boring wasps that make her so unaccountably angry. Even over the clatter of the shutter door running up through its cogs, I catch the sound of her jaws gnashing together like a rat trap. Lucky for her that horntails aren't nearly as dangerous as they look.

Before I dive back into the excruciating business of touting for work: coffee. Medically required. Anything to delay the desolation of the inbox refresh. Standing in the kitchen door, as the dark liquid drips through the filter and the aroma fills the air, I notice the oak boards from Ben's yard. Too heavy to haul up into the rafters without a good deal of trouble, they are still stood upright where the boys have left them. The dirty half-dozen leans against the wall, towering above a gang of short, tough-looking locals. Sycamore, elm, oak, and ash: the usual suspects. I'm tickled to see that even in such rough company, Ben's oak stands apart.

Like their little brothers, these midsized offcuts soon build up. Generally, they are between waist and chest height, of varying widths and thicknesses. Still too small for most jobs but, even in desperate times, far too valuable to chop up and burn. There are plenty of reasons that offcuts like these might find themselves homeless. For the native timbers, though, it is usually a surplus of character that keeps them out in the cold.

Trees have a hard time growing to maturity in Scotland. Struggling against bitter winters, scouring winds, exposed ground, and peaty, acidic soil. Limbs can be lost to the elements, torn off by gales, or weighed down to the breaking point by snow and ice. Roots must cling on for dear life, like desperate bony hands clawing at steep valleys and pitiless rock. It's demanding conditions like these that make the trees grow far more slowly than those that live in milder, more temperate environments. And just like with people, whether they are immediately obvious or not, these struggles always leave their marks. Rejected native offcuts are often so scarred and deformed, so garishly tattooed with knots and mineral streaks, or so shot through with deep fissures and *spalting*—the insidious, often beautiful gray track marks where fungus has made a meal of them—that they may never find a good home.

The reverse can be true too. Trees that have had it too easy can produce timber that has very little character. And though all hardwood is beautiful in its own way, to my eye the color and grain feature in timber imported from countries with less extreme climates can feel a little bland, even lazy, by comparison. But because it's bigger and cleaner, it's better suited for the sorts of commercial projects we build here, where stability and uniformity (and paperwork) are key. Rarely, though, does it have the same appeal as that which has fought for every inch.

While I am peering up into the rafters—the deep, broad, seldom-visited space in the beams above the kitchen and washroom where the longer lengths are kept (what Peter Temple's cabinetmaking lawyer Jack Irish would probably have called "*The Bank*"), I notice another reason the oak boards haven't found their way up there: there isn't much room. Leaving the coffee to brew, I drag over the aluminum roofing ladders, clambering up until I can lean my head and shoulders into the shadows. It's restrictive, awkward, and treacherous underfoot. But it's dry and warm and out of the way, built with doubled-up posts and beams to withstand the immense accumulated weight. The perfect place for timber to rest and continue to season. And, evidently, to hide.

Over to one side, where they are easiest to get at, half a dozen American oak and white ash boards are neatly stacked. Similarly sized, square-edged and consistent. Leftovers from our most recent jobs. With here and there a single slab of something older and more unusual from Africa or America. Black walnut, cherry, iroko, even purpleheart: the remarkable, iron-hard South American timber with its vibrant violet heartwood. Farther toward the back, though, where they are harder to reach, most of the boards look local.

It's risky to pull anything out alone. It wouldn't be the first time I'd lost my balance, too absorbed in the hunt, and I'm getting too old for leaping backward from ladders. Until the boys arrive, I can do little more—safely, anyway—than flip and investigate those nearest the surface. As I try not to crush my fingers—and to resist the temptation to shuffle the ladders along while I am still standing on them—I disturb tipsy-looking wasps and seams of ancient powdery sawdust. But even without hauling it all out, what I can see from here is encouraging. Many are live-edged, still bearing the bark and the contoured shape of the tree, and no two are quite the same. Some are obscure, wildly figured rejects, others impossibly wide monsters that time and again I couldn't rip down in good conscience. And in among it all is the timber-yard treasure: the boards I could not stand to leave behind but have never quite found a use for. Maple, sycamore, oak, olive-streaked ash, and elm. For nearly ten years this wood has been accumulating. A piece here, a piece there. The provincial and the exotic, comfortably coexisting. Some of it half-forgotten. And a lot more of it than I realized.

Climbing back down, blinking the dust from my eyes, I notice something else. Something short and wide, tucked in behind a clutch of longer offcuts. The neat flat-cut edge of its end-grain revealing the gently arcing lines of the tree's growth rings. Dark reddish brown, like burnt umber, or strong tea. With my feet now safely on solid ground, I drag away the timber that has been concealing it. It is a broad piece of one-inch elm, close to a meter long, with just a slight cupping to its width. Fine close grain tumbles down the board's length. And a tracery of spectral green streaks across it, like the northern lights. Toward the foot of the board, things become uglier. The tissue here is cracked and split, growing disoriented and deformed at one edge, where a frayed and melon-sized swelling flares out—as if it has been cruelly mashed with a meat hammer.

A burr begins as a mutation; a single bud gone haywire, often the result of infection, or some kind of trauma. Contorting, growing, twisting and compacting on the side of a tree, sometimes for hundreds of years, but never doing it any real harm. You've probably seen these great knobbly lumps bulging from trunks, perhaps never realizing that beneath the tightly knotted cauliflower-like surface, a myriad of swirling, almost impossibly beautiful clusters are hiding. That to some, what you are looking at is as rare and prized as a woodland truffle.

From the benchroom I hear the telephone's strange robotic monotone announcing Marisa's name. I catch it moments before the answerphone kicks in. She's still en route to college, and the station's garbled announcements are a harsh wall of sound in the background. Nothing, though, can disguise the current of excitement in her voice. "It's still available. Move-in ready. I spoke to the owner, got good vibes. He's showing us around himself—*tonight!*" Traffic noise, rustling pauses, and heel strikes tell me she's on the street now and hurrying, switching the phone from ear to ear to free up her hands. "I've been redoing the maths. God, I love a fucking spreadsheet," she says, and I can almost see the grin on her face. I keep quiet because I know that in a moment there will be another train to catch, and she will have to go. "The more I look at it," she goes on, winding up for the big finish, "the more I think we could really fucking do this!"

Click.

Even in hard times, this wellspring of optimism always manages to find its way to the surface. Its source is a mystery to me, but it's impossible not to be lifted by it. Her words charge me with energy, and once again I am seeing the interior, the faint outlines of the furniture beginning to take shape, our name being painted above the door. Hanging up the phone, I grin to myself as I head back toward the kitchen, and almost reflexively, I lift out the elm board.

Some large workshops have individual heavy-duty machines for surfacing and thicknessing: early-stage jobs both integral to the business of woodwork. But most modest operations (like ours) rely on a single combination machine—taking up less space and halving the costs. With a bit of clever hinging, a planer like this can skim the surfaces of rough-sawn timber flat, then transform to reduce its thickness and width very accurately. For scale, imagine three or four washing machines strapped together lengthwise. For volume and energy, imagine three or four hundred banging away on their spin cycles. With added razor blades.

At any planer's heart is a rotating metal cylinder—the cutter block—driven by a powerful motor and lipped with a series of long, thin, horribly sharp blades, called *knives.* Modern knives are usually made of high-speed steel (HSS); our planer has three of them, and moments from now they will all be spinning toward my hands a hundred times every second. Pulling on thin rubberized gloves for grip, safety glasses, and ear defenders, I throw the main breaker, fire up the whooshing dust extractor, and push the big green button. The planer's motor muscles into life with bone-crushing authority. Filling me, as it always does, with a shiver of dread.

Using a control lever, I carefully align the smooth cast-iron tables, subtly altering the levels and the gap between the two to reveal just the tiniest fraction of the speed-blurred knives. Even from two feet away, I can feel the air moving and the power vibrating up through the soles of my boots. Brushing off the grit and sawdust that has accumulated on the board, I examine its edges until I can discern the grain's direction. I want to plane *with*, rather than against the grain. Like stroking a dog's coat toward its tail.

Passing the board over the surface for the first time, I can feel the knives tearing into the fibers, gripping and biting, sending tightly curled chips hurtling through the extractor hose and into the collection bag's swirling maelstrom. A second pass, then a third, and a glance at the board's underside reveals a pair of inch-wide ribbons. Bright, clean, red-brown timber out at the edges, where the beginnings of a flat surface are starting to emerge. On the fourth pass the planer's pitch drops as the board flattens and the strips become wider, the motor straining to chew through more and more wood. Now I too must work harder, pressing down and pushing with greater force to keep the board and the knives from chattering together and trying to throw me off. With difficulty, I will myself not to think about the mere inch of wood that's standing between my hands and a brand-new career, and find myself thinking: how long has it actually been since I did this?

It's more than just a bit of rust making me jumpy. When I was a teenager, a machine just like this one tore itself to pieces, right in front of me—and things like that have a way of staying with you. The planer was about this size, but of a far greater vintage, with none of today's standard safety equipment. Cast-iron through and through, weighing half a ton at least. My father's, of course. The bite I was trying to take might have been too big, or a tough old knot might have jarred something loose. It's possible I just mis-tightened one of the knives' securing bolts. Too late now to ever know for sure, but it was probably my own fault. These things usually are. Whatever the reason, a knife slipped from the cutter block just a little, but it was enough. In a fraction of a second, the sharp edge caught the blunt iron lip of the out-table with extraordinary violence, again and again and again.

On any other day I'd have been staring down the barrel—point-blank range, or near enough to make no difference—and would have caught the full force of all that splintering metal in my upper body. This planer had no dust extraction, and with its feed rollers getting regularly jammed with shavings, nine times out of ten I'd have been dragging the boards through, as my father checked and fed them in. All the time with those terrible knives spinning toward me in a choking shower of chips and dust. But by chance I was working alone, feeding the timber into the maw myself when it happened. This meant the motor was hurling the danger away from me, instead of straight at me. So I was afforded the luxury of watching, rather than actively participating.

The next clear memory I have is being found outside by my

mother, a cigarette trembling between my fingers, mumbling about how upset dad was going to be—how much work we still had to do. And you know, I think every woodworker could probably tell you a story a bit like that, and I'd be willing to bet they were all a lot more careful afterward. That these things can bite is important to remember. It was certainly a lesson that the pale shaking lad sobbing into his mother's shoulder wouldn't soon forget.

The planing job doesn't take long, and it's with a sigh of genuine relief that I shut down the machine. With the motor's drone still ringing in my ears, I turn the newly exposed surfaces over and over in my hands. Pure milk chocolate. This, for me, is one of the most pleasurable moments in woodwork. Revealing the unique tones, shapes, and smells for the very first time in a clean, freshly milled piece of timber. A particular blend of characteristics that no one else has experienced before. Not for long, though, I think to myself, as I pull off my gloves to run my fingers over the swirling grain. We might finally have found you a home. All of you.

It takes me a while, but I finally track down the next things I'll need. Half-forgotten on a hook by the back door are dozens of slim, contoured templates. More than a decade's worth, strung together on a wire hoop like an enormous set of jailer's keys. They are thick with dust. They haven't been used for a *very* long time. I learned from my father to make and work from templates like these. Transposing the profile of each furniture component from full-scale drawings and shaping them in MDF. A material that works especially well for templates because it's cheap, thin, very flat, and grainless—so it can be shaped far more freely than real wood. Tailors do much the same thing with bespoke cloth suits: tracing and cutting the garment's individual parts using paper patterns. But instead of shears and fabric we use saws, bearing-guided profile cutters, and timber.

Using two or three of the rounded templates, and a long steel straightedge, I mark out the basic shape I'm thinking of. Sketching with a soft pencil directly onto a small piece of MDF. The profile I draw out, that of a small handheld cutting board or serving platter, is far too modest for sawing bread or carving meat, but it's perfect for little bites. Perfect, too, for little offcuts.

Having recently dispatched so many gnarly scraps of hardwood, the band saw's slim, strap-like blade is dreadfully blunt. Many of its teeth have been worn almost flat by dense balks of oak and elm, and probably the odd forgotten screw or nail. But I have no patience for changing it now. The boys will be here soon, and I'd rather they didn't see me stumbling over this. Luckily, the MDF is little more than densely compacted cardboard, and in just a few moments the template's basic profile appears. Finding that in my haste I am almost running around the workshop, I move swiftly to the sanding machine, and it doesn't take me long to pare it back until it sweetly meets the pencil lines.

Hacking out the rough forms in elm is far more difficult. The blade's dull edge screams and smokes in the cuts. But the wood is thin and dry and stable, so there is no real tension to contend with. And soon I have half a dozen blanks ready to be profiled. Because the boards are so small, though, I can't secure the template down with clamps to finalize the shapes mechanically. I won't be able to move the router—a handheld machine with a small exposed vertical cutter block, similar to the planer's—without banging into them. So instead, I resort to sticking the template and the elm together with spots of double-sided tape. Firming up the bonds with clamps but taking care not to overdo it. Knowing from experience that if I use too much, I'll never get them apart. I'm rushing again, making clumsy mistakes, and I'm far more out of practice than I realized. But seeing something come together, even something so small and simple as this—feeling the machines alive in my hands, and feeling useful for a change . . . I've missed it.

When Andrew clacks into the workshop, it's his cycling shoes that give him away. Woodshavings litter the floor around me, and my forearms are warm and faintly damp where a cloying layer of fresh sawdust still clings to them. The dust is in my hair and eyelashes, up my nose and in the air around me. It has a bitter, faintly peppery taste. But three small, smoothly shaped cutting boards are profiled on the bench. I have rounded over their edges and drilled neat holes for leather hanging loops in their corners. The boards must still be hand-sanded, fire-branded with the workshop's name, and sealed with food-safe oil, but they are at least three-quarters finished.

"You . . . are a filth *wizard*," Andrew says, cradling a cup of coffee, surveying the mess covering the floor, the bench, me. "Pull all the really short lengths of elm you can find," I say, removing my ear defenders and rubbing the dust from my lashes, feeling it flutter into my eyes. "Oak, beech, and maple, even ash if it's got olive heartwood. Nothing from up in the rafters, nothing really long or wide, but anything under a couple of feet that's interesting. Anything with character."

"Chopping boards?" he says, taking in the work on the bench and raising his eyebrows quizzically. "Chopping boards . . . for starters," I confirm, handing him the template. Immeasurably relieved that he has decided not to question my motives too closely. And this man used to safe-cracking complex cabinetry problems, to holding his breath as irreplaceable components of engineered metal, leather, crystal, gold, and glass are delicately combined into experimental one-off wooden artworks, he just nods thoughtfully, smiles, and sets down his coffee. Then, perhaps just happy to be making something at last, he raises both hands into the air, takes a deep breath, and belts out: "*Chopping boards it is!*"

A Brief Note On: Health and Safety

Using nothing more than good old-fashioned Scottish muscle, legendary naturalist, author, and beard enthusiast John Muir climbed high into the canopy of a mighty Douglas fir during a Sierra Nevada storm to, in his own words, "get my ear close to the Aeolian music of its topmost needles." The year was 1874 and the great man was (as usual) *very* excited about nature. As the storm raged on, he clung fast to the branches, settling into his front-row seat to ride out the tempest. Writing in *The Mountains of California*, he later noted that "never before did I enjoy so noble an exhilaration in motion." What he did not document, at least not in this account, was whether he also found himself gripped by the peculiar urge to hurl himself from the top of that great swaying tree. But I wouldn't be surprised.

Most commonly experienced at the tops of high buildings, cliffs, bridges, and ravines, *l'appel du vide*—the call of the void—the feeling that you should, nay, you *must* do the thing that horrifies you most, is one of the body's more eccentric warning systems. But we have probably all played out one scenario or another whenever real danger is close at hand. Jamming over the steering wheel on the motorway, pulling the plane's exit lever, stepping in front of the hurtling bus. It's not suicidal, at least not for most people. It's perfectly rational behavior.

These snuff films screened by our minds are designed, presumably, to scare us straight. Cognition using fear and imagination to crank up the volume on our vigilance. Such visions often occur in the workshop too, as I'm sure they do in any environment where perilous hazards are faced day in, day out, and where there is a heightened risk of becoming blasé. I can't imagine anyone regularly using a planer and not closely considering the implications of sticking their fingers in there (and in case you've ever wondered, nail guns really do *shoot* nails).

If you've been at it for a while, there may even be old classics. Vivid, toe-curling reimaginings that, unpleasant as they are, never get any less important to watch. In fact if anything they only become more valuable as time goes on, as the tools are taken more and more for granted. Coincidentally, for both my father and me these visions revolve around the band saw: a quiet, rather innocuous-looking machine that appears strangely motionless when running at full speed. And perhaps it is this illusion of harmlessness that means the warnings must be extra potent. My father's is simple, no frills: whipping his hand through the blade—*zzzzip*—and watching his fingers scatter onto the floor. And he really *wants* to do it. You have to, you see. If you don't believe it, it won't frighten you enough.

The manic film director in my head has the same goal in mind—safety—but he's cooked up something flashier, and considerably more final for me. More often than I'd like to admit, when I see a band saw running, I feel a desperate and terrible impulse to sprint in from a distance, leap headfirst to meet the blade fully horizontal, and split myself right down the middle.

The first time I contemplated this seriously, I was working in a timber yard, a dozen miles outside Hobart, Tasmania. The yard's band saw was a colossal thing, and despite being half-buried in a deep pit, it still towered overhead. Its blades were fully five inches across, with teeth like a bull shark's. Struck by its novelty, and clearly scared rigid, I made the mistake of describing this urge in fairly graphic detail, more or less as it occurred to me. Adding just for fun that, if it really was to be the last hurrah, ideally I'd be wearing a cape. My colleague—a strapping, humorless local whom I had only met a few hours earlier—looked at me for a long, long time. "Never occurred to you to do something like that?" I asked, earnestly. "My father even has a name for it. He calls it *Machine Tool Vertigo*."

7

"This stuff builds up so fast," Graham says, as curling local newsletters and takeaway flyers gather under the door. Stepping over the blizzard of junk mail, we follow him inside, where the smell of freshly painted walls hangs thickly in the air and the flustered alarm chirps in distress. Sixtyish, suave and tennis-court-trim, with close-cropped gray hair and a conspicuous suntan, I can't help feeling that Graham is a man whose shoulders are screaming out for a sweater. But he seems friendly, good-humored, and reasonably down to earth. And a good thing too, I think, as he stoops to punch in the code. You can't have too much of that in a landlord.

"Utility and washroom through the back, state-of-the-art alarm system, all just been redone," he says, displaying the kind of watch that's meant to be admired as he gestures around. Used as I am to the rough timber cladding of the workshop, the coarse brick and chipped, chalky plaster of our tired 1960s flat, the finishes strike me as dazzlingly neat. The gray, wood-effect flooring is carefully laid, free from telltale paint splatters despite its gleaming white skirting boards. There are no cobwebs or careless brush-strokes, even high in the hard-to-reach seams of its smooth white walls. And what little carpentry there is—doors, architraves, and simple plywood shelves—has all been smartly fitted. Renovation work like this is almost always slapdash somewhere: tedious snags that were never ticked off, awkward end-of-the-day jobs that clockwatching tradesmen never quite got around to. But Graham's team have cut no corners that I can see. I'm impressed.

Early evening sunshine streams in as we poke around, though in truth there is little we haven't already seen through the window. Indeed, as there are no shutters or blinds, inquisitive passersby have already begun to gather outside. Peering in, just as we did, drawn by movement in the vacant property. Graham and Marisa barely seem to notice, but I can feel the eyes scanning for intelligence. Watching us, as if we are actors on the big screen. And I can practically hear the rumor mill grinding into action. Out of the workshop, and thoroughly out of my element, the unwanted attention makes my skin crawl. Casting futilely about for blind spots and finding none, I decide that now might be a good time to investigate the back rooms. Thinking, as I hug the walls, that the place could really use some heavy curtains . . . and some bloody great big bits of furniture to hide behind.

Moving deeper into the property, for just a moment I experience a lurch of panic. Things are escalating sickeningly quickly. It's only been days since the idea first took hold, and already we're seriously considering taking on a second rental commitment—a third if you count our mortgage. Based on what, exactly? Pride?

Instinct? *Ego?* Steadying myself, I try to remember that hope is not a strategy. That we can't just keep waiting around for something to fall into our laps. That reckless and risky and downright foolish as this might be, with the boys empty-handed and the workshop's machines lying idle, every day that passes without a project to work on isn't just a day we can't afford—it's a day we'll never get back. Another week or two of sitting on our hands and it may be too late. Thinking back to the timber in the rafters, to the little cutting board production line the boys set up today, I push down the nerves and try to focus. Because it felt awfully good to be doing something at last.

A rush of cool air shivers past, softly drawing the inside door closed behind me, muffling Marisa's voice as I unlatch and open the back entrance. It's remarkably quiet in the old enclosed wynd, despite its proximity to the high street. Biscuit-colored walls of heavy stone are bathed in angled shadow. There are sloping slate roofs, a narrow flagstone path leading between buildings, and here and there the mottled glass of a bathroom window. Screwed to the masonry, where the entrance to a low enclosed passage leads back to the street, is a blue-and-white French street sign of polished metal, lending the place a touch of Gallic romance. The really striking thing, though, is the flowers. Pinks, reds, yellows, violets, greens, and blues—they spill from window boxes, hanging baskets, and dark wooden planters; climb yards of elegant trellis. An unlikely hidden garden, sprouting from the stone. The charm of the place, and the obvious care that's been taken with its details, feels to me like a good omen.

Stepping down onto worn gray cobbles, I am vaguely uneasy in what is clearly someone else's space. I busy myself hunting around for the small storeroom, mentioned in the particulars as just off the vennel. Finding it, I try the handle and the door creaks stiffly open. Its hinges, and the damp and chilly unlit brick space, feel long unused. It's empty. Closing the door, I look out to my right. Through the glossy black iron bars of a double gate, I can see the disembodied legs of pedestrians, obscured by the low ceiling holding up the flats above my head.

Back inside it's bright with the cold hard sizzle of striplights. As the door *whumps* gently closed, I can hear Marisa broaching the delicate subject of redecorating. Something that seems a terrible waste when the place has so clearly just been painted, but something we both feel strongly about. If we are really going to do this, we are going to do it right. No half-measures. I walk in just as she is sidestepping the issue of the various holes we will need to drill, doing her best to make light of it as her tape measure snaps violently home. Graham's eyes narrow ever so slightly. "What do you have in mind, exactly?" he asks, reaching out to touch his unblemished plasterwork with just a hint of regret.

"Minimal things," I say, picking up where Marisa leaves off with what I hope is an air of experienced nonchalance. Reassuring him that it's just a few framed pictures and a tasteful, traditional paint job. "It is a heritage area after all." I follow this up as quickly as I can with the mention of the hardwood details I plan to bring in. Knowing that this at least I can speak about with some confidence. "I was thinking Scottish elm for the shelves and the window seat," I say, with the wood from the workshop still clear in my mind's eye. The words are already out of my mouth before I really think them through, but I realize as they emerge that replacing the painted plywood with something handcrafted and locally sourced—something with depth and character—really will change the whole feel of the place for the better. That to my relief, I actually agree with myself.

Happily, at the mention of hardwood, Graham beams. Clasping his hands together in delight, his violated paintwork forgotten. In a languid voice that is pure public-school Scots, he pronounces this an "*excellent*" idea. Drawing out the word as if it is made of honey. Then, with a look that suggests he is taking us into his confidence, he levels with us. "I'll level with you," he says, steepling his fingers. "It's a great location and I've had some serious interest. But I really do like the sound of a furniture shop. It'll be good for the high street—and it'll be good for the town." He agrees to hold the place for a couple of days while we make our decision but says it's ours if we want it. And that as far as redecorating goes, as long as the work is neat and the colors tasteful, he's open to it. Then his eyes widen. "Hell," he says, with gusto, "I might even be your first customer!"

Another wave of nausea rolls up the beach. We are both meticulous planners, and this is such an unknown gamble. I glance at Marisa. She is flashing Graham that killer smile, but I know her too well. He's happy, so she's happy, but that doesn't mean she's not concerned too. I try hard to think clearly, to be positive. To push down the panic and visualize the endeavor as it *could be*, while I am actually standing here. Absorbing the quality of the finishes, Graham's friendly demeanor, the emotions it stirs to look out onto the street. And I think: if we are really going to do this, and God knows we have to do something, then to me this feels like a good place to do it. By the time we get home, turning off the engine and sitting together for a moment outside the door of our little flat, I know that Marisa agrees. Win or lose, it will be on our terms. We have both made up our minds. But of course, we're not the only ones with a say in this.

Friday's sausage ritual was born during the frigid winter renovation of the workshop itself. An overt bribe, conceived to cajole our troop of chilly helpers into action. It was quickly impossible to control. In just a few months we were ordering so many hot rolls from the local café that they added a special button on the till just for us. Eventually the orders became so expansive—and expensive—that neither the café nor petty cash could keep up. Operations moved in-house, and behind closed doors things really intensified. Innovation, craftsmanship, creative excess . . . What did we *think* was going to happen?

Fat peppery Cumberlands with caramelized red onion marmalade on toasted sweet brioche? Sticky salty chipolatas stacked together like tightly rolled cigars and crammed into oven-baked ciabatta? Blowtorch-flambeed halloumi perhaps, with baked eggs, chilli jam, and sun-dried tomatoes, folded into warm pita bread? Been a while since we've all been comprehensively ruined for the day by foot-long American-style franks in finger buns—with gherkins, mustard, and sauerkraut—and Springsteen, naturally.

Tupperware and microwaves were soon superseded by pots and pans, when Andrew, the gourmet of the bunch, dragged out a small electric oven from deep in storage. Blistered and scorched from its past life boiling oils and wax and even acid, it was caked in years of grime and filth, but he still pronounced it sausage-worthy. Over the years, sausages have become more than a sandwich filling; they have become symbolic. A tradition. An ideal. At some point the boys even bought a bugle. And rain or shine, deadlines be damned, once a week the five of us compete to coax ever more sophisticated results from the cramped confines of the workshop kitchen.

It's eleven a.m., and the whole team is out in the yard, all contentedly chewing. Today it's one of Tommy's heavy-duty vegetarian constructions, the startling mass of which belies its compact dimensions. I look over at Marisa and she nods. A tiny, all but imperceptible movement, like an auctioneer. Hoping that sausages will soften the blow, this is where we've agreed to break the news. This is where we tell them that the job they have been planning, prototyping, fretting over, and preparing for weeks—the one job they know we are all relying on to see us comfortably through for the next six months—is no longer going to happen.

Remembering how I felt when I first heard this news, and

knowing that with anything serious like this I find it next to impossible to keep the emotion from my voice, I try to deliver my words as carefully as I can. But as usual, it just comes out as a growl. "You guys might have already guessed as much," I say, with a rising lump in my throat that has almost nothing to do with Tommy's cooking, "but unfortunately, we won't be moving forward with the London job. The client has decided to go in a different direction."

Whether I'm delivering good news or bad, I always struggle to look people in the eye. And now I find myself staring at a spot high in the branches, and then down at my hands. I do my best to assure them it's no reflection on them, that the prototypes were excellent and well received. That the client's management team has simply changed. I make it clear that this *is* serious but, as Marisa and I have agreed, stop short of revealing the full extent of the financial implications. It's the truth, at least as far as I know, but to my ears it all still sounds terribly weak. "We're sorry," I manage. And then, remembering a favored saying of my father's father—*don't bring me your excuses, just tell me when it's done*—I shut my mouth.

Lying awake at night, listening to the wind whistling through the gaps around the windows and the snores rumbling down from the flats upstairs, I have played all this out in my mind a thousand different ways. Scripting every worst-case scenario in excruciating detail. Ashamed that we have let them down and put their livelihoods at risk. But only now is it dawning on me . . . it isn't just their jobs that hang in the balance—besides, they could probably all go and get another job tomorrow—it's the business we have fought to build together, the workshop and the team, *all this* that will go away. And it won't be our ideas, our willingness to take chances, or even our meager savings, and certainly not a few tables that will pull those things back from the brink. But the loyalty and the trust of the three men standing in front of us. Their willingness to believe in us. Without that, it's all finished.

For a long beat no one speaks. Spruce pollen swirls in the silent air, leaving a faint green dust on everything it touches, like chalk on the pavement after rain.

Robin leaps in first, as I'd guessed he might. The dogged cockney spirit tearing into the invisible foe, spoiling for a confrontation: a wrong to right. The others quickly follow suit, rallying round, offering support and reassurance, if a little more hesitantly. Andrew is always an open book, and he looks worried. Tommy gives less away. He is young and optimistic, but he is sharp and fiercely loyal so I know he will feel this keenly. From them all there is encouragement for us, and scalding derision for the client. But their words ring a little hollow. And not so very far beneath the bluster it's plain to see they are all concerned. Each of them has responsibilities, partners, families, bills, and futures of their own to worry about. There is bitterness, too; that much is plain. Paid or not they take great pride in what they do and how they spend their time. A big part of the reason the quality is so high is because they care so very much about the work. That the hard yards they have all put into the many fastidious stages of prototyping will now be for nothing cuts as deeply as I'd feared.

As the shock fades and the mood grows more subdued, and even Robin quietens down, Marisa seizes the initiative. I'm relieved. Keeping this from them and worrying about their reaction has been eating away at me, and airing the news has left me deflated. But there is more to it than that. The boys all know who really runs the show, and I'd guess they are all secretly looking to Marisa for a grown-up solution. I wouldn't admit it, but I'm with them. "As you can imagine," she says warmly, holding their gaze as I never can, "this leaves us with a *bit* of a window in the schedule." Then, like the born performer she is, she pauses for effect . . . and lays out our plan.

They react better than I'd dared hope.

"A *shop*?!" they all cry, their eyes widening like excited schoolboys. An exultant shout that comes in almost comical unison. Robin immediately pulls on his cap and tucks his thumbs into the lapels of his chore coat, giving us a frighteningly authentic imitation of a market trader. Tommy, something of an entrepreneur himself, grins broadly and rubs his hands, as if he cannot wait to get started. And Andrew, still struggling to fully hide his emotions, looks skeptical—but interested. Their questions come thick and fast and lively. Jokes are barked out, suggestions ranging from outlandish to excellent to just plain silly as the volume ratchets up. But although it is positive, theirs is a nervous energy too: frenzied and thin. Even I can feel it. Sensing the atmosphere changing, their need for something more tangible to hold on to, Marisa raises her hands, glances quickly at me, and gestures for them to listen. "You know this only works, this is only something we'll pursue, if you guys are on board," she says, with meaning. "We can't do it without you. So what do you say?"

Silence gathers again as the three of them exchange looks, but eventually it is Andrew who steps forward, appearing deadly serious for once. He takes in the yard and the trees, looking up at the sign above the workshop door, then back at Tommy and Robin and at both of us in turn, building to something. Then, closing his eyes and interlocking his fingers, he presses the tips to his lips. "I think I speak for all of us," he says, solemnly, "when I say that this . . . this calls for a *very* special cake!"

8

Four Weeks to Opening

In the week that's passed since Graham handed over the keys, every moment has been charged with high-voltage anxiety. Dreams are thrilling, and more or less harmless, but when solicitors get involved—when thick, serious-looking envelopes start thudding onto the mat and dreams begin to look uncomfortably like reality—everything changes. Because reality isn't harmless at all.

The inclusion of a "break clause" in the lease, grimly suggested by one of the street's long-term retailers on an eerily quiet Thursday evening in his own empty establishment, has effectively halved the length of our commitment. But we've still put our names to a two-year, five-figure financial contract. Sobering numbers in the current circumstances. With the timber hoarded in the rafters we do at least have something to work with, albeit a fairly eclectic mix. And by plundering our savings we have scraped together enough on top of the deposit to begin redecorating. But after that, and the first month or two of wages and rent, the bottom of the overdraft will once again become alarmingly visible. The shop had better start standing on its own two feet, and quickly. Or else, as my wife has so eloquently and repeatedly put it: we're fucked.

Tumbling all this in my head for the umpteenth time, I watch as my coffee mug shimmies ever closer toward the edge of the desk. For five minutes now, the mug, the floor, the walls, the tired old glass in the windows, practically *everything* in the office has been vibrating. All morning, too, we've been hearing the intermittent rasp of the chain saw, and the occasional fresh-apple crunch of heavy steel cleaving through wet lumber. What we haven't been hearing, as the two of us have tried vainly to concentrate on design, planning, council applications, and countless other unexpected fees and formalities, is the droning hum of the planer, or the metallic shriek of the table saw. And what all this means—this rasping, crunching, cleaving, and vibrating, this distinct absence of plant machinery—is that while we're in here, panicking, Out There someone is up to something. And I have a pretty good idea who.

"Bowls, man! Bowls like you've never seen!" Andrew yells manically when I finally collar him in the yard. On the hard-packed dirt at his feet, half a dozen short, chunky orange logs are strewn about. One is in his hand, while in his other he grips a very handsome hatchet. It's Swedish-made, with a hand-forged head, a hickory handle and, somewhere around here, a leather sheath. Pure axe porn. The scene is much as I expected, but I still have to bite my tongue.

I do dimly recollect discussing this with Andrew. I know, for instance, that he's had his eye on some logs of yew and cherry out in the woods for some time, that lathework is a particular passion of his, and that he's confident lathe-turned bowls and platters will fly off our newly installed shelves as fast as he can make them. But of course, he'll have to get on and make the bloody shelves first.

Andrew has the most carpentry experience, so we've tasked him with the shop's new hardwood details. These are important improvements that will significantly alter the way the space looks and feels. Encouraging potential customers who may be walking past to raise their eyebrows, rub their hands, and take careful note. I had thought, in fact, that most of this work was already close to finished. Passions, though, appear to have snuck to the front of the queue.

Lathes, for the uninitiated, are fairly simple machines, used to make profiled objects by revolving them at varying speeds so they can be pared away with chisels and abrasives. Lathework itself can be nerve-racking, physical and at times even dangerous. Never more so than in the beginning, when the blocky spinning object *appears* to be cylindrical, but most assuredly isn't. The business of jamming a long steel chisel into the mix goes considerably more smoothly if the wood being turned is fresh, and still packed full of moisture—or "green." (Wood, say, that has been cheerily gathered from the forest and split into workable chunks with a sexy Swedish hatchet.) But even with the greenest of timber, lathes can judder violently, and if they are positioned hard against a wall, they can even cause whole buildings to shake. This, of course, is what we have been experiencing all morning.

With assurances that the carpentry details are very much "in process," and that he is simply "filling time" between gluing or sanding stages or coats of oil, or something else wholly believable like that, I leave him to it. Slumping back down behind my desk with gritted teeth, the shuddering begins anew. And as paperwork, rolls of tape, pencils, books, and bulldog clips flutter and crash to the floor, I try hard to remind myself that it is not Andrew and his bowls, or Robin and Tommy shouting and laughing over their hysterically loud music, that's really bothering me. At least it's not just them.

With the decision made and the ink barely dry on the lease, fate has not been able to resist. We finally have our first real sniff of a serious corporate job. And in the end, it's come entirely out of the blue. Vague and experimental, requiring the use of materials and techniques that are entirely new to us, much of it would be a departure for our workshop. But it is interesting and creatively exciting, and it might just be our ticket back. At this early stage it's impossible to know if the job will come to anything; these sorts of things so often don't. But clients don't come much more high-profile, so if it does move forward, their pockets are undoubtedly deep enough to make sure it's done properly. To find out more and to throw our hat into the ring means traveling to London. Time and money we simply do not have. But with no certainty the shop will work as we hope, or that we can quickly find the customers we need, we really daren't turn our backs on anything, no matter how tenuous. So somehow, as soon as a date for a meeting is set, we shall have to find a way to get there.

Financially, four weeks is all we can stretch to, a deadline that's already looming fast. So what I should be doing right now is working with Marisa, developing concepts and drawing packages for the key pieces: the tables, desks, and cabinets that have the best chance of turning an honest profit. Giving the boys clear plans and sufficient time to handcraft them properly before we open the doors. Instead I'm in here, wincing at the price of train tickets, investigating experimental materials and byzantine fire regulations. Or else I'm arguing over paint colors, pleading with internet providers, or hunting around for old or half-finished furniture that might be reworked into something sellable. Either that or running from room to room scribbling down half-baked ideas on crumpled scraps of paper, laying out just enough track for each day, or even just each *hour*, to keep Tommy, Robin, and Andrew gainfully employed. The effect is paralyzing.

Often my eye wanders to the telephone, my mind to thoughts of calling my father. Other than Marisa, the one person in the world I really trust to weigh in on creative problems. Always ready with an answer for everything—and a brutally honest appraisal. And someone who could, in a heartbeat, resolve these shifting feelings of doubt and guilt and hope. For better or worse. Time after time I push the thoughts away. This is our mess, our mistake, and until we've found a way to fix it, it's still not a call I'm ready to make.

Even with clear heads, clear desks, and lower blood pressure, I'm not sure we'd be making much progress. Turns out it's been rather longer than we'd thought since either of us has tried to design furniture for people's homes. Furniture that can't just rely on elegant lines, clever details, and sumptuous materials. Furniture that's actually intended to be used on a regular basis. With everything so tight, and our timber stocks so precious, we know there's only one shot at getting this right. Hardly ideal conditions for creative ideas to flourish. Marisa and I must have covered sixty miles in a week, churning through ideas in the woods, hoping to kindle a spark of inspiration. If anything, we have almost too many ideas fighting for our attention. After so long designing for other people, it's hard not to think at times that we may have lost sight of what it is that *we* want to say. It isn't the objects themselves we're questioning. It's the style, the character, the voice that we can't seem to pin down.

Forty frustrating minutes later, having got nothing of value done, and with guilt gnawing at me, I find myself back out in the workshop. I'm pretty sure I didn't say anything too tactless to Andrew, but my face rarely keeps my feelings well hidden. Against the far wall, the core of the lathe is a whirling blur of energy. Behind a respirator and transparent plastic visor, Andrew's face is a mask of rigid concentration. It's unlikely I'll be able to muster much in the way of cheer, but even a nod or a smile, or just a few kind words about the work that the three of them are doing probably wouldn't go amiss.

I watch from a distance as ribbons of the timber's startlingly orange flesh stream from the point of his chisel, caking the knuckles clamping its spoon-shaped blade to the T-rest in damp shavings. The wood is very fresh, so there won't be much fine dust in the air, but I'm still glad to see he's wearing a respirator. You have to be very careful where sawdust is concerned. It's unpredictable stuff. Pine shavings' perfume is as bright and clean as a summer's day, and few aromas come as ecstatically close to perfection as the barley-sugar sweetness of freshly milled cedar. But even the merest whiff of iroko dust can send the most hardened woodworking veteran whimpering from the workshop as if they've been maced. And yew is properly toxic. (Its Latin name, *taxus*, may even be the root of the word.) Side effects may include: *inflammation of the nasal cavities, breathing difficulties, headaches, nausea, fainting.* Even a spot of *temporary blindness.* Two thousand years ago, Pliny the Elder documented the case of four soldiers perishing after drinking wine tainted by yew hip flasks. More recently, exposed for just a few minutes to sawdust from laburnum—another noxious hardwood, which is an ugly yellow color when cut—Andrew's forehead inflated like a balloon, until he had the obscene jutting brow of a neanderthal. Laburnum smoke is even worse; a lungful of that can put you into a coma from which you may never wake.

As he lifts the chisel away from the spinning log, shuts down the machine, and steps clear, I catch his eye and nod appreciatively at the raw-edged bowl that's beginning to emerge, giving him a thumbs up. Rearranging my hands into a T, I glance toward the kitchen. It's not much, but I hope the small gesture might help to ease any friction. He grins. I almost never stop to make the tea.

Digging out biscuits and filling mugs for the others too, I carry a tray through to the benchroom, finding Robin and Tommy working on a set of oak shelves. The narrow-gauge skeletal framework, with its wide, loose-fitting boards for each shelf, is one of the few things Marisa and I have found the time to design properly. Tommy has built a simple jig to help him align and cut the joints for the frame, and he is making progress. Robin too is busy, sanding and gluing together boards with heavy steel clamps on the bench next to his, making the shelves themselves. Beside them, racked on a high trolley, the blanks for dozens of cutting boards and serving platters rest between planing stages. And on the floor, an old, ex-exhibition coffee table that has until recently been in our living room awaits final refinishing. The work *is* progressing, but slower than I'd hoped. Hearing their voices, I notice again that their spirits, and the thunderous volume of the stereo, are very high. The atmosphere could not be more different to the one that permeates the office.

It's been like this for days. Relieved of the stress and intense pressure of a heavyweight client and a looming technical project, and with the novelty of making things almost just for fun—of having something tangible to do at last, no matter how basic—a mood of carefree liberation has blown into the workshop like a Caribbean breeze. Music and laughter have grown steadily louder, breaks have drifted until it seems they might go on forever, and at four-thirty *sharp* their cars disappear in a cloud of dust and gravel. With few of the major designs finalized, and having made the decision to keep the full gravity of our money problems to ourselves, there's really only so much we can say. But it isn't always easy to swallow. It's not as if I want them to be miserable . . . but would just a *pinch* of misery every now and then really be too much to ask? For solidarity's sake.

Back in the office, with the muse still maddeningly out of reach, the music and the lathe and the laughter throbbing through the walls, I can feel the thermostat in my chest beginning to rise. The simmering frustrations are threatening to bubble over, and I know I'm getting dangerously close to saying something I will regret. Seeing the look on my face, and probably able to hear my teeth grinding, Marisa takes me by the hand, whistles up the dog, and leads us out into the soothing embrace of the forest. Telling me: that's probably enough coffee for today.

"We've got to give them some serious work to do, and *bloody quickly*!" I seethe, kicking a stone into the bracken. Fuming that nearly a week has evaporated and we've still barely more than piecemeal accessories to show for it. Catching sight of the skittering rock, the dog wrenches desperately at her lead and sours my mood even further. "Breathe," urges Marisa, pushing through the trees. "I agree with you, but you're no use to anyone like this." Skirting around the muddy edge of the burn, with difficulty, I try to get hold of myself, following her up the trail in glowering silence.

Soon we have reached the site of a huge felled tree trunk, slick and half-rotten, part of the landscape. We're just far enough away that the music blaring from the open shutter door cannot find us. Pausing beneath the shadow of an immense spruce tree, I close my eyes and readjust the dial. Shuffling from screaming death metal to the softly tinkling *rushhhh* of the burn. I try to clear my mind, to feel and to hear the world around me. To be present, and to unclench my jaw. Gradually, the trill of woodland birds finds its way in, then the whisper of leaves and branches, the ship's-mast creak of the towering spruce deeply rooted in the earth. I breathe it in . . . and out. And slowly, slowly, my heart rate begins to drop.

I spent a lot of time in the woods growing up, and it stirred up many different feelings. A sense of adventure, exploring the shadowy timberline on the hill a mile above our house. Flushing startled pheasants and poking around in old stone ruins, eyes on a swivel for the farmer. Or stalking rabbits with my grandfather's .22 in the rhododendron-choked grounds of the nearby estate, becoming so aware of twigs snapping beneath my feet that it could take me an hour to creep a hundred yards. Terror, crab-walking through the darkness in the Highlands' vast and spooky monocrop forests. Mostly, though, in the straggle of windbreaking trees that bordered the end of our garden, solitude.

There were probably no more than fifty trees in all, their backs hard up against the countless acres of fields beyond. Rowan, sycamore, elder, holly, hawthorn, horse chestnut, willow, and Scots pine—with its deeply fissured hide like an alligator, and those woody cones that are practically begging to be lobbed at little brothers. But their haphazard arrangement, the uneven ground, and the knotted understory, made the place feel wild and secluded despite its size.

Trees get old and die, just as we do. But those that have not yet succumbed to the ravages of time, or to the decades of great winter storms that have battered them since I was young, are ordered now. Tidy and prettily situated in lush, carefully trimmed grass. Years of my father's fastidiousness have seen to that. Early on, though, when I was small and the woods were vast, when my father was busier and nature rampaged unchecked, it was different. And before the internet or mobile phones or more than a handful of television channels—before all the noise got out of control—I would hide out in there. No longer a shy, lonely little boy. But a pioneer, at large in the geography of my imagination.

There were mountains and ravines, lookouts, hidey-holes, pill-boxes and rickety sheet-iron forts, listing outlawed Nissen huts, smoldering bonfires, even a couple of weedy military vehicles: Land Rovers rotting away, slowly being plundered for parts. Then there was me, with grass-stained knees, trying to make sense of things.

Even at fourteen, when I was really beginning to get my teeth into the miserable business of teenage life, tortured by the many cruel maladies of adolescence and frankly loathsome, I would still squeeze myself up the narrow wooden steps to the treehouse my father had built for us at the bottom of the garden. So tall and stocky by then that I barely fit inside. I would sit up there with my back to the wall and stare out over the fields toward the horizon. Safe in the knowledge that up there no one would find me. And as the weather-beaten structure groaned under my weight, high in the branches and unsure of my place in the world, I would find some solace. Secretly dreaming of escape, and a life where I might hide out in the woods forever. (Just not in those fucking spruce woods.)

Opening my eyes and crouching with one knee in the damp earth, I place the flat of my palm on the ground, feeling the tangled web of corded roots. It's just a fraction of what's down there. The merest glimpse of the forest's dynamic internal system. Like the few visible veins on the back of your hand. "A tree is a passage between earth and sky," as Richard Powers has written. But much of it is well hidden. Hard to believe that, even now, moisture and nutrients from the soil are silently traveling along not so very far beneath my fingers, inching up toward the foliage high above. Making their own climb through the forest as we make ours. That the leaves and needles are cooking them up, concocting the sugars and sap they need to survive. That much of the oxygen we're breathing is simply a by-product—an airy sizzle in the pan.

"Better?" Marisa says, sarcastically.

"Hush you," I reply, hauling myself up.

But as I do, a jackdaw shrieks close by, and the dog, incensed, strains again at her lead. This time she catches me completely off-balance, threatening to drag me down the steeply banked slope. Instinctively, Marisa reaches out. One steadying hand finds my shoulder, the other, the trunk's sweeping curve. Looking up, I see her dark eyes glitter and narrow. "We're overthinking it," she says, giving my shoulder a squeeze. "We need to keep things simple, organic . . . like the Mack Chairs." Reaching out, I take her hand, and together, thoughtfully, we push on.

The chance to design the Mack Chairs came almost ten years ago. A competitive tender from the Glasgow School of Art, a venerable and beloved institution, with a deservedly prestigious global reputation, which happens to count Marisa as an alumnus. Entrants' concepts needed to be comfortable, stylish, stackable, and delivered on a challenging budget. Ideally, they needed to be contemporary too. And above all—because they would be sitting alongside countless original works by the legendary Charles Rennie Mackintosh—sensitively designed as well. We were young and broke, but it wasn't the fee that captivated Marisa. It was the humbling prospect of this connection to Mackintosh's work. It looked likely, in fact, that the winning concept would be the first newly designed bespoke furniture for the school since that of the great man himself.

Mackintosh was, for a time, an artistic force in Glasgow. And in addition to being the school's most celebrated son, at the age of just twenty-nine he designed its ornate faculty building, its furniture, fixtures, and fittings. With an obsessive eye for detail, extraordinary ambition, and prodigious talent to match, he had a hand in virtually everything outside and in, making him something of a hero to Marisa and her fellow architecture students. Who, like all budding architects, were also budding megalomaniacs.

The arts and crafts movement, which championed integrity, simplicity, and the skilled hand of the maker in the face of relentless industrialization, was highly influential. But it was art nouveau, then an emerging style, that was Mackintosh's true passion and the catalyst for much of the school's design. He reveled in its radical use of sensual flowing natural forms, exotic colors, and Japanese influences. He had an alchemist's touch with materials, painstakingly lavishing even the humblest and most practical elements of the building with care and attention. Pushing contractors to do things they would never normally do with stone, metal, ceramics and, of course, wood.

Having spent some six years surrounded by Mackintosh's work, Marisa was deeply inspired, and almost frighteningly motivated to win the commission, setting herself to the design challenge as I'd never seen before. She proposed constructing our chairs, which would be built mainly from white ash, around a brightly colored botanical cruciform, evoking the stamen of an exotic flower. We quickly realized that this tricky contoured component could not be made from wood and kept sufficiently refined, and so instead planned to sculpt it from solid aluminum—a material I had never worked with seriously before. I knew almost nothing about combining wood and metal, but I knew enough about proportion and style to be smitten by the form she envisaged.

On paper, it seemed a beautifully simple solution. Solid aluminum would make the cruciform immensely strong and rigid, despite its slender form—all at once forming the decorative core of the design and linking together the tapering legs, backrest, and seat pad. Avoiding structural leg braces would keep the lines clean and uncluttered, so the chairs could be stacked. The full-scale models I built only gave us more confidence. Seen in three dimensions, these had a graceful, almost Asian energy to them. Qualities we felt sure would only be enhanced by the use of warm, rich colors and sumptuous natural materials. Combining, we hoped, the nouveau with the new. Happily, the judges agreed and selected our design.

It was only then that the trouble began.

That we chose to use metal and rare, luxurious Swedish leather alongside the white ash I was familiar with would undoubtedly have pleased Mackintosh. Resorting to ballistics-grade adhesives, building forming jigs so large I needed the postman's help to move them, and badly scalding myself in amateur steam-bending attempts would surely have wrinkled his privet-mustache into a knowing grin. He was famously experimental with his own designs and material choices, and so far ahead of his time that, despite his illustrious name, legend has it many of the finest cabinetmakers of the day flatly refused to work with him. Often leaving him little choice but to resort to lesser-skilled joiners in the name of originality.

Still juggling teaching with architectural work, Marisa had only the evenings and weekends to develop the designs and manage the project—almost our first after moving operations away from my father's workshop. The rest of the time, I was alone. Weeks ground painfully into months, the heartbreaks punctuated all too rarely by breakthroughs, as I gradually mislaid more and more of my marbles. By the end, with the deadline looming and hundreds of hours over budget, I was virtually camped out at one end of the workshop. Surrounded by countless half-finished components, without a single straight line among them. Thoroughly unraveled. Two dozen chairs did eventually emerge, but they took a little of my sanity with them. And perhaps this explains why it's a job I've tried hard to forget.

Thinking of them now, though—seeing myself there again with those early prototypes, remembering the way the sweeping organic forms made me *feel* when they began to come alive—something starts to stir. The forest walls seem closer, more familiar, and I realize we have both stopped walking. All of a sudden, it is as if a spotlight has been switched on, illuminating fragments of the chairs' DNA, and of our own voice, long lain dormant. Of nouveau, Mackintosh, Japan, and arts and crafts, of beauty, integrity, simplicity, and soul. It seems to course up through the roots beneath my feet and rustle through the leaves. To emerge from its hiding place in nature's many sinuous connections. I am awake now to the dancer's curves in the trees' muscular transitions, to the elegant boughs and tapering stems. Everywhere I look there is strength and beauty, form and function, style and distinctive character.

And perhaps at last . . . *there is a spark.*

A Brief Note On: Finding Your Voice

Right now, today, this *minute*, there has never been a better time to explore the world of design. Historical, contemporary, futuristic, sculptural, mechanical and organic—there is an almost unimaginable quantity of exciting work out there. Work that, just a generation ago, would have been almost impossible to find. Use it. Pore over books and magazines, get online, read interviews with designers in different fields and discover, if you can, what moves them to do what they do. Scroll (God help you) through social media. Collect, curate, and digitally scrapbook. Train that algorithm to feed you something nutritious for a change.

Then get out there and track down physical examples. Learn for yourself that, like iconic artwork and architecture, and seriously beautiful people, well-designed and well-crafted objects have a magnetism that can really only be felt in person. And that the more of it you can expose yourself to, the better. Visit exhibitions, galleries, museums, and degree shows. Seek out country houses and design stores and expensive hotels. Get out into nature and into the Natural History Museum. In all these places and more, get up close, get down on your hands and knees if you have to, and look, *really* look. Unearth the things you love, the things that speak to you, and ask yourself *why* they work—not just how. Why the forms, connections, techniques, materials, details, and colors have been used and combined as they have, and why they are so special. Think about what's missing, underused, or ripe to be reimagined, and how these things might be applied to the kind of objects you care about designing. Seek out the seeds of inspiration, hybridize, and nurture your own unique creative voice. Then grab yourself a pencil, and a sketchbook . . . because you're going to need them.

9

"Proportion, proportion, *proportion*!" urges Marisa. Yes, *YES!* I nod, emphatically, as my hand scampers wildly around the paper. A graceful curve becomes a leaflike form, morphing into the supple bough of a young tree . . . gradually, a pair of sinuous, almost sensual table legs begin to emerge . . . then the lines start to muddle, and it's gone. Paper scrunches and another balled-up failure disappears over my shoulder.

Countless such sketches litter the desk or are already strewn about the office floor. Half are neat and deftly drafted, artistically hatched and shaded, depicting objects that clearly resemble tables, desks, cabinets, and chairs. Those are Marisa's. The rest drip with impatient energy. Their scruffy roiling flourishes scrawled with almost illegible block capitals, sometimes dozens crowded onto a page. Those are mine.

Off to one side, perched on top of a cardboard box, one of the Mack Chairs sits imperiously, as if it knows it's being watched. Dragged down from the dusty no-man's-land above the bench-room, out of its tomblike crate, I'm pleased to see that it's aged remarkably well. The timber has darkened a little of course, the grain's lacy filigree becoming more pronounced with age. The Nordic ice-blond of fresh-cut ash giving way, as it always does, to the brassy gold of Speyside malt. But it's no less handsome for it. The deeply curved back—made by pressing thin layers of ash, steamed to soften the fibers, into heavy molds—still feels impressively fine for something so strong. The cruciform's paint-work is vibrant and striking. And the leather-wrapped birchwood seat virtually begs to be sat on. Whether I have forgiven the chair for all those torturous months and misplaced marbles remains to be seen.

Glowing embers rear and flare as I throw on another chunk of oak. The heavy iron door squeals as it slams home. The stove roars and the dog stretches out, but in the rest of the workshop, only the mice and their shadows are stirring. It's late. The boys have long since packed up and headed home. For Marisa and me, though, the night's work is just beginning. We both felt it, out there in the woods . . . the edges of an idea. So we'll be in here until we can drag the bugger out into the light.

What we are trying to find is the table this chair was *meant* to sit beside. The desk to which it yearns to sidle. And to evoke, if we can, something authentic of nature's elegant forms. To do this, fumbling and frustrating as it is, we are sketching. Not simply because the "ingredients are cheap and disposable and don't intimidate," as A. A. Gill once noted, but because you can't just conjure a new design out of thin air (at least I can't). Instead, you have to spot it. And the best way to do that, is to draw it.

And draw it.

And draw it.

Sketching is a bit like humming or strumming, groping your way toward a new song or melody. It would be hard to describe precisely what it is you are listening for, or what is guiding you forward. But if you noodle around for long enough—if you know what you like and what you hate, and at least something of what it is you are trying to say—then a word, a note, or a couplet may catch and stick in your ear, tentatively suggesting a next step worth exploring. It could take hours or days, or even weeks for the whole tune to find you. It might present itself almost fully formed in just a few frantic minutes or slip between your fingers to vanish forever. The trick to unearthing something valuable on paper, as Peter Korn poetically suggests in *Why We Make Things and Why It Matters*, is to learn to recognize when one of your sketches "sings" to you.

Helping to guide our hands are a few invisible rules, rules that shape the objects surrounding us all every day. Because while we want our designs to be beautiful, and above all desirable, they will need to be functional, comfortable, and user-friendly too. We know, for instance, that the seat of a dining chair must be approximately forty to forty-five centimeters above the floor (or just below knee-level for an average adult). And that we want a little less from front to back, with a gentle backward lean for seat and backrest. We know that this, in turn, defines the ideal height of our tables and desks—somewhere between seventy and seventy-five centimeters. (Dead-level with the button on the average seated belly.) We know, too, that tops need really be no more than sixty centimeters deep, for few can comfortably reach much farther than that from a seated position, and that the same is ample elbow room for almost any diner. These guidelines can be flirted with—and God knows, I detest rules—but it isn't advisable to break them too drastically. Sleeping legs, crushed knees, cricked necks, spinal distortion . . . these are things that people tend to take very seriously indeed. And it doesn't take too long for furniture that falls outside these parameters to start causing problems. Simply put: it won't work properly.

So I draw myself a person. A balloon person. Torso, thighs, calves and feet down below, shoulders, action-hero arms, and a head up top. I sit him down and treat him to the little smoldering cigarette I give all my characters—because I know the levity will infuriate Marisa, and that his modeling career will be brutally short—adjusting and refining until he looks almost legitimate. One pencil stroke lays down the horizontal top of the table, just beneath his elbows, another the basic location of the vertical legs. The proportions are clearer and more realistic now, seen as they relate to the human body. Roots are still on my mind as I sketch in the gentle curves of the Mack Chair's form beneath him. The long back legs snaking up and in, as if from the forest floor, climbing toward the light. Finding the table's legs too rigid and harsh next to the chair's soft contours, I sweep them down and away from the vertical, so the figure can stretch his own legs while he takes a drag. Realizing as I do, that for the sort of large, heavy hardwood table we envisage, we could afford to make this angle really quite dramatic. To seat six or eight the top will need to be at least two meters long, and even with an almighty load on one end it's never likely to overbalance. The pencil scrapes and the legs blend into the footrail; the angles, curves, and transitions becoming more and more refined as the form continues to emerge. Lifting my hand from the page, I give it a long look, enjoying the way the construction's sleek, organic feel complements the chair's lines.

Switching to a plan view, looking down from above, I project faint guidelines, redrawing the figure as carefully as I can. For a moment I swither over the next steps, my fingers poised above the page. Reluctant to ruin what might be *something*. I chew my pencil (Andrew's pencil, to be precise), then, with the wishbone arch of sycamore seeds fluttering into my mind, I start back in, nature's inspiration guiding my hand. One curve, two, and I can begin to see it. This table wants to wrap itself around you . . . It wants to welcome you home.

Cold steel chain clatters through cogs and pulleys, and the wakening world outside inches its way in. Above the shutter door, the striplights hum softly. Like me, they'll take a while to warm up. With a yawn I can feel from the tips of my toes, I stumble into the kitchen. It's three a.m.

Coffee in hand, I push my way through the wads of discarded paper that still litter the office and drop back into my chair. Barely four hours ago, I had to virtually lift Marisa out of hers. Prising cramped fingers from the mouse and straightening her back into vaguely human shape. She is a CAD demon, a digital athlete, but she never does know when to stop. Clipping the sheaf of pages together, I hesitate for a moment, reluctant to leave the stove's lingering warmth. Perhaps I *should* just have slept here? Then robotically, I lever myself up and head back out into the workshop. Into the cold hard predawn chill.

With the table designed we have a centrepiece at last, and we can't afford to waste a day. We've got to get Robin onto this, and we've got to get him onto it immediately. But fate has a dark sense of humor, and it came as no surprise when, late yesterday afternoon, word of a last-minute diary change reached us. Midday today is now the only time the client can meet us in London for several weeks. And uncertain as it is, painfully expensive as last-minute rail travel might be, we couldn't afford to refuse. At least this way we'll know, I think, as I begin to gather my tools. At least we'll know sooner rather than later if there's really something in it. Better that, better anything, than more uncertainty.

Around eight a.m. the boys will start to arrive. First Andrew will zoom in on his bicycle, warm his vocal cords in the shower, then artfully drape his steaming undergarments somewhere nice and obvious to dry. Next, Robin's canary-yellow vintage Mini will skid to a halt in a cloud of dust and tweed and bluegrass, impossibly cool and improbably tiny on ten-inch rims. Then finally, in the dying seconds of seven-fifty-nine, the fat exhaust and thumping bass of Tommy's blacked-out lowrider Honda will reach us long before he does. Woodland creatures fleeing in all directions, as he sips a cappuccino, checks his messages, nibbles a pastry . . . and probably vacuums away the crumbs while he thunders through the trees. But by then, with luck, I should be long gone.

When I have ferreted out my templates, steel rules, masking tape, scalpel, the router's flat spanner, and bearing-guided cutter, I head into the benchroom. From here I grab the jigsaw, router, and speed clamps. Raiding Andrew's dwindling hidden stash (not the decoy stash, at the front of the drawer, but the one he doesn't think I know about), I slip a brand-new pencil behind my ear. Last but not least, I slide *Kind of Blue* into the CD player. Time to get to work.

Having developed the sketches, broken them down into individual components, finessed and finally worked up the line drawings into tight plans on the computer, Marisa's last act before I bundled her into the Land Rover was to print them out full-scale. Even at A3, this was something that had to be done on several sheets of paper, so a bit of careful taping will be the first order of business. I notice with a smile that, rushed and drained as she was, she's taken the time to add guidelines to each page so they can be accurately aligned. Five minutes of shaky-handed scalpel-work later, and I have the table's leg profile stitched together and fully cut out.

Lifting a clean, thin sheet of MDF onto a bench in the middle of the machine shop, out where I can move freely all around it, I lay down the paper pattern. The leg's form is starkly visible now, white and crisp against the pale brown background. The shape is almost as I pictured it, but the jump from the screen to the real world has had its effects, just as it always does. Surprisingly tiny changes can have a dramatic impact on the proportions of a piece of furniture. A radius being loosened or tightened ever so slightly, an angle subtly tweaked, or just a few millimeters on the width of a component, and it can become an entirely different animal. But it's a balancing act. Curves aren't usually critical to the construction, but aesthetically they mean everything. Whereas the angles, though often less obvious, are crucial. Over something so long and tall as this, even drifting from one side of a blunt pencil line to the other could be significant: dramatically amplifying mistakes in ways that will only become apparent when the parts are fully assembled.

In addition to the leg profile, I soon have the tricky Y-shaped component taped and cut out: the sycamore seed–inspired junction piece that will link the legs to the central footrail. This complicated mixture of compound curves took the longest to refine, and in truth until now I was anxious about its unorthodox shape. But seeing it like this, together at full-scale and interacting with the language of the leg, I can feel my confidence growing.

After drawing around the paper patterns as faithfully as I can, I begin to adjust the profiles, refining transitions and balance, working on feel and using trial and error. Sometimes this means adding a little extra thickness, or musculature. Other times rubbing out and redrawing lines to lighten things up. I follow old templates and manipulate steel rules to make longer flatter arcs and compound curves. Soon my makeshift bench is also littered with dinner plates, coffee cups, coins, and dustbin lids—seeking out those elusive shapes and bends. The computer work has helped, though. We've already built this once, digitally, and the components' forms are not so very far away.

When I have the profiles finalized, when all the angles are carefully checked, I cannot resist one last visual test before I chop them up to shape into templates. Measuring out the distance and taping down the paper template as a stand-in second leg, I lean the sheet against the side of the bench. Standing back, I can now see it as others will. As it will appear in the real world. It has swagger. Swagger, I like.

As the sun's first rays begin to filter through the trees, I am making good progress. But time is against me, and there is still much to do. Adrenaline and caffeine are helping, but fighting such heavyweight fatigue, it's a losing battle. The smoky, shuffling jazz drifting from the speakers is only making things worse. Miles Davis and John Coltrane adding to the soft, distant, dreamlike quality of sleep deprivation. Finding I am staring vacantly at nothing, with no clear idea how long I have been standing like this, I resort to physically slapping myself in the face. Pencils and straightedges, even scalpels are unlikely to cause me any serious lasting damage, but soon I'll be using very dangerous machines indeed—and I simply can't afford to be drowsy.

I've been lucky with routers, so far. But I've seen the scars on those who haven't. A friend of mine wears an ugly puckered trench on his forearm from an accident many years ago. A horrible mincing four-inch wound that probably would have killed him if he had not been patched up by a quick-thinking client with medical training. Something that happened fast, and a chance in a million. But a stark reminder that even the tools you know best are more than happy to bite you.

Two hours later, mercifully unbitten, and with just a few minutes to spare, I emerge at a dead run from the washroom. My hair is still wet from the weakly drizzling shower, and I am dressed now in blue cotton trousers, brogues, and a shirt that is badly in need of an iron. Fifteen seconds after that, I am peeling out of the yard.

With a cloud of dust at my back, I tick off the mental checklist: templates, cutting list, job sheet, annotated drawings—everything Robin should need is on his workbench. While out in the machine shop, every last piece of usable two-inch elm is piled up, ready for selection. More than enough to get him started on the table and, we dare to hope, the salvation of our business.

10

I open my eyes with a start. Groggy, confused, blinking at a world unspooling as if it's in a terrible hurry. Fields and trees, a startled deer caught out in the open like a bug-eyed fugitive, the rhythmic *thunka-thunka-thunk* of the rails beneath my seat. It isn't the place that's uncertain—the place I know intimately—it's my place in time.

Thirty years and a hundred such journeys struggle to order themselves in my head. I've spent a lot of time dead to the world on late-night trains, traveling east on the mainline from Edinburgh, covering the same ground as this, if considerably more slowly. A familiar rusting green footbridge whips overhead in a blur, waiting room doors flutter, and we snake violently between the platforms of an empty country station. A warning blast of the train's whistle shrieks, but it's not the whistle that's roused me. It is some old homing instinct.

Across the aisle, through the window and a quarter-mile up to my right, I can see the familiar dark straggle of trees, like an island adrift in an ocean of rolling fields. For just a moment, the red

brick summit of the water tower and the Scots pines' distinctive flat tops are faintly visible before our sprinting progress leaves
them far behind. My father is up there somewhere, though, bea-
vering away in his workshop. The workshop where I grew up. The
workshop where it all really began.

To peer into that long low room in the winter of '95, with the ice
rimed thick on the glue buckets and the dust-choked fan heater
belching flame from its scorched and disfigured vents, would be
to see a man galvanized by purpose, and panic. But a man secretly
enjoying every minute of it. It would be to see the coarse damp
whitewashed walls and sloping iron roof of a space scarcely big
enough to fit three cars end to end. Just a handful of antique
tools—rehomed and rehabilitated like battle-scarred pound dogs
that no one else wanted, a big brutal table saw, a hobbyist's band
saw, and a cast-iron planer (that I would later destroy), but little
else in the way of serious woodworking equipment.

It's hardly Alaska, but January in Scotland is plenty mean
enough to make working with your hands a challenge. And being
inside my father's workshop at that time of year always meant
being slightly colder than you would have been outside. Uninsulated stone buildings are rarely much fun, but the conditions
in there had as much to do with the floors as the walls. These
were concrete, a grueling material on which to stand for long, and
something I would later help him remedy with polystyrene and

sheets of plywood. The roughcast floor leached heat from your feet with pitiless efficiency, and drew moisture up from the rocky soil below. It was uneven, too, having never been quite the same since my father, in a moment of rash and uncharacteristic misjudgment, had tried to solve a chronic subterranean rat problem with a jar of four-star petrol and a lit match. (Got rid of the rats though, didn't it? he would doubtless insist I add.)

Despite the frigid conditions and his lack of facilities and furniture-making experience, he'd made good progress in the weeks following his redundancy. Grinding away long into the night with whatever materials he could find. The single-minded pursuit of keeping his family afloat helping to take his mind from the bitter chill at least. And by the time February slunk from the gloom, he had a small collection of pieces to show for his efforts. There was a simple pine blanket chest, lined with fabric by my mother, a pair of small oak milking stools, and a growing assortment of wooden accessories: picture frames, live-edged mirrors, doorstops shaped to look like split thistles, breadboards, key rings and the like. It wasn't much, but it was a start. And as it turned out, it was enough to catch the attention of a local gallery. They were impressed. They wanted more. More, my father was always happy to do.

Though he was still very green when it came to many of the more technical aspects, he was by no means unskilled with his hands. Long years of heavy-duty building work had seen to that. When my parents initially bought the ruin of our house from my grandparents, at the start of the eighties—part of a derelict farm steading they were selling off to fund their own renovation, just next door—they lacked the money to pay tradesmen, leaving my father little choice but to learn. He always knew the only way he was going to put a roof over his growing family's head was to build it himself. Luckily, he relished the prospect.

Hardworking, fastidious, and inventive in whatever he did, and tall and broad as a second-row forward, building work was a natural fit for my father. Working evenings and weekends, and eventually even condensing his week's office work into four long days the better to cram more in, he'd soon chalked up the sort of hours that only really the very young can. So by the time I emerged into the world in the harsh winter of '81, kicking and screaming from the comparative comfort of life's green room, he was already up to his neck in it.

It likely surprised no one who knew him well when, in among all the ditch digging and demolition, the dry-stone dyking and concrete mixing, the plumbing, plastering, painting, hammering, sawing, leveling and kneeling (building is all fucking kneeling), he discovered a taste and a genuine flair for the trade that went well beyond necessity. Or that when, as they so often did, my parents found themselves in dire need of cash, it was to building work that he turned for some extra income.

With every year that passed, his skills caught up a little more with his ambition. And though, until redundancy hit, he never stopped making his living as a landscape architect, or chipping away at the house room by room, the few freelance building jobs he took on grew ever more sophisticated. So much so that by the time my sister arrived when I was nine or ten, he'd even put together his own little ragtag building crew and progressed to planning and managing whole projects, as far afield as the Hebrides and the Highlands. All of them ostensibly in his spare time.

Landscape architecture did far more than put food on the table, though, even if I didn't realize it then. It was the reason the trees we encountered were never simply oak, ash, or monkey puzzle, but *Quercus petraea*, *Fraxinus excelsior*, and *Araucaria araucana*—his favorite. It was the reason our overgrown garden was forever being molded into fantastic little worlds we were too young, or simply too accustomed, to perceive as designed. The circular folly around the elder tree, with each salvaged brick meticulously cleaned and laid just so, whittled away again brick by brick to be laid into swirling paving before the fruit was even dark on the branch; the system of underground pipework, channeling the gutter runoff beneath the lawn to trickle musically into the duck pond from the old brass tap; and the two-story treehouse he built for us, with its pitched roof, mullioned windows, and zipwire escape route. And it was the reason he understood, and always cared so very much about the materials around him.

The gallery's early interest in my father's work gave him an outlet, a small income, and an excuse to keep going. And that was all he needed. But from then on, he was always on the lookout for an extra pair of hands to speed things along. At eleven, my brother Bobby was probably just about old enough to lend him his. But Bobby had a dreamy, artistic nature, a brightness and a musical aptitude that kept him, and his valuable hands, safely tucked away in his bedroom. My sister Jen, though capable and rugged, was still only seven. Which left me—surly, socially awkward, already close to six feet tall and with all the clumsy strength of the heavy-set teenager—squarely in my father's foresights. And skilled as I'd become by then at vanishing into thin air whenever there were chores to be done (and I really was quite extraordinary at this) there were times when escape was impossible. So weekends and afternoons, probably as much to keep me out of trouble as for any real aptitude or interest I might have shown, my father relieved me of the burden of having nothing "useful to do" and pulled me in to help. Though perhaps *help* is pitching it a bit high.

I remember all too well the choking, eye-watering hours spent fire-branding dozens of slim wooden key rings. The terrible yellow resinous smoke filling the air as the big iron door key, ground flat, welded to the handle of an old potato masher and heated glowing red with the blowtorch, sizzled and squeaked its way into the timber. The searing inescapable pain of losing the skin from the tips of my fingers to the sanding machine—and the panic of accidentally bonding them together with superglue. I filled the house (and my lungs) with fumes from his stove-boiled finishing oil concoctions, clubbed, smashed, splintered, and burned my hands, hyperextended my thumbs, clogged my sinuses with sawdust, grazed my corneas, and watched (you really can't believe how fast this happens) as scraps of my clothes disappeared into the workings of machines.

Naturally I resented being made to work out there in the cold—and on the *weekends*. What card-carrying sullen teenager wouldn't? Complaining bitterly, and more or less continually, if generally under my breath. But there was nothing about the work that was particularly foreign or unusual to me. Of course I know now that workshops and building sites are treacherous places, for an adult let alone a child. Just as I know that seeing my father hurtling off toward the hospital with quantities of blood, flesh, or fingernails missing, or hunting around in the meat of his hand with a gore-stained magnet for a sawblade's tooth, was not the usual childhood experience. But I didn't know that then. Then, and for as long as I could remember, my world had been one of chundering cement mixers and stuttering hammer drills, fire breathing butane torches and showers of glowing orange grinder sparks. Of fetching and carrying, hunting down tools, following my father around with a shovel or a wheelbarrow. We'd been playing these roles for a long time he and I, and secretly, somewhere very deep down and in ways I was careful never to let him see, it felt special to be included. Besides, whether I liked it or not, there was a job to be done. And as I'm told I succinctly put it at five years old, when asked if I'd like to come in from the garden (sighing and leaning on my little spade), "I can't right now . . . I'm helping my daddy."

Traveling without Marisa is never any fun. But locked inside a fast train for the better part of five hours I console myself with the thought that at least I can relax for a while. Except, of course, that I can't. On the little fold-down table in front of me, my laptop glows expectantly. Emails, bills, press entreaties, and design work.

A deluge of neglected admin. Soon my phone will get in on the act. Messages will begin to appear the very instant Robin has digested the drawings. (Robin is a fiend for detail.) The red pen will be unsheathed, ruthlessly slashing through mistakes and miscalculations I have almost certainly made. There will be questions and clarifications. And that's not even to mention the trail of destruction I've left in my wake. For that too I shall be called to answer.

But the messages never come. And alone with my thoughts, my head pressed against the cool glass and the rails singing through my back teeth, I think again of those early clumsy days. The mixture of pain, pride, and insecurity. Never wanting to admit to my father that I was out of my depth. Trying to show him I could do it on my own, to earn his respect, and to build some for myself. Even after all these years, full-grown and with a workshop of my own, nothing has really changed.

At eleven, the nicotine-cream of London brick begins to appear. Rooftops, razor tape, and graffiti replace the fluttering green fields as the city thickens. In what seems no time at all I am on my feet and pulling my bag from the rack, fumbling for my ticket, stepping down onto a station platform that is all echo and thunder and pigeon.

On the tube I try to mentally prepare, to get into character. Building trust and asking the right questions, establishing, in no uncertain terms, that I'm the one who knows *exactly* where to hit it with the hammer, that's what all these miles and hours are about. But try as I might, I can't seem to tap into it. Soon I will be sitting down with one of the most powerful people in British retail, with a chance to close on enough high-profile work to make our money problems disappear. To get our feet back under the grown-ups' table. This, I tell myself, is what you *do*. And I try hard to believe it.

Arriving with half an hour to spare before my meeting, I can't sit still. So I wander. Drowsily ambling, exploring the store's many extravagant floors. It's not the goods I'm looking at, though there are clearly some spectacular products on offer, but what Marisa might call the "interior architecture." An almost endless array of finely crafted fixtures and fittings, made from virtually every luxurious material I can think of. Creating these sorts of sumptuous display cabinets, trunks, and presentation cases was, until very recently, the way we made our living—so I am looking with a professional eye. Running my hands over wood that isn't really wood, brass that isn't really brass, chrome and steel and countless yards of faux leather, I try not to be bitter. But the taste is still there, no question.

About a month ago, we received a very polite, if rather unbelievable, email. There was a photo attached and a message that began: "Can you tell me what this is?" It seemed a strange thing to ask, but we read on, intrigued, recognizing the object in the picture as a finely crafted encasement of hardwood and leather because, a year or so prior, our workshop had made it. Curious to know how it had found its way into private hands, we pressed for more information. But the emailer would say only that they had "acquired it." This seemed odd—the piece having been commissioned by a large luxury retailer a lot like this one, and never intended for private sale—and just mysterious enough to suggest something nefarious, some sort of in-job. Always eager to leap to criminal conclusions, Marisa for one smelled a rat. So we dug deeper. And here's the knee to the crotch: weeks of work, some of our finest, using exquisite natural materials, and the mysterious emailer had bought it for a low, *low* price . . . at one of the high street's most well-known discount surplus stores. A trinket, with no explanation, just a brand name and a fancy box. A fancy box it had never even been taken out of.

Nursing bruised professional pride, for days I tried to understand why this was so unsettling. We'd been paid to make it, and paid reasonably well. But it hurt. I came to realize that the incident had brought something disagreeable out into the light, something I'd never really let myself think about before. All the time and care we've invested into making things like this for big brands over the years, believing they were important and that they mattered . . . where did I really imagine they had all been ending up when the store's interiors were refreshed? Something that happens in retail as surely as the changing of the seasons. This one at least had found a new home, hadn't been turned into landfill. But what about all the rest?

As I drift sleepily over polished floors, and more and more examples of finely crafted furniture and fixtures seem to swirl together until it is almost dizzying, I know in my bones that I don't want to be here anymore. That as much as we might need this work—that I will take this meeting and do whatever I can to secure the job— what I *really* want . . . is to be as far away from all this as possible.

11

Three Weeks to Opening

It's like digging out a splinter, I tell myself. It'll only hurt for a moment, but ignore it and it will fester. It doesn't help. And just as it has been all morning, my finger stays poised above the email's send key. In between grinding bouts of redecorating, design, planning, and pitching in with the sanding and oiling, long hours of research have gone into the London project, and I have finally discovered exactly how to do it. Regrettably, I have also discovered myself right out of a job. The perfect team of designers and makers does exist . . . but it isn't us. Hard to find, indeed almost digitally invisible, but highly experienced, there is a team of specialists in London who would make a far more professional job of this than we could. Reluctant to act as middlemen, realistically too inexperienced to offer much in the way of support, and truthfully more than a little concerned about spreading ourselves too thin, Marisa and I have made the difficult decision to step back. Making it up as you go along is all very well, but it's a small community, and who knows, this crowd may need the work as much as we do. It's the right thing to do, I'm sure of it. But sending the message still feels a lot like failure. I know too that the second I do, *everything* will ride on one big bet.

Tuning my mind away from the discomfort, I close my eyes and press the button. And just like that, our future looks a lot less certain.

Out in the machine shop, I chat to Robin. After ransacking the rafters' treasures, he has almost enough elm for the table's construction, but the final stages of machining have revealed some questionable spots in the two-inch stock for the legs. He sucks his teeth and gives me a look that says: "It's up to you, but *I* wouldn't." This wouldn't bother me too much if we were working to a more standard design. For something simpler, chunkier, with straight legs and braces, say, we might be able to stretch it. But the beauty of our table lies in its sinuous organic connections; and in the pared-back lines and flowing sculptural one-piece form there's nowhere to hide. A single weak point, just one risky fault in the grain that may dry and crack in the warmth of a client's home, and the whole construction won't just be compromised, it will be unsalvageable. With that in mind, and frankly glad of the distraction, I shake off the office and climb back behind the wheel to see if I can track down some alternatives.

The yard I have in mind used to be one of my go-tos for hardwood. It's under new management these days, specializing in cladding, fencing, and firewood. Ripping thousands of yards of fresh-cut softwood for outdoor projects every month. But I know they still have the kit to process hardwoods and dabble in kiln-drying from time to time, so I'm hoping they may have something stashed away. In any event, the yard is close by, and it's been a while since I visited. Intuition tells me it's worth a poke around, and necessity agrees.

Five miles east, a slag heap marks the turning. Of the nineteen that survive locally, it's one of the smallest, but as I weave the Land Rover between the farm track's potholes it still looms up like a great Martian dune. Iron-ore-red and flocked with a tight buzz cut of moss and lichen, it dwarfs the cluster of sheds and agricultural buildings that huddle about its gritty foothills.

When my great-great-grandfather was alive, this area produced more shale oil than anywhere else on the planet. A hundred-and-twenty bubbling, despoiling works, plundering six hundred thousand barrels a year from the ground beneath my tires. Sixty years was all it took to pile up two hundred million tons of waste. Literal mountains of cracked and boiled bloodred rubble, forever changing a landscape that just a generation before had been nothing but sleepy farmland.

The yard's high palisade fence lends the place the quaintly fortified feel of an old west stockade. I half expect to see rifle barrels poking between the rough-sawn boards, to hear *"That's far enough"* and a warning shot from behind the ramparts. But today the gates lie open. And over the whine of the saw and the gasp of the extraction hopper, the only greeting that comes my way is courtesy of a bounding collie dog.

"Aye well, there could be some left over in the far shed," shouts

Alan, the head man, removing his ear defenders and waving to his mate to keep cutting. Stepping away from the shrieking saw, he tries and fails to collar the excited dog. "She's only young," he tells me. And she looks it. A lithe wriggling bundle, fizzing with energy. "Mine's developed the nasty habit of trying to bite the machines," I say, as we distance ourselves from the racket of the saw. Alan nods, sagely. "Aye, they do that . . . until one day something wi' bigger teeth bites back! . . . Oh Jesus, *WILLOW*!" We watch as the young collie evaporates, covering two hundred yards in the blink of an eye, rematerializing on top of a ragged stone wall at the foot of the yard. As Alan lumbers off in her direction, he shouts back over his shoulder: "After the bloody farm dogs again! She's in heat! You a'right just to have a dig through yourself?"

Grabbing my tape from the cab, I make my way down to the far shed—second to last in a row of old refrigerated containers, tucked in beside the brick walls and terra-cotta tiles of a crumbling farm outbuilding. The exterior is faded blue, with main power routed in for lighting and a small radiator for the winter months. The great advantage of repurposing refrigerated units for storage is that they come ready-insulated. But this one's seen better days. Without airflow or a touch of warmth now and then the moisture content of the timber inside is at risk of gradually creeping back up in the colder weather.

The door squeals open and the light flickers on. Beside one wall is a waist-high stack of boards. Long and dark and dirty, messily piled atop one another on the scarred plywood floor.

Shuffled more times than a deck of prison cards. Propped against the other, a dozen or so live-edged slabs stand vertically. Slim pickings. But the short boards look good and thick—two inches at least—and plenty wide enough for our purposes. Under the striplight's synthetic glare it's difficult to get an accurate read, but if I'm lucky the smudged rifts I *think* I can see are just a shadow's tricks, and not the warning signs of wood that's home- less for a good reason. To be sure, though, I'll need to get them outside.

I am bent double, scratching away at the surface of a board with the edge of my knife, when Alan reappears, conspicuously dogless. "Find what you're looking for?" he says, breathing hard. I've whittled it down to three, and the lineup slouches against a high stack of stickered air-drying timber, just outside the contain- er's open doors. But though natural light is honest, it's not X-ray vision, and with such grubby specimens as these, it's not at all easy to tell. "Maybe," I say. "You?" He rolls his eyes and laughs drily, pulling on his ear defenders. "I'll leave you to it then."

The slab I keep coming back to is almost two feet wide, thicker than the others—closer to three inches than two. Its grime- darkened surfaces are peppered with the dusty boot-prints of earlier prospectors, and it occurs to me that some of them might very well be mine. But even if it is a little dirty, it's dense, flat, and reassuringly heavy. And what little I can see of the grain figure looks clean. My moisture meter, though, is swithering, unwill- ing to commit. A good moisture meter—one that bores down deeply into the wood's surfaces and costs more than a pack of cigarettes—would be a sensible investment for this sort of thing. But as we so rarely use timber that has not come from a big commercial supplier, more or less assured to be good and dry when it arrives, mine is small and cheap and thoroughly untrustworthy. More like a cracker prize than a piece of technology. Flipping the batteries, I try again, pressing the two sharp metal teeth into the wood's flesh like a vampire bat. This time it reads a healthy nine percent, but others it's been up as high as fourteen. Which, for fine interior woodwork that won't shrink and crack in a warm, dry house, is either good or *almost* acceptable . . . depending on which reading I'm inclined to believe.

The color too, and any hidden rot or spalting, are far from certain. The only way to know for sure what's hidden under there will be to skim away the first couple of millimeters in the workshop, and by then I'll already have bought and dismembered the thing. And what's that going to cost me? Wood is sold by the cubic meter, sometimes the cubic foot depending on the yard, so pulling out my tape and phone, I do the math: 0.05 cubic meters, or thereabouts, at a couple of grand a cube *if* Alan's feeling generous. This means I'm looking at roughly ninety pounds, maybe an even hundred, to find out exactly what it is I'm buying.

All at once it hits me: the costs, the risks, the responsibility. What if this is all a terrible mistake? I feel the nausea rise and the white noise begin to rush in my ears. I have to reach out and steady myself on the door of the container. Then a quizzical, whimpered yelp, and something softly hitting the dirt behind me, pulls me out of the nosedive.

Turning, with my heart still thudding, I find Willow, the little collie. Her pleading eyes dart back and forth, looking first at mine and then at the stick at my feet. Her trembling lip is curled into something approaching a grin. And I think to myself: all over Britain today, people are dragging themselves to jobs they hate, being crammed into trains and buses, stewing in traffic, watching the clock and seeing their days tick slowly away. And here I am, on a farm in the sunshine, panning for gold.

Pulling out my phone again, and taking a deep breath, I punch in the number. I've been putting this off for far too long.

In the background I can hear the keening of machines and the twanging adulterous croon of Robert Cray. As always, my father sounds almost indescribably annoyed to have had to answer the phone. I don't say hello—I never do—I just get down to business. "What would you say if I told you that, instead of doing that big commercial job we had on the books, the one that pays well and was going to last until Christmas, we were going to open our own furniture shop instead? On account of that big, well-paid job being canceled at the last second, the bank account being empty, and there not being another scrap of serious work on the horizon . . ." There is a pause as the mechanical drone fades away. I wait for the rebuke, or worse, the sigh.

Slide guitar and silence, for just a moment.

Then he says: "So what can I do to help?"

With just those few words—knowing that my father is at last part of the team, that I was a fool to ever imagine it could be otherwise—the fist that has been clenched so tightly in my chest for days relaxes its grip. I begin to believe we have a chance. And finally, I can breathe.

"Look at *this* guy!" Robin shouts, gleefully wielding a table leg cut from the newly acquired elm, revealing a tattoo on his forearm of a spokeshave. He's shirtless under the machine shop's clinking tin roof, surrounded by the usual mountains of drawings, notes, jigs, and measuring tools, sweating in the heat. Piled beside him on a wooden trolley are the neat profiles of the table's legs, rails, and structural braces, and the unusual Y-shaped junctions. And tucked into the back of his shorts, unless I am mistaken, there is a bright pink hot water bottle. "Chilly?" I shout back, inquiringly. But before he can answer, there is a blast of heavily fanned air, and Andrew staggers out of the benchroom, similarly underdressed. "Andrew can't handle much more of this, he's losing it, man!" he bellows—the heat near shimmering around him. Robin rushes over and seizes him by the shoulders, violently shaking some sense into him. Revealing, as he does, that Andrew too has a hot water bottle slipped into his waistband.

As if to underscore the high pressure, a long spell of unusually fine hot weather is forecast, and already the mercury is climbing dramatically. Unsurprisingly, serious cold is much more challenging. Pipes freeze and flood, finishing oils thicken and struggle to penetrate the timber's pores, adhesives refuse to cure, making joints brittle and unreliable, and even when you're wearing gloves, fingers feel like lumps of frozen meat. And that's just assuming we can physically make our way into the workshop through the ice and drifting snow of ungritted forest roads. But working with your hands at the other end of the thermometer is far from ideal either. Timber and sheet material curl up, almost as you watch, sunlight quickly bleaches the silhouettes of mislaid objects onto wood's surfaces, and glues and oils dry so fast that you barely have time to work with them before they have set or cured. More than anything though, because much of the work is manual and laborious and must be carried out under the muffling embrace of ear, eye, and respiratory protection, it can just be very uncomfortable.

The heat doesn't seem to be bothering Robin. Though if it were, we probably wouldn't know about it, so rarely does he complain about anything. All we really have to worry about with Robin in these sorts of conditions is stopping him from knotting a handkerchief onto his head and dragging a paddling pool onto the roof (as he keeps threatening to do). Andrew, on the other hand, has a thermostat finely calibrated for the high island latitudes of Scotland. Where, because of the Gulf Stream, it almost never gets seriously hot or cold. Anything that strays beyond fifteen degrees will make him sluggish, and well into the midtwenties, like today, he begins to break down completely. Last summer, when stubborn oil-based paint refused to dry on a time-critical piece he was finalizing, but when fans or ventilation risked kicking up dust and grit, we had to shut him into a small, sun-baked room with heaters and dehumidifiers blasting day and night, until the job was finished. The Andrew that emerged wore the wild-eyed, haunted, near-naked look of a castaway, and I'm not sure he's completely recovered from it yet.

I watch as the pair of them switch out their chilled hot water bottles with fresh ones from the freezer, enjoying their theatrical squeals, then I look in on Tommy, curious to see how he is faring. Tommy detests the cold above all things, and for him this sort of temperature is still on the chilly side of acceptable. Sure enough, though the benchroom's heat is withering, he barely seems to notice. Components for a piece that Marisa and I have taken to calling the "Dram Table" are arranged in neat piles on his scrupulously clean, almost clinically white, benchtop. The Dram Table is a simple design, small and round-topped, with sinuous legs inspired by the big table's. Made from solid oak, its surfaces will eventually be "fumed" with strong ammonia—a reaction first discovered in cow byres, when the beasts' urine turned the beams black over time—rapidly bringing forth the rich dark tones that lurk within all tannin-heavy timber, especially oak. The parts feel delicate and skeletal on the wide expanse of his bench, and with his clipboard like a medical chart, there is something of the operating theater about the whole scene. Though you might think twice if your surgeon was wearing a vibrant orange sweatshirt and Nike trainers, holding a burned croissant in one hand and a razor-honed marking knife in the other, I daresay Tommy would make a neat job of it. "Happy?" I ask.

"Happier than Andy," he replies, grinning broadly as he looks over my shoulder.

On his own scarred and stained workbench, Andrew's head

and shoulders are concealed inside a great wooden box. This too is oak, though it won't be fumed but left raw and finished with layers of penetrating oils, accentuating its natural golden color. The large statement doors and fine-boned interlocking leg structure are still far from complete, but it's good to see that the carcass is going together. "I'm not coming out!" groans from inside the box. Then, as I watch, a hand emerges, feels around among the chisels and the saws and the sandpaper, until it finds, clasps, and drags back a water bottle. "Leave me . . ." he says. "I'm *finished.*"

The top, bottom, and sides of this cabinet are being miter-jointed, like a very deep picture frame, so the grain will run uninterrupted right around the exterior. Dividing the storage space inside and helping to keep the carcass firmly locked together, a thick, dovetailed central upright will eventually be slid into a flared-bottomed slot from the back. Something that Andrew will have to fit before the rear panel is screwed on. It's clever; even if the glue fails the dovetail's wedge-shaped ends will grip in the joints, meaning—in theory anyway—that it can never come apart. It's fiddly though, and it will really only work if the joints are a perfect fit. Piling on the misery for the man sweating in the box, it's also a detail that will be hidden away inside forever. Never to be seen.

On a trolley beside him, clamped together with evenly spaced stickers, the thin panels of solid elm that will eventually form the cabinet's dramatic doors await their next phase of machining. Even without finishing oil deepening their color, their grain roils and churns like turbulent water. Essentially these are our own thickly cut homemade veneers, and making them will have been a job that neither the boys, nor the band saw, will have enjoyed very much. Elm is incredibly hard, dense and fibrous, with grain that often swirls in all directions at once. Even with a powerful table saw, it's tough to slice through cleanly and straight. Harder still with an underpowered band saw like ours. They'll have been cutting right at the limit of the blade's height, where the motor and the tensioned strap of finely toothed steel needs to work hardest. The blade will have tried to wander off course, screaming and smoking, requiring another set of hands, and possibly wedges, to keep the cuts open. Nevertheless, it has meant they can cut far more deeply, and with far less waste, than the table saw can manage, keeping the door panels as broad as possible and making best use of the material. These "book-matched" feature panels, when they are finally joined, will appear to be mirrored, creating rich topographical Rorschach patterns, like the wings of a butterfly. "All good?" I ask. And a thumb emerges shakily from the cabinet.

Seeing the troublesome timber makes me think for a moment about my father. Three weeks isn't long, and fifty miles away, in his own workshop, he'll already be getting to grips with slabs of Scottish wood a lot like this. He hasn't told us yet exactly what it is he's planning—what his carving chisels may be conjuring for the shop—that would spoil the surprise. But for character, theater, and drama, nothing else comes close to elm. So as challenging as it is to work with, I'd be willing to bet he's cooking up some way to use it.

12

Ten Days to Opening

"Starting to feel pretty fucking real," Marisa says, tearing a piece of scalding pork with her fingers and taking a wild bite. She is perched beside me on a driftwood log, wreathed for a moment in charcoal smoke, a saucy smear coloring her cheek. Grunting assent, I take another long pull on my beer, looking out over the scattered rocks to the denim-blue water beyond. Half a mile back along the coast, past the tidal flats and the widening mouth of the burn, the craggy outline of the castle looms out into the Forth. At our backs, the sun is beginning to sink. While inside my head, excitement limbers up for its nighttime battle with panic.

Four miles away, the shop is really starting to look like something now. All that shuffling, sanding, taping, painting, and endless bloody kneeling is paying off. The dry weather has had us outdoors for days, but with the newly fitted window blind giving us some yearned-for privacy at last, we've spent the afternoon inside, hidden away from prying eyes—*peepers*, as we have taken to calling them. Seeking to bring something of the forest to town, we've elected for green, outside and in. It is the chalky gray-green of grand wooden gates in crumbling walled gardens. Liter-for-liter as expensive as Champagne.

"The boys are on track," I say. "Barring any major issues. Getting a bit tight with the desk still to finish. Might have to get in there myself and help this week . . . if I can remember how." As I talk, the dog's black eyes never leave my plate, her nose quivering. "Need to get the pricing nailed down tomorrow too." Marisa licks her fingers and arches her eyebrows, throwing a scrap to the drooling hound. "No coffee for you then."

She's right to worry. Even without the amplifying effects of caffeine there's a good chance that things will get heated. Balancing our own gut feelings for what the market will bear with the hard facts of costs to be covered is always a conversation fraught with danger. That's partly why it's taken so long to make firm decisions. Insecurity and anxiety are running high; we are both so tightly wound that misplaced words could flare up fast, and neither of us wants that. Whichever way it goes, the things the boys are making will certainly be expensive. And who knows how people in town will really react? I mean really, *who knows*? Estate agents notwithstanding, there is literally nothing else on the high street that even comes close to the kind of prices we're talking about. Not remotely. Sometimes it makes me giggle like a madman just thinking about it, so that I have to bite down on my knuckles if anyone else is in earshot.

Constantly threatening to push up those costs are the extra

details, because, even when I'm trying to be restrained, and even when I know I shouldn't . . . they always have a way of creeping back in. A clever joint here, a custom-made handle there. Precision hinges, leather linings, carefully aligned and polished brass screwheads on the *backs* of cabinets. Caring about these things has been a big part of my job for such a long time that if I see something—anything—that can be improved, I just can't stop myself. We've been lucky with materials for these first pieces, but moving forward it won't be cheap to buy more, and the pricing must reflect that. Add to the mix a team of craftsmen who have their quality setting permanently fixed to HIGH, and the prices really begin to mount up. And that's before we've added anything in for the shop's costs and overheads, or even a penny of wages for ourselves.

From the start we've both agreed that we need to keep the furniture as accessible as we can. But I'm all too aware that after years of doing the kind of work we have, our definition of accessible is probably a little different than most people's. And because I'm *terrified* that we'll price ourselves out of reach, even as I add more complexity with one hand I keep trying to slash prices to the bone with the other. Marisa, with her own far more sensible hands, keeps calmly trying to make sure we cover our costs.

"It would be different if we could make some of these things in small batches. Even just the components, unassembled, but they're all one-offs . . ." I say, feeling the panic rising again. Hearing it in my voice. We've been through all this a hundred times and a dozen different ways before, but once again Marisa tries to be positive. Uncharacteristically, as I gather the dinner things, kick sand over the coals, and corral the dog, I find myself listening to what she is saying.

"Take coffee," she says. "To make a cup of coffee at home, even a *spectacular* cup of coffee, will probably only cost a few pennies. In cafés, it's pounds. The markup is *hundreds* of percent, and it's an experience that's over in minutes. No one complains—they're lining up every day. Our furniture won't just be beautiful, it will endure for a lifetime. If you can help people understand the time and the effort, if you can explain the work that goes into making it, they'll listen to you. People will understand the value, and the quality. You'll see." Her confidence makes me smile, just as it always does. But something niggles in my ear. "What's all this 'you' stuff? *We*, surely?" There is a pause . . . and the ghost of a smile.

It's temporary cover, a couple of extra days' teaching a week. She hasn't said yes—yet. But we both know there isn't really a choice. We can certainly use the extra income, and I know she loves to teach. But it has taken us ten years to get to this point, to working together pretty well full-time, designing and making objects we really care about—to living our dream. All of a sudden, it feels as if we are sliding backward. And once again it is Marisa who must make the sacrifice. This must hurt, I think, more than she will let me see. It had never even crossed my mind I might be manning the place more or less alone, and frankly just the thought of talking to all those people brings me out in a cold sweat, but I can't very well complain about it, can I?

"Well then," I say. "It's just lucky I'm such a born salesman."

A Brief Note On: Marketing

Two and a half centuries ago, Thomas Chippendale—easily the most renowned furniture maker of his or any other day—issued a bound and richly illustrated catalog showcasing the full range of his extravagant designs. Until then, furnishings had been shown as dull, two-dimensional schematics, but Chippendale changed all that. With over a hundred finely drafted perspective drawings, vividly brought to life with texture and shading, his catalog threw open the doors to a cabinetmaker's workshop as no one had before. What followed was a raft of plagiarism, naturally. With such detailed plans so easily to hand, copies were churned out by lesser workshops as far away as America. But there were sales too, and some fairly serious ones at that. Chippendale's name was out there, no question, and it wasn't long before the first furniture advertising of its kind found its way into the hands of the eighteenth century's influencers: the aristocracy. And the rest . . . is history.

Of course the internet, press, and social media have made it far simpler to get your work in front of incalculably more people. But some things haven't changed so very much in two hundred and fifty years. As Chippendale himself discovered, there's nothing that brings in the customers quite like aspirational imagery.

Bombarded as we are on a minute-by-minute basis with glossy content, these days it is often an image rather than an object that can change your fortunes. So, difficult and disagreeable as it is to some, to promote your own woodwork you need to take its presentation seriously. You must design the tone and mood of your photography, just as you would with anything else that leaves your workshop. Applying the same standards, being precious about the quality, and keeping things consistent. Because, like it or not, the things you choose to share—and the way you choose to share them—will do much to shape your reputation. And remember: the internet never forgets.

Twenty minutes late, the vintage Range Rover finally rolls into the carpark and crunches to a stop beside me. If not for the seagulls squabbling over chip wrappers at the edge of the muddy rugby field, we are alone. The driver's window buzzes lazily down, and a head emerges—all beard and hair and London lumberjack style. The voice is snootily affected: Bertie Wooster in Nigel Cabourn. "You there—you look suitably rural. I'm looking for a woodyard . . . have you seen such a place?! Been driving around for *haars*. Don't you go in for signposts up here?"

"Where we're going, they barely go in for *roads*," I shout across, tapping my watch and motioning for him to follow. As I start my engine and the window creaks closed, behind the tinted glass I can hear Benedict howling with laughter. I pull out onto the quiet backroad, and ten minutes later, reflected in my rear view, I watch as he pilots the beautiful old four-by-four beneath the looming Scots pines.

"Bloody *HELL*! They don't want you finding this place, do they?" he says, his eyes wandering over the firewood pens, the chickens, and the ancient Land Rovers' corpses, coming to rest on the jumble of mighty logs. "Jee*zus*, would you look at the size of those big bastards."

It's early, still cool in the shade of the yard, with just an edge of the swirling mist that seems to reside here. Clearly no one has informed the Highlands about the hot weather the rest of the country is experiencing. "Ben, meet Benedict," I say, as the two men size each other up. Between them, it's hard to pick a winner in the fashion stakes. Ben is attired today in filthy red overalls, yellow fisherman's wellies, and a threadbare woolen bobble hat. Benedict, in voluminous denim dungarees, Henley, and handcrafted leather boots, has a monstrous tripod slung over one shoulder.

It's elm that brings me back here. Elm and marketing . . . and a slice of serendipity. By chance, Benedict was in the area, and by good fortune an editor he knows expressed an interest in writing a feature on the shop at precisely the right moment. He put the two of us together, and soon, we hope, he'll put us between his hallowed pages. Benedict will be back in Scotland in a week or so to photograph the furniture and the newly decorated interior. But first, to give the piece a little authentic flavor, I have agreed to bring him here. To the most authentic place I know. (With strict instructions not to give too much away.)

Despite his absence, the specter of my father looms large. Turns out I was right about his plans for the shop, and having begun exploring the slabs from our last visit more closely, he wants more—much more—and he's terrified someone else will get here before he does. As Ben and I try to decipher his shopping list, Benedict bounces around. He fiddles with mountains of gear, measures the light, fires up a laptop, and pulls on more layers. I watch from the corner of my eye as he squeezes into the drying sheds, getting in close on hanging chain saw blades, wild woodgrain, and treacherous boule logs. Captivated.

"Ahh, yes. Kellie Castle, in Fife. D'you know it?" Ben asks, seemingly oblivious to the flashes and hoots emanating from his woodshed. "Those boards came from a big old elm from the gardens there, must be ten year' ago now. Good eye, your father."

Tracking them down, we drag out the topmost slabs and stand them, one after the other, against the rim of a tractor's wheel. Though I am easily twice his size, Ben's strength outmatches mine. The best of the boards are two and a half inches thick, Y-shaped and massively broad. Almost as wide as they are long. They are remarkable specimens. But two will have to be enough—it's all the cash I have in the world, and this place doesn't take plastic.

I spot Benedict rummaging in his truck, and in a moment he is at my shoulder, screwing on a lens as big as a pint glass. "Now *that* . . ." he says, "is a piece of WOOD. What the hell *is* it!?" I begin to explain, but then Ben appears—materializing like a sprite from among the stacks—a smoldering roll-up between his lips. ". . . Poets, artists, and great writers used to visit that castle. In Fife it is. Yes. Robert Lorimer, the architect, he spent summers there as a child. He probably walked under this very tree. Makes you think . . ."

With the charismatic sawyer soon in full flow, I stand back and watch as his words sink in. Benedict is clearly charmed, but it is more than that. It is the yard, and the timber itself, the spirit and the history. And I realize in a flash that *this*, in essence, is our marketing strategy. We have never been able to afford to pay for advertising, investing instead in creating beautiful objects and letting them speak for themselves. But now it is not just the objects that will affect people, no matter how beautifully designed or crafted they may be. It's the wood, it's the people who live by it . . . and it's the stories that are locked inside.

Sipping coffee by the open shutter door back at the workshop, I am still thinking about Ben's words. Half-watching as Robin sorts through boards for the tabletop, seeking that perfect combination. It isn't always obvious, but there is a great deal of care and experience being brought to bear in the top of a piece of furniture—especially that of a big table. It's gratifying work too. The top is always the star, and the key point of tactile interaction. Revealing the face and doing much to define the character of the furniture.

The timber of course has much to say, but communicating something of the work's identity is also within the maker's control. As a whole, does the design feel rustic, reliably rough around the edges, even a little raw in places—wearing its scars with pride? Or is it clean and flawless: a supermodel airbrushed to perfection? The difference between heavy, steadfast, and rugged on the one hand, and slim, elegant, and refined on the other may be as little as a few millimeters of thickness. Just one knothole preserved or discarded. These considerations might have been clear since the lines first scurried into the pages of the sketchbook, they could be something that only crystallized once eyes and hands were laid on the timber, or they may have been quietly evolving in the background as the furniture's true form and character emerged on the bench. But it's not just the scale, style, and figure of the individual boards that must be weighed carefully as the timber is selected. Because the top will be made from several boards—their carefully straightened and glue-jointed edges fitted together as seamlessly as possible—it is the way they will work as a team that really matters.

Chosen boards must be roughly cut to width and length on the table saw, because the smaller they are, the easier they are to handle and to flatten out. Always trying to make the best use of material, while avoiding or retaining problematic or especially beautiful flaws. Then, gradually, they must be planed down to their final thickness, allowing enough time for the wood to move between heavy machining stages and taking care to mill consistently from both sides. When the time comes to actually join the boards together, assuming the timber has been through-and-through sawn, there are two main considerations: stability and aesthetics.

Stability is straightforward, but it can be frustrating. The two sides of the board will look very different, because one has been cut through the crown—the upper, outer side of the growth rings—and the other has not. You can see the shape as a gentle smile in the end grain, becoming more pronounced the farther the boards get from the pithy heart of the tree. And because every board is trying to curl back into the shape of the tree as it dries, you can't (or at least you shouldn't) joint too many boards together in the same orientation. Over-under is the rule, but because the crown side is generally prettier, sticking to that rule isn't always easy.

Aesthetics, on the other hand, is anything but straightforward. As confounding as any artistic composition. Should the boards be arrayed as symmetrically as possible, with the strongest feature running down the middle? Or should the most prominent figure be gathered at one side, giving the ensemble a more natural look? Carefully manicured or wild and authentic? And where should the grain align, tricking the eye for a moment, making several individual boards appear as one? Seeking that elusive quality of a tree that has been rolled out flat. Or what my father would call *balance*.

As if he can hear my thoughts, Robin turns. He does his best to grin, but I know it's written all over my face. That as I stare at the wood he's shuffling through, it's taking everything I've got not to meddle. If I were in his shoes right now, would I want to hear it? To be reminded of things I already know? Slugging back the bitter dregs, I glance once more at the timber, grin back, and head for the office, leaving him to compose his own story.

They say that every room in the world has a tone: a specific musical key that seasoned musicians can find and identify. That if that note is played, the room will reverberate in a special, unique way. For workshops it is more of an energy, and walking into ours I can feel it at once. Everyone is busy, focused, moving like clockwork. The whole place hums with it.

Insistent hip-hop rattles under the door of the leatherwork room. Leaning inside, I find Tommy with a glittering blade gripped between his fingers, nodding to the beat. He is carefully upholstering a thick birch plywood panel: a stable core of engineered material for the newly designed desk's top. A material we have chosen as a nod to old writing desks, to feel comfortable under wrists and laptops—and because we have completely run out of hardwood. He inclines his head toward the components he's wrapping in rich forest green leather but does not stop cutting. *What do I think?* The leather is from the Tärnsjö tannery in Sweden. More offcuts. Not Scottish, then, but in some ways even more appropriate than local material. Unlike most commercially produced upholstery leather it's been vegetable-tanned, rather than chemically. So, like all the timber we're using, it will age and change, developing its own distinctive patina over time. Where the hide is bonded to the plywood, I can see that the surfaces are taut and flat. The edges sharp and precise. Tommy really is an artist with a razor. I nod back appreciatively.

I hear Andrew before I see him. But pushing open the door to the finishing room, it is immediately obvious that the drunk-in-a-gutter singing belies the meticulous work he's doing. We've used American white ash to build the sculpted base of the desk—which borrows much of its organic language from the table's design. Far paler and more consistent than native ash, the bone-white timber is left over from a big commercial job, and most likely came from a forest in New England. For a while it bothered me slightly that, unlike the rest of the furniture we've been building, we haven't used local, handpicked wood. But with money so tight, we simply can't afford not to use everything we have. In the end we've decided to lean into this uniformity of color—accentuating the pale tones with a wax-based white-tinted oil, to give it a ghostly, ethereal appearance. It's beautiful, but because oil like this is so much thicker than other, more penetrative finishing oils, it must be carefully and thinly applied, layer upon layer. And despite the racket he's making, Andrew is attending to it with the delicate care of a portrait artist.

To my relief, the desk itself has come together quickly. The design and construction being so similar to the table's has helped. The oak cabinet, too, has come together well, though it has been decidedly more work than anything else we're build-ing. There are more components in each of its large statement doors—composites of stiff, aircraft-grade honeycomb alumi-num, thinly cut elm, complex hinges, and custom-made brass pulls—than there are in the *entire* desk. Each of the doors lies drying for now, jutting out above Andrew's head on slim metal racking. Their surfaces, in contrast to the ash, are being enriched with multiple coats of Danish oil, exaggerating the tone and feature.

Out in the machine shop, the only place where there is enough space to assemble something so large, Robin has both ends of the table's skeleton glued together. Each comprises two tapering legs, a single Y-shaped connecting piece, and a straight upper rail. Smooth, organic contours that would have been almost impossible to clamp if not for the small blocky steps he retained for a time on the legs' profiles. These are cut away now, and the shapes are becoming more sinuous all the time. Seeing me approach, he lays down the router he is using to soften the edges and blend the transitions. The cutter whirrs quickly into silence, as the motor's safety brake kicks in.

"Put it together if you like, won't take a minute," Robin says, probably glad of a breather. Truthfully, I have been delaying this moment, looking in now and then when no one was watching, and scarcely able to believe how good the table looks. It's not in my nature, but I've tried to delay the gratification of seeing it properly until he has it fully built. Worried I may jinx it. Now, though, I hesitate for a different reason. Unsupported, each end of the table is incredibly top-heavy, their profound lean keeping them unstable until the long base and upper rails can tie them together. And seeing them in this precarious state is stirring up an unpleasant memory.

The chair I had built was ready to assemble, shaped, and sanded—weeks of work. But it is always wise to try one last dry fit before getting wood glue involved. That was *part* of the reason, anyway. Really, after all that time working on individual components, I just wanted to put it together and look at it for a while. It was, after all, the most impressive thing I had ever made by myself. Something Marisa and I had spent long hours designing for our first exhibition. Alone in my father's workshop, I eventually tried to take it apart again. And as I did so, the chair's back legs—its delicate, gently tapering black walnut back legs, with their steam-bent curving backrest loosely fitted between them—got away from me. I actually howled: a hysterical pleading *"NO!"* But it didn't help. With the front legs still grasped in my hands, the rest of the chair slipped from the frame's mortises with a soft *thhwock*. They teetered for a long, agonizing moment, just out of reach, before slowly, slowly toppling. Bouncing onto the floor with a terrible, splintering (and, as it turned out, irreparable) crash.

The late stages of jobs are always nerve-racking. There are just *so many* operations that have to be redone, in sequence, if something goes wrong. All it takes is a single lapse in concentration, just one careless slip of the hand. A final trim of a table edge and the blade might catch on a fault line, splintering off the side of an otherwise perfectly finished top. Resin might be too old, or simply too cold, and the day would be spent picking the sticky uncured goop from a knothole—like digging toffee from a tooth cavity. Or the razor might slip and a whole leather top would need to be stripped and refinished. Hardly thoughts to steady trembling hands.

But already Robin is fitting the long, heavy base rail into the first pair of legs, and before I can even lend a hand, he has the other end fitted. Revealing for the first time the lithe shape and form of the finished table. "Get this glued up today," he says. "Top to shape and sand and we're ready to start oiling. Day to spare at least. And you were *worried*!"

But I can barely hear him. I'm listening to something sing.

13

Opening Night

I am obsessing about plastic wineglasses. I have to obsess about something, but until this precise moment I didn't know exactly what it would be. But lurking here in the shop's cramped back room, fitting the bases onto their transparent plastic stems, I feel as if I am loading bullets into a gun. Robin applied the final coat of oil to the tabletop so recently his reflection is virtually still visible in the lustrous sheen, and just the thought of putting anything, let alone wineglasses, on the still-curing surfaces is enough to make me feel physically sick. But how would that look? Telling people they must not, on any account, actually *use* the furniture—on opening night?

Blame the photographer.

"Let's get them out into the woods," he said, "we've got to get them into the trees!" A manic grin spreading across his face as he hoisted his tripod and all but skipped into the forest. Ignoring the trio of worried craftsmen shaking their heads and pleading with their eyes. But if you have a world-class photographer on hand, you do as you're told—even if it is threatening to rain.

What must we have looked like, I wonder, to woodland passersby? Stumbling over roots and mud and thickets of weedy grass, dressed to the nines in our best *rugged portrait* gear. A man at either end of a gleaming dining table, a bulky wooden cabinet, and a bone-white, leather-topped desk. Chocking them up with pine cones, branches, and twigs—as my father, crouching, made frames with his fingers, providing unsolicited photography advice to a nodding Benedict.

For a thoroughly tense hour we watched the darkening skies, making minute adjustments, poised with cloths to dart in and wipe away those first few scouting raindrops. More finishing oil all round was nonnegotiable after that.

Already these past weeks the walls in here have felt closer, warmer. But filling the place with the last pieces of furniture has changed everything. The space looks smaller, and the furniture looks bigger—just as it always does when you get it out of the workshop. As of a few hours ago, when all this finally came together, our visitors will no longer enter a jumbled building site, or a packaging-strewn storeroom, but a carefully curated space. Instead of the pungent metallic odor of new paint, they'll be met by the heady, luxurious scent of freshly oiled timber, beeswax, and leather. But the first thing they'll actually *see* . . . is puffins. A triptych of playful birds, feature panels carved by my father. Teenage memories from the Shetland Isles, captured in oak. Gamboling now, not on Muckle Flugga's rocky cliffs, but on top of a radiator disguised with narrow laths of vertical ash. (Because you never do know when those perfectly uniform offcuts in the racks will come in handy.)

Below the puffins' feet, we've placed the low circular dark oak Dram Table. And to their left, above as many plants and wildflowers as we could pilfer from the flat and the woods, we've hung a pair of oak-framed panels—each packed with carefully composed offcuts of ash, walnut, oak, cherry, iroko, yew, and elm. Artworks, of a sort, that also serve to showcase the variety of hardwoods we most commonly use. To the right, beyond the deep new elm window seat, with its glass demijohns of ferns and fragrant spruce boughs, small accessories are displayed on elm shelves built into the alcove: Andrew's live-edged lathe-turned bowls, cutting boards of varying sizes, timbers, and styles, and delicate, colorful, blown-glass vessels—from the workshop of our friends at Gillies Jones in Yorkshire.

In the middle of the room, flanked by two Mack Chairs, is the star of the show. And with its flowing organic transitions, to me the grand elm table feels more like a sculpture than a piece of furniture. To one edge of its mighty top, among the swirling purples, reds, and greens, there remains just the tiniest taste of the tree's true form. A handsbreadth of live edge and finely sanded bark, still visible in the straight, sharp, otherwise regimented lines. A perfect imperfection—a signature—like the crimped pie crust or the fingerprint in the clay. And right at the back, just through the wall from where I sit (and fret), the bone-white desk, the complex feature-doored elm and oak cabinet, and a long, wall-mounted rack of coat hooks: polished brass knobs, lathe-turned and mounted on a slim panel of fumed oak and forest green bridle leather.

All in all, not a bad showing in the time.

Out front, Marisa dusts and buffs, tweaks, fiddles and fine-tunes. Rotating flyers and business cards until they are perfectly square. Peering out from my hiding place, I can see her standing between the table and the long side wall, a duster in her hand and a look of bafflement on her face. Soon that spot will be filled by a set of slim oak shelves, displaying design books and small accessories. But the shelves remain half-finished for now, so instead the whole wall is dominated by just one object. An object that, unless I miss my guess, she is trying to decide how on earth to polish.

"Let your imagination run wild," we said. "It's time to show the world what you can really do with your carving chisels!" This is what happens, I think to myself. This is what happens when you let him loose.

The osprey my father has carved is as tall and thick and broad as a tombstone. Made from a single block of three-inch Scottish elm. His great feathered wings are arched, and a writhing trout is clutched in his mighty talons. And he's bolted to the only stud I could find in the building stout enough to hold him up.

It's just friends and family tonight, and I *know* the furniture looks good, but my nerves are still jangling. As I unscrew the cap to pour myself a steadying dram, over the whiskey's sweet vanilla I catch a waft of beeswax polish. The place is so thick with the stuff you can almost taste it. But the whoosh of air that carries it my way is a signal. The street door has been opened.

It has begun.

The boys clatter in first with wives and partners, closely followed by my parents, then Marisa's and Andrew's families.
A handful of curious, well-wishing locals—shopkeepers and
residents—soon make up the numbers. In no time the place is
half-full, then packed. Scored, as these things always are, with
stilted small talk. There's no room for me, so I stay out of the
way. Fiddling with the music, pouring the wine, passing plastic glasses out into grasping fingers. And realizing as I do that
what I really should have done was leave the bases off the bloody
things entirely—that way nobody could have put them down on
anything.

It is always so peculiar to see the boys in their street clothes.
Except Tommy, who always looks as if he has just stepped out of a
music video—whether he's in a workshop or a nightclub. Robin
is spruced and buttoned up like a turn of the century Kentucky
coal miner out for an evening's carousing, and already he is fend-
ing off advances from Marisa's single friends. Andrew is fidgeting
with his collar, ill at ease in dress trousers and a smart blue blazer.
He has the look of a wild ten-year-old forced back into school
uniform after a long summer of freedom. In truth I too am finding it odd to be back inside a clean shirt. After a month of labor
of one kind or another—of woodyards and workshops and grimy
redecorating—I've slipped easily back into the well-worn clothes.
To working with my hands again, and to feeling genuinely useful
from time to time.

Of course none of us looks nearly so uncomfortable as my

father. Social situations, cold sober at least, are not his strongest suit. And for him, wearing anything he can't cover in glue and sawdust, bloody entrails and two-stroke oil at a moment's notice is tantamount to torture. I watch him bear-hug Marisa, then gravitate nervously toward the boys—because he knows they speak his language. His fingertips slide softly over the tabletop as he passes. The jacket he's wearing is leather, new, to me anyway. But the thick green shirt beneath it is threadbare, old and familiar.

And I know exactly where I have seen it before.

The opening night of my father's first furniture exhibition came just two months from his redundancy. It was held in a modest craft gallery, where early examples of his work had been on display, in a small nearby market town. He had sold a handful of pieces by then, but nothing really substantial, and throughout the short, bleak month of February had been busying himself preparing for the show. My parents have never been keen on spending money they do not have. It's why the house took more than thirty years to build, and why every car that was ever parked on their neatly laid paving was falling apart. And by then, financially at least, things must have been getting horribly desperate. The leather jacket he wore that night was old, in need of replacement, but the thick green shirt was new. Bought, I suspect, without his knowledge—and specially for the occasion. It was the first time we'd seen him in anything even remotely clean since Christmas.

The snowdrops were out, and the salt crunched underfoot, and granny held tightly to my arm as I helped her into the back seat of my parent's weary Volvo. Wrapped in a navy blue wool shawl, her eyes were bright, and she smelled strongly of lavender. On moonlit roads, we made the five-mile journey over the hills to Haddington. And while, up front, her son hunched over the wheel nursing frayed nerves, in the back she winked at me. A glimpse into her handbag revealed the distinctive purple foil, and the source of the twinkle in her eye. Dipping in and out, we spent the drive palming down chunks of rich, velvety milk chocolate, covering our tracks with sham yawns and stifled giggles.

Skulking in a corner of the gallery—fat, fourteen, and ill at ease in my own skin—I soon realized I was not the only one hoping the frosty ground would swallow him up. I could feel the discomfort radiating from my father. His tall, bulky frame hemmed in and painfully awkward among the tight bustle of people and loaded glass shelves, struggling to make small talk. On anyone else, this rabbit-in-the-headlights look might have been reassuring—made me feel a little less abnormal. But on him it was unsettling. Starkly contrasting the way he was at home, in his workshop, or when he was building something with his hands. I'd never seen him look like that before. Exhausted, frustrated, angry—certainly. Haunted, even. The ghosts of his own brutal boarding school incarceration still looming large on the rare occasions when he had to cross the threshold of one of our schools. But in there he looked utterly terrified.

As the evening progressed and the glasses of wine went down, and the first small pieces of work began to sell, his mood lightened, though, until he almost looked to be enjoying himself. I listened: an awkward invisible teenager. And as people cooed, fondling the furniture's smooth surfaces, I even felt the warm glow of a little pride blossoming. It wasn't my father I was proud of but myself. *I* had sanded many of those surfaces. *I* had felt the rough timber slowly graduate to the texture of polished marble beneath my fingers. It was *me* that had branded those key rings, and *my* eyes that had stung with their terrible resinous smoke. And like the dreadful callow adolescent I was, whenever the opportunity arose I said as much. Not that anyone was listening, or even looking terribly closely, come to that. Because that's one of the strange things about exhibitions: most people don't look—not *really*. Even then it struck me as terribly disproportionate. The sheer amount of work that went in and the time most people spent looking. Hours, days, weeks of energy had been poured into everything, but most visitors gave the furniture only the briefest of glances.

Work sold though. After a tough few years the economy was on the up, and with the internet still very much in its infancy, shopping local wasn't so much a movement as a practical necessity. My father's prices were low—which helped. He simply couldn't afford to risk making them otherwise. And with the gallery taking their own cut, he can't have cleared much. But unbeknownst to me, his enjoyment stemmed from more than just a few small sales. One or two of the people I saw him talking to were interested in commissioning their own furniture. There was even talk of a whole bespoke kitchen. Something that, with his building background and contacts to draw on, he could comfortably oversee from cabinetry to plumbing to electrics to remodeling. Months of potential work and, as it turned out, something he would go on to specialize in over the coming years.

It was only a small exhibition then, at a local craft gallery, but it was the start of something. Something that saved my family. And something we are all still feeling the ripples of today.

"I *know* you've got something decent to drink back there—and a *real* glass," my father says, poking his head around the door. "Pour me a dram, get yourself out here, and let's have a drink while you tell me how great I am." Steeling myself, I straighten my collar, take a deep breath, and finally join the party. And of course, it's not terrifying or teeth-grindingly awful. All that is just in my imagination. Instead . . . it's rather wonderful.

Thoughtful people say thoughtful things—people I care for and people I barely know. There is genuine warmth, enthusiasm, and optimism. A tingling feeling of family and community. I share the boys' smiles, watching as uneasy pride spreads like dawn sunshine into wide grins, as details they have sweated over are discovered and appreciated. Hearing things like: "This one's mine!" and "When I win the lottery!" Tucking them away for later.

Andrew's father and my own soon find each other, as I'd guessed they might. Inhibitions numbed, the old man will be drawn to a fellow storyteller like a moth to a flame. Like his son, the cheerful, loquacious Shetlander has a wealth of extraordinary tales that no single evening can hope to contain. But I know from experience that he'll give it his best shot. I put my arm around my father's shoulder and steer him away, and together we take in his wild osprey carving. "You know," I say, as seriously as I can, "that this . . . *this* is far and away the stupidest thing I've ever seen."

"It is not. It's brilliant. Everyone says so . . . but the scar through his face!" He grimaces theatrically. "It was *such* a disappointment!" The scar slashes down through the head and beak: a hidden flaw in the timber. Something that makes the epic raptor look even more menacing, but something that, having bored down deeply into the thick elm, he wouldn't have known about until it was already too late. The extravagant depth and severe undercut of the huge wings, the way the elm's dramatic grain feature has been selected and arranged to give each individual feather the look of the real thing—it really is a remarkable object, and he knows it. But I still tell him as much. "The scar gives him character," I say, slapping him on the back and shaking my head in genuine wonder. "And isn't it *lucky* that the grain aligned in the feathers like that."

Suddenly overwhelmed by it all, I need air, and a moment alone with my thoughts. The storm doors are closed, to discourage the uninvited guests who always try to drift in when even plastic glasses are chinking. Pushing my way outside, I find Marisa and her father on the street. They are watching, in undisguised amusement, as one visitor—who has been crowing all evening about his new car's fancy onboard computer—is finding it has been a bit too clever for its own good. As he inches forward and back, forward and back, trying vainly to extricate himself from the impossibly tight space it has parked him in and growing more and more irate by the minute, I join them in their laughter. Swigging the last of my beer and trying hard not to see this hilarious moment as an omen, I put my arm around Marisa.

As her father giggles his way back through the door, I pull her to the edge of the pavement. From here, in the gathering dark, the window is brightly lit. From here we can take it all in. Inside, the hard-core are still milling and laughing, still fondling the furniture and taking pictures. We watch for a long time in silence, holding each other close, before looking up at the freshly painted gold lettering above the door. Our name is up there, and with it the fate of our business and the exhilarating prospect of the unknown. We smile at each other, but we don't speak.

We don't have to.

Part 3

Connections

People confuse me.

—*Anthony Bourdain,*
KITCHEN CONFIDENTIAL

14

Excitement, disbelief, and then, nanoseconds later, blind panic. Like realizing midair you forgot to pack the parachute. But the purse is already out of the handbag, the card poised expectantly. The scarlet nails are raising it aloft like a wand. "It is for sale . . . isn't it?" the lady asks again. "It's *perfect* for my new flat." I know my lips are moving, but no words seem to be coming out. Of all the scenarios I've run through these past few weeks, this one, in all honesty, had not occurred to me.

I mean, how does one actually sell something . . . in a shop?

Packaging, wrapping paper, tape, bags, ribbons, receipts . . . a pen. Why are these things only now occurring to me? Worse, we've got no cash to make change (who carries cash anymore?), and as neither Marisa nor I have ever tested the digital card reader properly, there is a small but nonetheless very real chance we may have no way of taking payments at all. I glance over at my wife. Reliable, prepared, steadfast. She will know what to do.

Bugger.

Luckily, Marisa recovers fast. Ushering me into the back room and grabbing the card reader, she nudges the door half-closed behind me and takes the lead. Peering outside, where the muffled talk is all optimism, cheer, big smiles, and gratitude, I breathe a sigh of relief. Hunting around for something to parcel up the wooden coat rack, it's also a relief to find that Tommy made two of these things, otherwise I'd be out there unscrewing the display model from the brickwork. Packaging is a problem, though. There really isn't anything back here to wrap it up with. At over two feet long and close to an inch thick, solid oak with handmade brass hooks, it's hardly going to fit in her handbag.

Bin bags? Newspaper? . . . Toilet paper? Half a dozen sheets are already off the roll when good sense prevails. Toilet paper doesn't feel professional. It doesn't feel *luxurious.* The clock is ticking, and the panic is beginning to surge again as I haul down the first of the stacked storage boxes. Too late I feel the lid slip and watch, helplessly, as the plastic wine glasses clatter to the floor. One shatters on impact, while another finds the water hazard—splashing into the toilet bowl. The clock keeps ticking.

I don't think this is how it's supposed to go.

Sneaking another look through the cracked door, I can see Marisa pressing the little black box up against the window. She must need a signal to process the sale. I still have time. "Just up for the weekend." "New flat in Twickenham." "*Love* the shop." It's all still sounding very positive, but I know that intense look on my wife's face. I've seen it too many times before up at the workshop to be mistaken. I'd recognize her "*FUCKING INTERNET!*" look anywhere. A sure sign that technology isn't cooperating. But

I've got my own problems. It's a quarter-mile round trip to the supermarket for birthday wrapping paper, or twice that distance in the other direction to the post office. Think man, think . . . Leather! *Yes!* We have leather swatches, big ones, desktop samples rolled up in the oak cabinet out in the shop.

"All going according to plan?" I ask, as jovially as I can. Marisa's eyes bulge a little as I hover in front of the cabinet. The street door is open now, the card reader thrust out into the air. The customer is still browsing, killing time. She doesn't look irritated. Yet. Grabbing the leather, I retreat to the safety of the back room, kick the door closed behind me, and unroll it. It. Is. HUGE. But there's no time to worry about that now. Digging out the scissors—small, cheap, blunt—I begin to hack away at the hide. It's heavy going, with each finger-straining bite chomping through another ragged inch. I don't think the scissors are going to make it, but after five long minutes I finally have something I can hold up for inspection. Not great. But fully wrapped I'm sure it will look fine. It is, after all, at least forty quid's worth of full-grain cowhide. Not to mention, my only option.

Casting about for a means to fasten it all together and coming up empty, my dejected eye falls to the floor. To my good shoes: the brogues with the leather laces . . . One foot up on the counter, I yank out a lace and dust it off. It will have to do. Triumphantly, sweating now, I roll and wrap and truss up the coat-hook like a butcher's joint.

Out front the place is packed. Four more people have appeared. It is a very small shop. They point and stroke and exclaim, reading the little explanatory messages I have written—the hundreds of handwritten words detailing the timbers and techniques—with what looks like genuine interest. Yet *more* people are huddled around the door and window. Drawn, presumably, by the gathering crowd. Marisa looks up, beaming. "Tiny IT hiccup, but it's sorted now. And can you believe it, Sarah here is going to take this whole set of cutting boards too!"

While this latest packaging challenge sinks in, another lady—tall, blond, tastefully dressed—thrusts another cutting board in my direction. It's a two-footer. Like a great fat cricket bat, with a beveled base so your fingers can get in underneath, and a little leather hanging loop secured with a polished brass pin. More of a serving platter than a cutting board, really. And it's expensive; it took a long time to make. "Is this *really* the same wood that's in the Aesop boutique, in Stockbridge?" she asks, a mix of curiosity and wonder coloring her voice. Fumbling with my tongue, I tell her that it is, and then, warming to the subject, wade into a long meandering story about the wood's provenance: sycamore, wild, local . . .

When I finally stop talking, I find that she, and the two people next to her, are still listening intently. "Amazing," she is saying, "just *amazing*. I'm obsessed with that store. I'll take this, *and* this." Pointing out an ash and walnut knife block, stroking its polished curves. I know I'm grinning, but I don't care. "Thank you," I say, "*thank you*." And I really, really mean it.

The first month's rent has just been paid.

But it doesn't stop there. Another smartly dressed couple are patiently awaiting my attention. They too, look intrigued. With one hand on the undulating lip of a lathe-turned bowl, the man breaks the silence . . . by offering me a cherry tree. He just comes right out with it. "Tree surgeon was just going to chop it up, but it seems an awful waste," he says. And they both shake their heads, looking genuinely pained at the idea. Maybe, they suggest, there's something *we* could do with it?

How to handle this? If sales keep going at this rate we'll be out of stock before the end of the week, but we still can't be buying whole trees. It would need to be uplifted, sawn and seasoned, and unless we, quite literally, turned it all into bowls, it would be years until we could actually use it. Bracing myself, I try to explain. "We can't really pay much . . ." But they cut me off. Just knowing the wood had been put to good use, that a tree that's stood in their garden for years has not just been tossed into the fire, that it has, I suppose, a chance at a second life, is payment enough.

This is interesting.

Saving their address in my phone, I watch them wave goodbye, having made plans to visit their home after we close for the evening. Hot on their heels, two more happy customers leave, with promises to return, and treasured (if largely unwrapped) wares clutched beneath their arms. The place feels strangely empty when they are gone. But I am buzzing. I want more of this. *Much* more.

It's not to be.

Adrenaline fades, fades . . . and the door stays stubbornly closed. Until at last I finally blink. And suddenly, the late night, the wine and the whiskey and the weeks of anxiety are like a millstone around my neck.

"Coffee? Celebratory muffin?" Marisa suggests. Caffeine and sugar to restart the engine. I could certainly use it. But it isn't going to happen. "You're not leaving me here . . . *alone*!" I yelp, barring the door. Incredulous. I saw the trouble she had with the card reader; I can't handle that sort of pressure. I'll crack, I know it. Anyway, it's going to get busy again any second now.

Any second now . . .

People are fickle creatures. For an hour and ten minutes—I'm timing it—not one person crosses the threshold. Outside, the sun is still shining, the street is still busy, nothing appears to have changed. Just beyond the window, couples and families, buggies and dogs and gaggles of teenagers still wander up and down. Many pause to peer in, some with their hands cupped against the glass or looking right at us, even going so far as to reach for the door handle. But seeing an empty shop repels them all. No one seems to want to be the first. Perhaps that's it?

For a while we try pretending to be customers ourselves: conducting animated conversations beside the window, lifting and handling objects as if in deep and ponderous deliberation, pointing thoughtfully, pulling out our wallets. But none of it makes a scrap of difference. And eventually I find myself retreating to the back wall, hands clasped behind my waist, adopting a fixed grin. Neither of these postures is familiar to me, and my shoulders, spine, and face soon begin to ache. Sitting down, though, feels terribly unwelcoming. And so, becalmed, we smile, and we wait.

And wait.

Finally, when I have all but given up hope, mere moments before we're about to call it a day, the door swishes open again. "Don't mind me," the man says. "Just waiting for the bus."

Squinting around, he sets his shopping bags down on the big elm table with an ominously heavy thud, adding with a laugh and raised hands that he's: "not going to *buy* anything!" I look at the man, the shopping bags spilling onto the brand-new table, and inside my head I can actually hear the cartoon shriek of a steam whistle. With my blood pressure rocketing, I open my mouth to speak, but Marisa is too quick for me. Before I can react, I'm being hustled unceremoniously into the back room.

A mixed bag then, day one, I reflect as we walk west along the high street to inspect our new cherry tree. One or two small things to work on—taking payments, handling goods, customer service—but on balance a success. Four sales on our first day is better than we'd dared hope. Good sales, too. Not huge, but not tiny, and reason to celebrate. It is a fine summer evening, the tail end of a beautiful afternoon. And as I curl my toes to keep the flapping shoe on my foot, passing thronging benches outside already raucous pubs, my mind keeps drifting back. Replaying the day's highs and lows. The way people looked at the furniture, seeming to be drawn by the wood itself, compelled to caress the surfaces; the looks in their eyes when they opened the door and drew first breath, when they heard the stories behind the work. But of course, I'm only really half-thinking about any of those things. The other half of my mind is churning, fulminating. Fixated.

"You're still thinking about him, aren't you?" Marisa says.

"Well aren't *you*?!" I erupt. "The time, the effort, the care. I mean . . . how could he? Right on top of the table. The bloody scoundrel!"

15

Well before seven the next morning, we are already slithering over wet grass, feeling tightly packed shale crunch like broken seashells underfoot. To know at last that there might just be a way out of this—that digging deeper might actually have revealed an escape route—and to have slept all the way through the night for a change, has us both fleet of foot. For the first time in weeks our morning run through the forest is upbeat, half a pace quicker. Sensing our mood, the dog bounds ahead, her tongue lolling from the side of her mouth, straining at her harness. When she glances back over her shoulder, it is with the manic look of a particularly unhinged Nicolas Cage character. Oh, great, I think to myself, I can't wait to walk *that* along the high street.

Regrettably the town does not wake up so quickly. I watch from the shop's window, like a housebound pet looking out for an owner's return. Expectantly twitching at every movement, all but wagging my tail. But the morning grinds along, Sunday-slow and lazy. There are moments of excitement, but all too often they are dampened by disappointment. An enthusiastic visitor returns with her husband in tow, only to cringe apologetically as he loiters by the door, visibly uninterested, virtually clutching his wallet to his chest. A shrink-wrapped neighbor, clad head to toe in bright Lycra, bounces on the spot, running through a veritable shopping list of furniture needs, before revealing she "prefers glass and metal to wood." And a family of fondling American tourists handles every last thing we have on offer, lingering tantalizingly beside the giant osprey (which is, by some distance, the most American thing in Linlithgow, let alone the shop), before telling us we ought to *"open one of these in New York!"* and leaving empty-handed.

There are sales though, and more reasons to celebrate. Another good-sized cutting board and one of Andrew's lathe-turned bowls head out of the door. Wrapped now in brown waxed paper and bought by a pair of charming sisters. The two ladies pore over everything, genuinely interested, warmly assuring us that this is "just what the high street needs." That they will "tell their friends." And that they will "be back!" But after the adrenaline rush of our opening day, the pace feels sluggish and listless.

Lunchtime, and it's a ghost town. But I still cannot bring myself to walk out the door. Knowing that the very moment I do, someone will arrive to change the course of the day. I refresh emails, polish, dust, clean, pace, fret, overwater the plants, guzzle coffee, and stare agonizingly out of the window. Willing someone— anyone—to walk through the door. Soon Marisa can stand no more, and she heads off to explore the street, leaving me alone.

And then, all of a sudden, he's just *there*.

"Did you do this?" the man says gruffly. He must be sixty at least, but he is lean and hard and tensed like a muscle, and despite his shock of gray hair, he looks like a middleweight boxer. "*Did you?*" he repeats. Pointing first at me, and then back toward the carved osprey. It doesn't feel like a possible sale . . . but what would *I* know? If it is, it's exciting. We're not taking a big cut, certainly nothing like a serious gallery, but our commission on this work would be almost four figures. Dad would do well too—very well. "My father's work," I manage, stumbling over my words, and wondering where to go next. I needn't worry. On hearing I am not the craftsman the man visibly relaxes. "John Donaldson," he says, holding out a bone-crushing hand. "I'm a woodcarver myself."

Damn.

John and I talk for a while, and I discover that much of his own carving work is done for historic buildings: complicated large-scale friezes, decorative panels, and heraldic work for castles and the like. Some of it taking years to complete. He reveals that, if it is to be painted, some restoration work is carved from materials like MDF, and seems impressed, if a little surprised, that anyone should choose to use elm—just about the toughest, most fibrous and fickle wood there is to carve with—rather than something softer, stabler, and more lenient, like a sensible person. Why not use one of the more grainless fruitwoods: lime or pear or apple, even oak? Why make life so very difficult?

It's a sort of sickness he has—is what I want to say. But I get the feeling I will be the only one amused by this. So instead, fumbling around for an answer and looking up at the work—feeling its vitality, the way the grain has been used to animate the mighty bird, giving it depth and movement, bringing it to life—I simply say this: "To see if he can."

Marisa returns and, having spread our meager profits around the high street, we nibble muffins and drink good coffee. The rest of the afternoon passes quietly. There are a few kind words, and a few really quite extreme peepers, but most must be enjoying their Sunday lunches or their football, or whatever it is that people do on weekends. I am just about to lower the blind and pull over the storm shutters, to head outside for the first time in close to seven hours, when a lady hurries past the window. Tentatively, she opens the door and leans in. "Are you still open?" she asks. "I'm sorry it's so late." She strikes me as kindly and friendly, if a little anxious. She will not hold my gaze for long. It's a trait I know I share, and immediately I feel a connection. "Of course," I say, and welcome her inside.

In a softly lilting Scottish voice, the lady introduces herself as Catriona, another neighbor, who has been meaning to "pop in." She does not stare, as most do, at the looming three-foot osprey. Does not linger by the smaller, more affordable items. Catriona only has eyes for the table, and her hands are caressing its smooth elm top almost before she knows that she's doing it. Instinctively, she draws them back as if they've been burned. Looking up, she asks, as no one else has, if it is alright to touch. "*Please*," we say, almost in stereo. And as she reaches again for the timber's sculptural form, running her fingers along the top and down the contour of the leg, beaming, the day's minor disappointments fade away.

Catriona does not say the next words we hear—she breathes them. "*I love it.*"

Perhaps it is the lines of age on Catriona's hands, their shape and tenderness as she reaches out for the polished timber. It could be the deep red color of the elm, her snow-white hair, or the covetous twinkling in her eyes. But something about the interaction jolts me—stirring up a memory from deep, deep down. It is a memory I keep locked away, as if it were tightly sealed in an iron-wrought chest, buried in the murk where I cannot see it. Without warning, the chest is loose and bubbling up from the depths. And as the form ascends, tumbling toward the light, an overwhelming giddiness fizzes through my lungs. It is a powerful, thrilling, terrible feeling, as if I must burst, or cry out. Or cry.

It is pain and pride and grief . . . and love.

When I was young, I was sure that if I watched and listened for long enough, I could crack this whole socializing thing. Surely, I thought, there must be some code, some design, *something* I was missing. And if I could only puzzle it out then life would be a lot less worrying. What must it feel like to be comfortable around other people, I wondered to myself, my face pressed up against the glass, peering in from outside. Pretty fucking good by the looks of it. But I hadn't the faintest idea how to do it.

We were out in the sticks of course, miles from the nearest town, and there weren't many people around in the beginning to practice with. So on those rare occasions when I was dropped into heavy social situations, generally I froze. Watchful and confused, chewing my metaphorical pencil under the teacher's desk, with my literal back against the wall. This is crazy, I thought. These *people* are crazy. Could I have missed the day when the instructions were handed out? To my lasting regret, by the time I understood that everyone feels a bit like this sometimes—that the trick, if there is such a thing, is to stop thinking about it and just get on with it— I'd missed my window. The habits were already hardwired.

Isolated or not, I wasn't alone. Far from it. I had a loving family and a few little pals I'd grown up with. I had my granny, too: my father's mother. The quintessential sweet old lady who lived next door, distrusted foreigners, and liked to make telemarketers cry. However bad things got, however confusing the world might seem, I could always race round to her warm kitchen, hunker down on her sofa and share her milk chocolate. I'd help pick fruit from her garden, tend bonfires smoking white with wet leaves, and take my life in my hands riding shotgun on her supermarket shopping trips. From the day I was born, her house and garden were extensions of my own. Vibrant, integral landmarks of my childhood geography. She was my partner in crime, and she was my friend. But she was more than that, too. Artisans all need patrons; granny was my first.

It started with small things, little jobs she'd find for me to do. The base for an embroidery, a picture frame, candleholder or breadboard, a simple footstool for her porch. It was a way to give me some pocket money, and perhaps to teach me a few things. I'd been tagging along beside my father since I was old enough to carry a shovel—first as a toddling builder's laborer then as an unwilling weekend woodworking apprentice—so I knew my way around the simpler tools well enough. But these jobs were different. They were my own projects, and I think she understood the power of that. Dad kept an eye on me just the same, and until I was old enough to fire up the really big machines, he quietly did the heavy work for me. But as I got older, and my skills developed, and the commissions got bigger and more challenging, I did more and more of the work myself. At least that is how he made it seem.

There was a little side table in ash: a basic, but properly mortise-and-tenon-jointed frame, with straight legs, pegged joints, and arched upper rails. I remember I fitted a low shelf of slim ash panels, very thin and each the width of a playing card, for newspapers and the washboard-sized slabs of milk chocolate granny was never without. A detail that developed because I had all these perfect offcut strips left over after the legs were machined and I wanted to find some way to use them.

Then came a larger, more elaborate coffee table, also in ash. The top of this piece had arched support rails too, but I scooped them in as well as up, then tried the same trick with the profile of the top. Giving the whole thing a slightly pinched look that I thought terribly clever. Some of the edges I rounded over, others I kept sharp; the tops of the legs I left protruding just above the table's surface, specifically because I knew I shouldn't. And to finish it off—entirely on a whim and without really giving it too much thought—I set upon it with a router, hacking a pair of sweeping curved channels right into the middle of the top. These I filled with contrasting strips of vibrant orange yew, bent hard and pared down flush with a hand plane. This last flamboyantly daubed brushstroke might have ruined the table completely— and I think in my father's eyes it probably did—but I couldn't know for sure unless I tried it for myself.

All of these were simple enough projects, and they were never completed without a good deal of my father's assistance. But they were by some distance the most complicated things I had ever attempted to design, plan, and execute on my own. And though I didn't realize it at the time, I was learning a lot.

Time passed, and life cooked up fresh challenges for both of us. But life can always be relied upon for plenty of new things that need escaping, so well into my teenage years her kitchen remained my bolthole, and we remained close. Then came the biggest project we'd ever discussed: a pair of bedside cabinets. This was a serious job. I had to survey her bedroom, figure out the heights and depths, and puzzle out the complexities of building and fitting multiple drawers. No mechanical runners in my father's workshop, these were piston fit—each one perfectly sized to ride smoothly on nothing but wax and a cushion of air.

In line with our usual arrangement, I was given an entirely free hand with design before we refined and tweaked the details— scheming and plotting together at the big table in her kitchen. The proposal I sketched out was a simple affair: boxy rectangular carcasses, made using thick panels of solid timber, assembled with the most basic of housing joints. Tongues cut onto the sides, fitted into channels in the top and bottom, locking it all together. Each unit would have a plywood back, recessed into another slim channel that ran right around the carcass. Something I knew from watching my father would help me keep them square during their assembly.

I was in my late teens by then and had been helping out on bespoke kitchen builds with my father for quite a few years. Kitchens, certainly his custom-made epics, develop just about every skill a maker will ever need. But this was just cash-in-hand, weekend muscle work—lifting and sanding, dragging and oiling—and rarely was I called upon to do anything terribly complicated. Even from the sidelines, though, I felt I had absorbed plenty of skills and techniques I could replicate. Things, to be clear, that I was keen to try and pass off as my own.

My father and I skirted round each other carefully. The workshop was his space—like an extension of him, really—but I had grown up in there, and felt entirely at home. I had a hair-trigger temper, but the muzzle wasn't directed at him so much as at everything. Myself included. We didn't fight or shout, it wasn't a wild blaze. Rather, I would brood and glower, warning twists of smoke drifting into the air, as beneath the surface, stoked by a bottomless insecurity, the fire never fully went out.

He liked to say: "I'm just making it up as I go along." But he always seemed to know exactly what he was doing. Something that was, by turns, reassuring and absolutely infuriating. Originality, experimentation, that was fine, applauded even, but he abhorred laziness, and couldn't stand to see things done sloppily. So even though he *knew* what would happen, when impatience got the better of me, as it so often did, God help him, he'd wade in.

Granny and I chose elm for the cabinets, I don't know why. Perhaps there was some of it lying around that I had my eye on. I don't think I would have had the wherewithal, or the budget, to select my own timber from a woodyard, and I certainly wouldn't have blinked at lifting anything in the workshop that wasn't nailed down. Always desperate to jump straight into the fine details, I skimped on the design phase and rushed into production. Nevertheless, they still took months of work.

With my father's support, I planed down the elm—insisting that *I* would be the one to feed it into the machine, all but ruining the first boards in the process. The stock I didn't destroy was beautiful, almost a dark rose pink, with swirling green galaxies of feature. I sawed, jointed, and glued the main pieces into broad panels. Ignoring my father's advice about "balance" and instead making the joins as dramatic and obvious as I could. And then for days—it may even have been weeks—I just stared at them. I wandered around the bench, pondering my next moves, unwilling to ask for help. Risky as it was, I balanced the panels together like an immense house of cards, hoping the answers would reveal themselves. Hoping I would just *see it*.

Wanting more than anything to withhold from my father the satisfaction of seeing me fail because of such inadequate preparation, gradually, making small steps, I moved things along.

Nothing happened quickly, but whenever I focused down and made some grand leap forward—when my father had something particularly unappealing he wanted me to do, say, and I could play my trump card—granny would tour the workshop and check in on progress. Seeing her reaction always spurred me on.

I was tremendously proud of the drawers. They were solid elm, and even if they were little more than screw-fixed wooden boxes, there were eight of them in all, and that's over a hundred individual components. I'd strengthened the junctions with neat little recessed lozenges of darker elm, another detail I thought tremendously clever and had lifted, wholesale, from my father. Granny thought this wonderful, and we both loudly agreed that they were far, *far* better than anything dad had ever done.

Then very suddenly, granny moved. Quickly, and for reasons I did not entirely understand. She left the house she had helped build—the house where, for all my life, she had been a constant fixture—and the next time I saw her it was in a small, ugly, identikit bungalow in the nearby town where I went to school.

She moved close to the railway station, so I visited her often. Making my own way down the quiet road from our house and traveling the ten or so minutes out to the coast. The new bungalow felt foreign and restrictive to me. Set on a manicured lawn in a manicured cul-de-sac, it was just one in a flock of a hundred clones. I always felt as if I was going to break something just by moving around in there. It was hot and stuffy, and almost unbearably tidy. But granny's bed moved with her, so work on the cabinets continued, and with the main construction soon nearing its end, I could finally indulge myself. Rubbing my hands with glee . . . it was time for the *details*.

By now I was recessing strips of starkly contrasting timber into more or less anything I could find, so I welcomed the opportunity for more: adding bigger, square-ended stitches to the carcass's joints. Dark elm in one and pale maple in the other. This wasn't so much to strengthen them—they were already practically indestructible—I did it simply because I could. On the lathe, I turned round chunky feet that would never be seen, and low down on each side I scorched my initial. Branding a sizzling "C" with a ground-off section of plumber's copper pipe, glowing red from the blowtorch. One detail had me stumped, though, and it was an important one: the handles.

Dad kept a box of hardware samples in a cupboard in the workshop, and this I dutifully carted along to granny's new house. Always excited to catch up on progress, she nonetheless seemed smaller, more diminished somehow. The result of living in a centrally heated box in a town no doubt! Together we tried every option going, covering her carpet with years of sawdust and woodshavings in the process. Brass and stainless steel, round and square, hinged and recessed—nothing was quite right. I found it hard to believe that something so trivial as handles could make such a significant difference to the furniture's character. But the evidence was right there in front of us. The wrong handles aged the cabinets terribly or made the drawers feel too modern, masculine, or military. I didn't have any clear idea what I wanted them to feel like, which didn't help, but unbeknownst to me, I did have one great advantage: not once did it occur to me to look beyond my father's workshop for inspiration, and too much choice can be paralyzing. It was hardly surprising then, that a few days later, his workshop is where I found my answer.

Shaker peg-rails were designed, in part at least, to hang up chairs during the day. To the Shakers, discouraging sinful sitting when you should be working—i.e., during daylight hours—was almost as important as keeping the place tidy. My father loved this, of course (why he never took to locking away the chairs, and the televisions come to that, during our daylight hours is still something of a mystery to me), and he had turned dozens of his own mushroom-shaped wooden pegs on the lathe. Using different sizes to make cupboard handles, doorknobs, and cup hooks for a kitchen he was building.

I destroyed a lot of good timber trying to make those eight perfect knobs. Dark elm for one set and maple for the other. Something always tore or broke, snapped or exploded. Or the shape simply got skewed out of proportion. All too easy to do with the long, spoon-shaped chisels. You really wouldn't believe the hours of work that went into them, and each no bigger than a cotton reel. But eventually, there they sat. And with this last main job out of the way, all that remained was final fitting and finishing.

What I didn't know, as I sanded and oiled and patted myself on the back, anticipating the gleeful look on granny's face, was that this would be the last project we did together.

I was surprised, on delivery day, when we continued on past her turning, drawing up five minutes later in the familiar carpark.

The low white buildings were flanked by thick green bushes and holly trees. I had been in the little hospital before, for sprains and stitches. And dad was a regular fixture, always having something patched up, set, or sewn back together. Mum looked grave and sad, but warm as she turned to me. Strengthened by a faith I envy but have never possessed. She put her hand on mine.

"She'd like to see you . . ." she said.

One half of my brain lit up, and before the other half had a chance to weigh in, I was already in motion. Out of the car, not thinking, just acting. Emotion surging up like a rogue wave. Mum caught on fast, holding open the doors. And to the consternation of the nurses on shift, and anyone else who happened to be at large in the hospital's hallways, a determined young man with a face like thunder strode through the building, laboring under the weight of a chunky wooden cabinet.

Granny had always been a big, strong lady, full of life and devilment and dessert. She wasn't afraid of anything. It took me flat aback to see what the illness had done to her. Stricken in that hospital bed, dwarfed by it, she looked wrung out, gaunt . . . and frightened. Her health had been worsening gradually for months, though up until then I had been too blinkered to see it. But things had taken a turn for the worse, and by then there were really only weeks left. Looking up, seeing me, she brightened. And sunken as they were, shrouded with the dark bruises of fatigue and fear, there was no mistaking those twinkling eyes. I was tongue-tied, honestly. Shocked into silence by the first really sick person I had ever been so close to. Choked up, I set the cabinet down and sat timidly on the edge of her bed. She touched my arm, and in a moment turned her attention to the cabinet. Then, laying a pale, emaciated hand on the elm's polished surface, she looked back at me, and grinned.

Closing the storm doors behind Catriona, I turn to find the dog is watching me. I am used to her many faces: greed, rage, impatience—often all three. But this is different. Sitting in the middle of the floor, her head cocked to one side, she is watching me intently with something like curiosity. It is almost as if she can see something she does not understand. Can she sense that I have been away, burrowed deep down in my past? Perhaps she simply knows that I am sad.

With those brown eyes still puzzling me out, I lock the memory away again, the stinging afterglow of grief's first real scar still livid in my chest. But just as I am about to give it a final push down into the depths, I pause. I have missed my granny, and it was good to see her again. To see that mischievous, avaricious smile, to smell the gooseberry patch and the lavender perfume and the wet leaves on the smoldering bonfire. To hear a real professional tease my father. And to watch as her gentle hands caressed something we had planned and schemed together. What harm would it really do to open the chest from time to time? To remind myself what it can mean to make something special for someone. To show them, even if I cannot tell them, just how much I care.

16

Weekday mornings are the worst, I know that now. If I had my way, we'd never open in the mornings again. Not on weekdays, anyway. Don't get me wrong, I love the mornings; I am a morning person. But almost without exception the only visitors we've had before eleven a.m. have been strained mums dragging troops of sticky-fingered children, conversation junkies, the bored, the lonely, and those waiting for the bus. But the afternoons . . . the afternoons do sometimes glean something interesting.

It's Thursday, it's two p.m., and I am trying, oh I am *really* trying not to get too excited. Run the client checklist: she doesn't seem crazy, she hasn't told me she could "do it herself if she had the time," suggested I recycle something wooden she already has, or put her coffee cup or her wet umbrella or her child down on any of the furniture. All green lights so far. "It's not that I don't like this furniture," she says, looking at me, and then around at the shop, smiling warmly. "It's beautiful, it really is . . . but this table is far too big, and the style just isn't quite right for our home." Bespoke then, we can do bespoke I suppose. Though with just the thought of the word, of starting again with a blank sheet of paper, I can already feel any profits slipping between my fingers. The only thing that's nagging at me is the folder under her arm. She has already alluded to its contents: a series of clippings and design ideas, taken from interiors magazines. Indeed, my toes are already tightly curled in anticipation. My visitor's name is Mary. She is sharp and direct and has short, precise blond hair, and she and her husband Jim live on the outskirts of town. Clearing a space, I brace myself as she spreads the folder's contents widely on the table . . . then sigh inwardly with relief. Now, I can get excited.

"The room isn't huge," Mary says, "but there are times, like Christmas, when we'd need to seat eight or ten." I'm listening, but I am also leafing through the images, my pulse quickening with every page. Almost all the tables are large, high-end statement pieces, from designers whose work I respect and admire. None of the lines is anything like as sinuous as those we have chosen for our own collection, laying to rest any thoughts I had of suggesting a resized variation, in fact some even verge on farmhouse—rustic tops on tapered legs. But all are clean and considered with a contemporary twist. One in particular gives me pause. It is a Benchmark piece. Sean Sutcliffe and Terence Conran's legendary workshop in Berkshire: one of the finest cabinetmakers in Britain since the late eighties. "We thought . . ." she goes on with a gleam in her eye, "what about two tables that can fit together somehow? More versatile, more practical."

It is an interesting thought. The idea presents challenges, and it's challenges that so often push creativity into unexplored realms. Already there are half-formed ideas jostling excitedly for attention in my head. But then budget bursts back in, uninvited, like a stranger barging into the saloon. We are running a business, of course, or trying to, and budget is a crucial consideration. But I still feel uncomfortably mercenary even thinking of money at this stage—let alone mentioning it. After years of commercial clients, it's my first really hard-edged reminder of just how different it's going to be talking to real people about the costs . . . people whose own money is on the table. People who may take it personally.

Budget is never really about scale, though inevitably the price of materials plays its part, it's about components and processes. Budget is about the maker's time. And the problem with a pair of tables—even if they are similar or even identical in design, and even if they spend the majority of their lives fixed together—is that they will take far longer to make and finish than a single piece, and inevitably this will drive up the costs. Already I know beyond doubt that whatever we come up with will feel expensive. But if it's two tables rather than one, compared to the other pieces she has researched, it could end up being *very* expensive.

The examples in her folder are not cheap, though, I can see that. In addition to the Benchmark piece, several more are British-made and finely crafted from quality materials. All are designer. And this bodes well. I am about to broach the subject, waiting for my moment, keying myself up, when she says: "We have two grown children you see, and we know something handmade and special like this will outlast us. This way there will be no arguments. One," and with this she dusts her hands together, "for each of them."

This sentiment so endears me to Mary and Jim, and to the project, that in a moment my budget worries are shoved hard back out of the swinging doors. In their place is an unfamiliar sensation. The tingling edge of something, something I haven't felt for a long time. A reminder of just how special this kind of work can be.

"It could literally say *anything*," Marisa says, squinting, hamming it up, as thick hedgerows bully the Land Rover and we creep along looking for clues. I'll admit the map I've drawn is not my finest work (though not to Marisa, obviously), but it can't be that bad. Risking a glance away from the road, I cast an eye. It isn't good. Right, here . . . maybe?

We are late. God, how I detest being late.

This is familiar territory, that's the problem. The tangle of winding backroads is closer to the workshop than it is to town, so I had assumed that instinct alone would be sufficient. Technically, I suppose this is the Bathgate Hills? It's rippling and heavily wooded, and reception is certainly no better than at the workshop—which of course means no satellite navigation. Through a process of elimination and, yes, a crackling phone call between my increasingly exasperated wife and Mary, ten minutes later we are sipping coffee in a stylish, light-filled dining room.

Great care has clearly been taken with the interior. There are hardwood floors of real oak, and neatly painted walls in a rich midnight blue—a blue so dark it is almost black. The few, neatly framed paintings, and what objects there are displayed on shelves and side tables, feel carefully curated. Looking around the room, it almost feels like an art gallery, or a magazine spread. On the table in front of us, the contents of Mary's inspiration folder are neatly arrayed, and I can see that more images have been added. So with coffees in hand, together, we get down to business.

We talk materials, laying out and discussing samples of elm, oak, and ash—durable, hard-wearing local timbers, well suited for working tables. We talk sizes, making a basic survey and photographing the room as we do, so that Marisa can build the space on the computer and drop the concepts into position. We talk detailing, the idea of incorporating flashes of color, rich, deep wood stain, and polished metals like brass, copper, or steel. And we talk chairs, just in case they may be considering buying something new and the scale and style may factor in. (Chairs with arms, for instance, can cause storage problems, because they will not fit under tables with chunky constructional braces or rails.)

As Marisa continues to take down notes, I excuse myself, holding up my tape measure by way of explanation. Two relatively small tables will be far easier to carry in from outside than one large one, but it is always worth checking the route in. Tight corners, awkward stairs, and narrow doorways are usually navigable with a bit of careful wriggling, but there are always those instances where nothing can be done. Once, years ago, the mirrored lift to a brand-new penthouse apartment comprehensively caught my father and me out. A lift that had seemed so very big when we initially glanced in, but that in the end left us no option but to cut the piece apart and rebuild it five flights up—in front of the client. Wandering back down the corridor toward the stairs, I can't help but notice the avenue of neatly framed family photographs. I pause beside one in particular. In it, a younger Jim and Mary are posing with two beaming girls.

It makes me smile too.

Contrast is LOUD, contrast is dramatic, and it is all too tempting to indulge. To pair walnut, ebony, or fumed oak with sycamore, ash, or maple. To amplify complex technical joints, decorative peg details, and exclamation-point inlays by pairing the dark oh-so-starkly with the pale. No degree show, portfolio, or exhibition would really be complete without at least a handful of harlequins. But over the years I've come to think there is something wonderfully sophisticated, something so much more *adult* about using complementary timbers and tones. Subtler combinations, that feel no need to shout.

Ebony black for the table's legs, that's what we've got in mind. Stained solid oak, finished perhaps in a semimatte wax oil to flatten and subdue, and to give them a more contemporary look. This tone will echo the chalky walls of Mary and Jim's dining room, making the legs feel suitably considered. Elm for the top— it almost goes without saying. Laying down the sample, I knew, even before they spoke. Few can resist its charms. But it is the perfect match. Durable and incredibly hard-wearing, despite its rich, dark sumptuous colors. And if the legs are going to be muted, a serious slice of flair is just what we need.

In the office, I swivel to look over Marisa's shoulder, and let out a low whistle. "Oh, I know," she says, rotating the three-dimensional model on her screen with a practiced flick of the wrist. She's got every right to be cocky; this almost never happens. She's put one right in the middle. It's a bull's-eye. If she had a mic, this is where she would drop it.

"Talk me through it."

A Brief Note On: Inspiration

Horace Goldin cut his first victim in half in 1921: a hotel bellboy, dismembered with a giant whipsaw. He cut hundreds of people in half after that, all over the world, and was soon so proficient, and so infamous, that he even started selling instructions. A born showman, it wasn't long before Horace grew dissatisfied with a mere handsaw and began to tinker with the idea of using a giant buzz saw instead. Louder, faster, and infinitely more theatrical—just think of the time it would save. Just think of the box office!

While Horace Goldin didn't actually invent what is arguably the world's most iconic illusion, it's fair to say that few alive possessed his wealth of hands-on experience. I'd go further. I'd say that no one will ever know quite as much as Horace Goldin did about cutting people in half. But what he could never have known (as he hacked all those people to bits) was the influence his work might one day have on the struggling proprietors of a tiny rural furniture shop . . .

While I have been tinkering with timbers and hunting down images of existing tables, searching for ideas, Marisa's attention has been elsewhere. Stripping back the concept to its essence, forgetting about the technical—the timber, joints, and craft—she's been trying to find the seed of something truly original. It takes practice to do this, and discipline (which may explain why I have such difficulty with it), but it's a good reminder of how a real designer operates. Instead of worrying about the minutiae of actually building a piece of furniture, she's looked instead at objects, rituals, nature, and eventually even early-twentieth-century stage magicians, seeking a novel means to split one object into two. And the lesson here is this: design inspiration can come from anywhere.

There is something of the farmhouse, or medieval refectory table in the shape of the dark legs she has drawn. These can be refined later, but right now they are chunky at the shoulder, square then cylindrical, lathe-turned and simple. Playful profiles that undulate, tapering in like tight-ankled jeans at the base. Six of these legs support a large elm top. Or at least that is what they *appear* to do, until she reveals the table's party trick. Using one of the graphics tools, Marisa pans and rotates to expose the hidden break line, dragging one half away from the other. It is as if the central pair of legs, and the tabletop itself, have been sliced neatly in two, right down the middle. Cleaving the midlegs like split logs—or a magician's beautiful assistant. But there is more. Where the break line is revealed, the curvaceous flat faces of the parted legs, indeed the whole sliced-through sections of the table, are covered with shimmering gold. A theatrical flourish worthy of a table that will bear the name *Goldin*.

"Getting the brass machined from your drawings shouldn't be a problem, but it won't be cheap," I say, slipping straight into production gear. "But without CNC [computerized woodworking tools] matching those profiles on the lathe is going to be an absolute bastard."

"How big is the lathe?" Marisa asks. But I am already up and halfway to the door, thinking the same thing.

Passing the benchroom, I catch sight of Tommy putting the finishing touches on the set of fine-boned oak shelves at last. His head is nodding to a beat I cannot hear. He looks focused, utterly tuned in to what he is doing. The shelves are looking good.

Out in the machine shop I survey the lathe. Its bed is over a meter long, and I know we'll only need two-thirds of that to accommodate the leg of a standard-height table. And though it's only a fairly small machine, from the bed to the spinning center point of its headstock measures 150 mm, so technically—if not entirely advisably—we could turn a leg almost a foot across. Far more than we need, and certainly more than enough to shake the workshop walls.

"What are *you* doing?" Andrew asks, suspiciously. Emerging from the kitchen as my tape measure snaps home. "I could ask you the same question," I reply, narrowing my eyes at the contents of his hands. "I'll have you know that these are bespoke ice lollies," he says, taking a lick from the vivid layers of color. I open my mouth to speak, but any further discussion is lost in a wall of noise, as Robin appears and all hell breaks loose. Stalking back to the office, I can hear him exclaiming behind me: "They worked, they *really* worked!"

"More than enough room," I tell Marisa, who looks up from her computer and smiles as I come in. Then: "Did you know about the ice lollies?" Her eyes widen and her chair scrapes back.

"Didn't *you*?" she says, virtually running for the door. "It's pretty well all they've talked about for days."

It's nice to see them all in such good spirits, and in the quiet of the empty office, alone with my thoughts, I allow myself a little smirk. But it doesn't last long. In truth, I'm worried. For the time being, they have things to keep them busy, but there is still nothing bringing in an immediate income. And though Mary and Jim's table is beginning to look like something, the job is by no means certain. After a strong start in the shop, I can already feel the money beginning to dry up again. The clock has never really stopped counting down of course; the clamor and excitement simply drowned out the ticking. If one of the large pieces doesn't sell soon, we'll be into the last perilous hours again before we know it.

After lunch, with the bulk of the conceptual design work behind us, I leave Marisa in the office, heading into town to open up. I have made and drunk the first of what will be many coffees when a young woman cautiously pushes her way through the door, asking if we're open. "Only my father would very much like to see the woodwork, if that might be alright?" I can see him sitting outside the window, his hands crossed in his lap, pointedly looking the other way. "He doesn't want to be a bother," she says, and I get the strong feeling these are his words.

The old man nods a curt greeting as his daughter helps him inside, then he makes his way methodically around alone. I try to be discreet, glancing up past my laptop screen only now and then, when I think my curiosity will go unnoticed. I catch him once, lifting a simple cutting board to his face, running a thumb like a hammer's claw along its smooth edges, exploring the thick leather hanging loop, turning it over and over in his hands and staring into the swirling feature as if it is a photograph of an old friend. It is field maple—cat oak or whistle wood. A tree that makes its home in thickly tangled hedgerows. A fighter. Now his fingertips are caressing the top of the Dram Table, the glossy surfaces and the leather-wrapped edge, the handmade brass cleat detail that Tommy so cleverly incorporated. After a long moment the hands disappear beneath the top, groping around for the good stuff. The construction. A wry smile breaking on his lips, and an expression that says: *caught you*. More than anything, I notice how closely he looks.

When at last he seeks me out, his grip is like a vise, and it does not let go easily as he looks me in the eye. His knowing smile still lingers at the corners of his mouth, giving me the strangest sensation that I have passed some sort of test.

That he was "a joiner, man and boy," I think I already knew. Even before his hard hands rearranged the bones in mine there was something altogether too familiar, too intimate about his interactions with the wood. The way he instinctively sought out the connections and the hidden surfaces, places only an old hand would know to reach for. It all hinted at a long acquaintance.

Sunlight streams through the window, casting the wavering shadows of ferns and spruce branches onto the floor. We talk easily, falling into stories of the things professionals always talk about. Where we've worked and what we've made, how we came to be in the trade, memorable scars, close shaves—and our fathers. I discover he's been itching to visit since our sign first went up but didn't like to intrude. Passing today, though, and seeing me inside, he simply couldn't resist. He seems genuinely moved to speak to someone else who has spent their life in and around "the trade." Someone else who is interested in what he has to say, and in doing a "quality job" for its own sake.

His respect for the craftsmanship verges at times on reverence, leaving me clumsily fumbling to find the words—to tell him that it wasn't me who built these things. But as we trade dog-eared tales and his mind reels back, reliving his own treasured moments of effort, achievement, fellowship, and the pride of a job well done, it is clearly more than just the work on show that's affecting him. As he hears again the clamor of industry, the shriek of the saw, and the teasing trill of happy workshop banter, a change comes over him, that seems almost to lift him from his wheelchair. It charges the air around us like thunderheads before a storm, and I can feel it fizzing from the fingers that find and clutch my arm as the memories come spilling out.

And I find myself wondering: if this man had spent his working life folded in behind a desk, or fielding telephone calls, if those powerful gnarled machines on the ends of his wrists had been put to work tapping at keys rather than making fine shavings curl from timber, would he feel this way? Would the same searing frustration inhabit his voice and his steely grip? The same heartache? Would I be able to sense this almost physical pain that his working days are well behind him? I think the old man would happily stay and chew over old times until the sun goes down. But unlike anyone else who has visited so far, he soon begins to look uncomfortable. If anyone understands the value of time, he does. The stoic air returns and, as if on cue, so does his daughter.

When he leaves, an afterglow of pride remains, making me stand a little taller than before. Energized, I decide to move some things around, hoping perhaps that a change of feng shui might deliver a change in our fortunes. I turn my attentions to the window. Up until now we have filled this space with greenery, delicate branches, ears of barley, and wildflowers gathered from the woodland, arranged in one-gallon glass demijohns, and some of the smaller pieces of furniture. The Dram Table and Mack Chair, cutting boards and bowls. But after my encounter, my eye begins to wander around the shop with rather more audacity.

Could I?

Shuffling the big oak cabinet across the floor alone is not entirely straightforward. It would be far easier and safer with someone on the other end. But what I have to do next is downright foolish. What the hell, it will be over in a moment—best not to think about it too much. Bear-hugging the carcass, leaning back dangerously until the toes of its interlocked wooden legs find purchase, by some quirk of fortune or muscle memory I somehow manage to get it up there without damaging either of us. So there it sits, filling the window, blocking out the light. From inside, then, it is not ideal. But after heading out into the street, I know I've made the right decision. Framed like this, and viewed through the glass, the door's wild elm grain feels like some wondrous ancient map. The boys really have done a fine job. It is as much a work of art as a piece of furniture.

I am making minute adjustments, down on my knees on the floor with my tape measure, trying to get the cabinet central in the space, contemplating what else I might cram in there with it, when the door swishes open again. The stranger regards me with the boggled eyes of a frog. They dart away, hunt around, circle back—as I imagine his tongue might pursue a fly. I watch as he takes silent inventory: green walls, green skirtings, green doorframes, green doors, green blinds, slim laths of blond ash boxing in the radiator and already beginning to bulge in the close dry heat. A light scattering of furniture, all moderately askew. One perspiring shopkeeper, kneeling, breathing heavily. Still in fine fettle from the old man's visit, I nod hello and give him my little speech—as polished by now as any of the furniture. In return, he gives me the thin, tight-lipped smile. The one that says: "I'd very much like you to stop talking to me now."

Leaving him to his browsing, I straighten the furniture, and assume my position at the rear of the shop. Arms folded behind me, grin firmly fixed, ready and waiting to answer any questions he may have. He feels my eyes on him and treats me to another blast of the thin and tight stuff. I'll get no questions from this guy, and that's fine with me, I just wanted him to know that I am paying attention. I busy myself trying to disguise the gap the cabinet has left, dragging over plants, tweaking and adjusting. And that is when I hear it.

The gasp is not a gentle thing, but a proper, hammed up, vaudeville spider-in-my-soup number. Spinning on my heel, I'm thinking: *please* don't be clutching your chest. With one palm flat against the paintwork, he's physically supporting himself on the wall. The blood has drained from his face, he is slack-jawed and plainly in some sort of shock. And he's clutching something alright, but it's not his chest . . . it's the table's price tag. Almost visibly shaking now, he looks up from the offending item—the little story and the sum I have carefully handwritten on the square of bridle leather—fixing me with an expression of such disbelief, such towering contempt, that it takes my breath away.

What I want to say is this: forget for a moment the weeks it took to handcraft this fine solid elm table, forget the years of experience brought to bear by the maker, the thousands of hours of training and practice, the costly mistakes, the electricity, insurance and overheads, the team of arborists who brought down the tree, the sawyer who milled and dried the boards, the man in front of you, rooted to the spot, who painstakingly selected each one before handing over many hundreds of pounds for the privilege, and think on this—this table might last a hundred years, it might last *four* hundred. Your children's children might still be sitting around it when you are but a memory. A vaguely amphibian headshot gathering dust on the mantel. All this and more I want to say, but of course I don't. I probably couldn't. My jaw is clenched so tightly that it might as well be wired shut. The stupid fixed grin is still there. But behind the scenes, whatever fragile confidence these past few days have nurtured is fast evaporating.

It's not me that stands staring into space long after the man has indignantly huffed and puffed his way back out into the street. It's someone else, someone numb and detached, mechanical in his movements, who draws the blinds, grabs his dog, and locks the door behind him.

Traffic thunders past, and the unpleasantness plays over and over on repeat. The things I should have said but couldn't. The clawing shame that just one look, just one negative reaction could affect me so much. That I didn't stand up for myself, for the team, and for the work. There is anger too, simmering just beneath the surface. And something else, something I must keep moving to get away from.

Doubt.

Part 4
Shaped by Hand

There are obvious crossroads in your life—births,
deaths, marriages, emigrations—but there are
others, perhaps more compelling, that are hidden,
that seem nothing at the time, tripwires that later
you realise set off everything that came after.

—*A. A. Gill,*
POUR ME: A LIFE

17

It was the first half of the first year of a brand-new century. The world had not ended, as some had feared it might; the sky was still up there overhead, though at nineteen I could barely see it through the clouds of gloom and cigarette smoke. We were seated around the breakfast table. Me pale and dehydrated, picking through the tattered remains of the previous evening's entertainment like a gumshoe rummaging in the bin for clues. My father mopping up eggs and bacon with thickly buttered bread. He had been quietly making a name for himself for almost five years by then and had just been offered another big kitchen job. The job promised months of assured income but it would be difficult to handle alone. As I lurked behind the cereal boxes, he cleared his throat and made his pitch. I was no stranger to the workshop, I knew something about the work too, and with me he knew what he was getting into. Was I interested in joining him full-time? he asked.

Whether he was actively trying to lend some direction to my rudderless months since leaving school, or he genuinely couldn't have done the job single-handed, I can't say. Though the truth is probably a little of both. In any event, the offer was there, hanging above the curling toast and the cornflakes, waiting to change the course of my life.

Having already spent more than my fair share of time propping them up, it was predictable, if not entirely healthy, that I'd found work as a barman. I was still living with my parents, and though on occasion I did lend a hand with his projects, day to day I was firmly ensconced in the comfortably numbing drudgery of pub life. It was an easy way for a teenager with no degree, no previous experience, and no real direction to make a few quid for beer and tobacco and room and board while he figured out what he wanted to do with his life. The local hotel was hiring, I was looking, and it was close to home. So close that, on frosty nights before I was born, as they made their way back from the primary school where my mother worked as a teacher, my parents would often stop in for a warming dram in front of the fire. Secure in the knowledge that the last few miles were well enough out of the way to risk driving even after a couple of drinks.

Months had passed in this way. My stomach had grown, and my spirits had withered, as any aspirations I may have had were drowned in the ready supply of pilfered beer. I'd tried to tell myself that the camaraderie, the new friends, and new substances I was discovering were making me happy. But even stumbling along, I was increasingly aware that each day was melting into the next. That I wasn't simply serving the locals—men who'd been occupying their barstools long enough to see my father's face in mine—I was turning into one myself. I knew that there must be more to life than watching it pass by through the pub's dimpled windows. Unbeknownst to me, I wasn't alone in that opinion.

I'll think about it, I'd told him, before I sloped outside for a cigarette. And that is what I did. Rolling up the last of my tobacco, sitting on the bench at the edge of the woods, looking out over the green wash of fields and the little line of trees that always made me dream of faraway places, places I had never seen. I'd let university slip through my fingers, I'd no plans or ambitions, no prospects at all really. And though I'd no real notion what working with my father, or with my hands, would really be like on a full-time basis, I had just enough sense to recognize an opportunity. And as the ugly lung-punch of the day's first draw slammed into my system, I made up my mind.

Whatever I might have thought I knew about making things, the unpleasant reality didn't take long to reveal itself: I knew next to nothing. Worse than nothing, really. Because after years spent around the work, I *thought* I understood far more than I did. And woe betide anyone who tried to tell me otherwise. Sparks flew daily, and the dusty air crackled around me as I scowled and snarled my way to six o'clock. Cold beer time.

I was always just furious that these things that should be so easy, things I saw my father do all the time, were somehow so far beyond my own capabilities. It drove me crazy, and in turn I'm sure I drove *him* crazy. But if he regretted his decision to hire me on, he kept his concerns—and there must have been many— tactfully out of my earshot. By then it was too late anyway. I had left my job at the pub, and the kitchen had blossomed into an extravagant design. A project that, even with the two of us working full-time, would go on to take over six months to complete. Filling every inch of the cramped little workshop in the process.

School, regrettably, had bred in me a deep and abiding mistrust of authority. As coincidentally it had in my father—though his experiences were *considerably* rougher than mine. Ironically, though, it was a childhood spent left more or less to my own devices, and the stubborn independent streak it forged, that made it so very hard for me to take instruction. I bridled at the idea of asking for help, and this was a serious problem because (not to belabor the point) I knew almost nothing. Despite the conceit, clumsiness, and near-pathological impatience of his surly new apprentice, the natural teacher in my father cared too much about his subject to risk souring it with bitterness. Dad didn't just want me to help him, to learn new skills, and to find some direction . . . he wanted me to love it all as much as he did.

So he did what he always does: he got creative. Rather than giving me direct instructions, he would list the jobs that needed doing, and then leave me to figure them out for myself. Or at least that is how he made it feel. He would highlight ways that something might be done better, or make useful suggestions, but never explicitly tell me what to do. Guessing that I would improve more quickly, or at least try a good deal harder, if there was a point to be proved, he exploited my ego (a powerful ally) wherever he could. But knowing my sensitivity to criticism, how short was the fuse that led to detonation if anything even *approaching* a negative comment slipped from his lips, he was always careful to tread lightly. It must have been like handling nitroglycerine.

But he persisted.

When I blunted his knives cutting through abrasive paper, left deep scratches in finishes, lazily allowed oily brushes to dry out rather than cleaning them, or snapped yet another drill bit, he'd shrug it off or make a joke of it. Making sure that the next time he needed sandpaper, I saw him folding it over a steel rule, giving it the cool flick of the wrist that so neatly tears it into sections. Or when he was sanding something himself, casually mentioning the need to climb through the abrasive grades—from coarse to fine— and the practice of raising the wood's fibers with a damp cloth to obtain a near mirror finish, as if these were things I already knew. And while there were times when even he couldn't hide his exasperation in the heat of the moment, the brief storms soon passed, as an opportunity to learn something or to innovate occurred to him. Problems to my father, like broken tools or building projects, were always just challenges waiting for solutions. No matter how bad or how thoughtless the mistake, whatever the implications or the sheer number of backward steps it forced him to take, he never made me feel stupid or ashamed. If I worked hard for it, if I racked my brains and found my own solution, even if I failed, he treated me with respect. That meant a lot to me. More than he knew.

Nothing, of course, is more mundane or prosaic than the job your father does. I never really saw myself as a woodworker, a cabinetmaker, or a joiner. It was something I did, not something

I was. I just needed to bring in some cash while I figured out what I wanted to do with my life. Yet in spite of all my bluster, every once in a while, I'd find myself being drawn in. My hands would instinctively know where they were supposed to be, without my mind having to tell them. One process would automatically lead to another, and almost by magic the job would be done better than I expected. Or a joint would go together so sweetly that, pulling it apart again, it would pop juicily—a sure sign that the fit was *perfect*. With new skills not learned so much as earned, and the feeling that, however minutely, I was finding my own answers rather than following the rules, there was a freedom that caught my imagination and slowly started to take hold.

Handling them every day, I became more intimately connected with the characters of different hardwood species. Getting to know their particular qualities . . . and their quirks. Oak, for instance, is heavy, sharp and bristly. Its fibers catch and prickle like an old man's stubble. Few timbers possess its strength or durability, but it has to be worked and machined very carefully or it can shear out and tear, exposing the razor-sharp fault lines that may be hidden within its grain. Once, smoothing the fine oak edge of a cabinet with a sandpaper-wrapped block, I punched a splintered fragment into the tip of my right index finger. It happened fast: a sickening moment like a belt from an electric fence, burying itself so deeply I couldn't even see it. Only after a week, with the finger looking sickly and gray, did it begin to show itself, peeking coyly from its puncture wound. Using a pair of needle-nosed pliers (and scarcely able to watch) I dragged it out—the whole half-inch of it. The splinter was so arrestingly three-dimensional and perfectly preserved, and the damage it had done to the edge so obvious, that I reattached it with superglue. The fit as seamless as a puzzle piece.

I learned about the different sorts of adhesives and finishing oils, discovering firsthand the effects that temperature and the timber's varying densities can have on their efficacy. And that oily rags can, and do, spontaneously combust. I began to make my own boiled linseed oil concoctions, heating and thinning the viscous, fragrant liquid with artist's turpentine to deeply penetrate and bring out the wood's lustrous color. I saw how iron and steel from chisels and clamps will react with oak's natural tannins wherever moisture is involved, staining your hands and the wood's surfaces with an inky blue-black that is next to impossible to remove. I struggled to put an edge on tools, found that drill bits get screamingly hot when you use them, and that an angle grinder's sparks will melt window glass and get you into terrible trouble. As an employee, albeit a thoroughly insubordinate one, I was spared the daily stress and worry that comes with having your name above the door. But working with him full-time in such a confined space, living and breathing the experience as he did, I learned a lot about my father too. Up until then, I had always existed in a peculiar limbo somewhere between awe and intimidation—not of the man, but of his capabilities, his standards. But gradually, as I came to better understand the things he was trying to do, I began to see that he was fallible. That there genuinely were plenty of times when he was making it up more or less as he went along. That what I had been missing was the effort and the grit that meant he never stopped, never gave up until the job was finished properly. As I began to get a taste of what that meant, of just how hard it was to push through and find a solution, to make something thoughtful and new and beautiful, and to do it quickly . . . I finally started to learn some respect.

Then, one day, a few years in—I'd like to believe because he had quietly started to value my efforts, but probably because he had too much to do himself—my father handed me the drawings for some complicated oak desks, telling me that I would be responsible for building the frames. My skills had improved significantly by then. Given the time and space, there were plenty of things I could do to a fairly reasonable standard. I'd built kitchen cabinets, worktops, drawers and doors—or significant parts of them at least. But with just the two of us in the workshop, I had really only ever played second fiddle. It was my first time, and you never do forget your first time.

With traditional mortise-and-tenoned frames, floating panelwork to allow for seasonal movement, tooled leather tops, and banks of piston-fit drawers, the pair of writing desks were grand affairs. Heirlooms of tomorrow. My job was to cut, machine, joint, and dry-fit the skeletal assemblies, before the panels and the drawers went in. I would be making the desks' bones. Not long before, we'd expanded our workspace—pushing out into the vennel, covering it over with a curved roof and more than doubling the size—so I was left alone in the "old" workshop to puzzle out the drawings. Next door, where he could be heard but not seen through the wide double doors, my father was working on the drawers, the carved panels, and the fitted library shelves that completed the commission.

Only subtly different in their detailing, the desks were a matched pair for a husband and wife; meaning the basic construction for both was the same. This simplified the framing job but meant I had to make two of everything. That and devise a system of marking and keeping track of each near-identical oak component, in sets that ran well into three figures. It took me a long time to plan the job. Not least because of the struggles I have always had with two-dimensional plans. For Marisa and my father, and many of the best cabinetmakers I have worked with over the years, technical drawings like these seem to leap off the page. They can walk around inside them and implicitly understand them with the merest glance. But for all the use they are to me, they might as well be written in a foreign language. I could almost hear my father sighing as I painstakingly redrew my own crude, cartoonish versions of his plans. After that there was a long week of sawing, planing, and cutting—precise but reasonably straightforward work—to get the many oak lengths machined to size. Then came the tricky part.

Mortising machines make square holes: their spiral-grooved auger bits are tightly fitted into hollow chisels that travel down just behind the point of the drill, crisply squaring off the holes. Anxiously, I clamped the first leg onto the machine's wide bed, to begin cutting the joints. Knowing that if I got this wrong, all I'd have made in a week would be some very expensive firewood. My father's mortiser was Victorian-era, cast-iron and almost comically massive. It had once been steam powered, though for the years it occupied a good fifth of his workshop it was two large electric motors that turned its many *whapping* leather drive-belts. Perched on the swivel stool, adjusting giant handwheels and pulling the sorts of levers you might expect to find in a railway switchyard, I fired it up. The workshop shook, the chisels sliced into the oak, and the drill bits screamed in their smoking-hot steel housings, and little by little the mortises began to emerge.

After the better part of a week, I had the mortises and the tenons—the simple shouldered corresponding joints—completed. Each one individually sweetened with a file, until the fit was perfect. Finally the moment had arrived when I could test the joints for a whole desk. A full dry-fit. Something I did alone because I wasn't at all sure they would work. While my father was still up the hill with the dogs, I headed out to the workshop early in the morning. Arming myself with a rubber mallet and a set of long steel clamps, I cleared my bench and set to work. It was tricky to get them all in there by myself, even risky for a moment, but it happened fast, faster than I expected. The joints *thunking* gratifyingly into place. And then, suddenly, miraculously, there it was. I watched it happen. I *made* it happen. Something that, just moments before, had been a pile of inanimate sticks now had life and form. Two dimensions became three—and nothing would ever be quite the same again.

18

For five years I worked side by side with my father. Together we hand-built kitchens, staircases, cabinets, gates, beds, doors, benches, tables, chairs, and a hundred other things besides. He taught me a lot. Enough for me to think, with all the misplaced confidence of youth, that I actually knew what I was doing. But I still had no clear idea who I was—or just what it was that I really wanted to do with my life. And so at twenty-four years old, determined to find out, and certain that the answers lay out there on the road, I decided it was high time I saw the world. I would be back, I told him and meant it. But it probably hurt. I would just have been becoming useful. What few tools I had accumulated did not travel with me. I gave no serious thought to what I was going to do for an income, but furniture making was not high on the agenda. It was time for a change. Time to spread my wings.

Several beery weeks later, having burned through most of my cash and just as the southern winter was giving way to spring, I washed up in a quiet beachside suburb on the windswept coast of Christchurch, New Zealand. As far as the eye could see in either direction the waves frothed and grabbed at its scrubby strip of sand, and it wasn't rolling fields but snow-dusted peaks that filled the horizon. The place felt wild and half-forgotten, rugged . . . and affordable. Just what I was looking for. With a couple of friends, I found a house for rent—unfurnished, uninsulated, and unloved—just beyond the dunes. So close to the water that, on big days, the rumbling surf could be heard from inside its crumbling fibro walls. We signed a six-month lease on the spot. I had somewhere to live, oceanside no less, but I was running out of money fast.

I remember well the sinking feeling, as I stared down at the cursor blinking on the blank computer screen. Alone, and suddenly very far from home, in the tired internet café. "Onetime barman" and "unqualified furniture maker" were going to make for a very compact CV. Worse still, the only reference I could really rely on was from my father, and his word was hardly likely to hold much weight with a prospective employer. Even *you'll* struggle to pad this out, I thought to myself, as reality started to close its jaws.

The classifieds didn't inspire much hope either. Pulling pints and rinsing glasses, cleaning out ashtrays and listening to day drunks witter on? I'd had my fill of that and more. Office work was out too. With no degree, they probably wouldn't have had me anyway. And having always lived a stone's throw from a railway station, and never seeing the need of a driver's license, I couldn't make deliveries. Sales? A shop assistant? Really? I was supposed to be spreading my wings!

If the realization I only had one marketable skill wasn't enough, the stark evidence of how everyone else was required to make their livings being laid out in front of me really got me thinking. And sitting there, looking back over my time in the workshop, it finally dawned on me. Woodwork wasn't just the trade I knew best, the one job outside of slinging beer where I had some practical experience . . . it was the only thing I could actually see myself doing. It was the first time I had ever thought of working with my hands as a vocation—as a calling, even.

Regrettably there wasn't much joinery work going at the salty end of Christchurch. There *were* carpentry jobs, but it would mean more travel. Even without tools, I could ship out to one of the remote job sites in the mountain villages of Franz Josef or Fox Glacier. A hired screw-gun, fitting doors and windows in the snow. These places were crying out for willing hands, and their romantic names did stir something intrepid in my soul. But I'd just signed a lease, and I was getting to like Christchurch. So before I pulled on my steel toecaps and mucked in with the laborers, or relented and trudged around the local bars and hotels, I thought I'd try my luck at a few serious woodworking workshops. My chest—though now adorned with the ubiquitous whalebone necklace—was still puffed out with the false confidence I'd carried from home. I knew a few things, and even if they weren't advertising, once they knew who they were dealing with, I felt sure they'd change their tunes.

Unannounced and with no real idea of what I was going to say, I bused and hiked out to a couple of local outfits. Having only ever been in one job interview—one that required little more than a pulse and a working arm to pull pints—doing any sort of preparation didn't really occur to me. The first workshop was on the other side of town, a fine cabinetmakers, and all told it took me nearly two hours to reach it, which didn't bode well if they did offer me some work. I needn't have worried. With no tools or references, portfolio, qualifications, or official training, I was quite literally laughed out of the door. I'd probably been asking for it, and my ego certainly needed a spanking, but boy, did it hurt.

The second place was far more promising, and it was only ninety minutes from the front door. A wiry, tough-looking woodworker with a dust-mask hanging around his neck considered me carefully. He even offered me a bit of work, sanding on an upcoming project. But as this wouldn't start for a few weeks, and even then it would be sporadic and part-time at best, I thanked him for his time and kept on looking.

Poring over the job pages in the beachside library, where I'd discovered that newspapers could be read for free while looking out over the marching waves, something finally caught my eye. Newly advertised on a crisp page of newsprint, it read: "*Cabinetmakers wanted. Skilled and experienced bench-hands sought for full-time positions.*" And that is how I found myself, thanks to three buses and a long dismal walk through the light industrial district, chatting amiably with Paul—a friendly, rangy Kiwi.

Thankfully, Paul shrugged off my on-paper shortcomings, as all around us loud music, and the rip and clang and roar of the biggest workshop I had ever seen colored the air. He'd traveled and worked all over the world himself, and after we'd talked and I'd showed him a few printouts of projects I'd worked on with dad, he seemed happy enough to take me at my word. Still chastened by the stinging memory of the earlier cabinetmaker's laughter, a meeker attitude probably didn't hurt.

Pulling out a sheaf of drawings, which to my relief looked straightforward enough, he talked me through the work. "No antiques in New Zealand," he said, with a strong accent. "So there's always a good market for well-made oak reproductions. French provincial . . . sort of." I nodded and half-studied the drawings—a long console table—struggling as usual to make sense of the two-dimensional plans. "The oak we bring in by the container-load from France," Paul continued, indicating a huge cache of boards stacked toward the rear. "Always oak, always hand-finished." In retrospect I should have paid more attention to these last words, but I was trying, from the corner of my eye, to make some sense of the workshop's layout.

As we walked through the place, we skirted between benches and hulking, whirring machines, many of which I didn't recognize (though this I kept to myself). Six or eight sinewy men in singlets and T-shirts wheeled trolleys piled high with components, purposefully hand-planed timber, and hammered together frames and carcasses on small, scarred workbenches. None of them so much as looked up as we passed.

Back in the office, a stocky, muscular, good-looking guy with a shaved head gave me a theatrical double take. "*Jeez*," he said.

"Look at the fuckin' size of ya!" This, as it turned out, was the boss, giving me the once-over. I didn't ask what the job paid, and I didn't really know how I was going to make such a long and awkward journey ten times a week, but by then I was too desperate to care. I can do this, I thought, and five minutes later, handing me a short list of hand tools to buy, the boss agreed.

That first morning I walked the mile of cool sand shoeless, feeling it smooth as flour between my toes, to meet Tim: a lean, dark cabinetmaker who lived nearby, and who had been tasked with my transport. It was the sort of workshop that starts spectacularly early in the morning, and as I made my way along the empty beach with my boots slung over my shoulder, the sun was just peeking its head above the distant Southern Alps. A filament of blazing orange. We talked little on the road; Tim, I would discover, wasn't much for talking. And just shy of seven, I marched through the open shutter door, into the workshop that would be my home away from home for the next six months.

I should think it took about fifteen minutes, though it could have been less, for me to comprehend just how far out of my depth I was. How utterly, comically underprepared. Eighteen hours was the target, Paul said, as he broke down the drawings in detail. The first piece I would be working on was the same long console table I had been shown during the interview. Dovetailed drawers, tapered legs, cleat-ended top, and solid oak construction . . . in *eighteen hours*!? It was something I'd have spent two weeks or more making at home, and—I realized to my horror—something I would have had a great deal of help with from my father.

"You're new, so we'll cut you a bit of slack at first, but don't take the piss," Paul said, as he directed me to a bench I could use for the day. I would be moved around until a proper space could be found for me, but I got the feeling they wouldn't be making room until I proved I could stick it out. And with that, he left me to it.

Peeling the oiled paper wrappings from my new purchases, I unpacked the cheap jack-plane, spokeshave, and chisels I had bought with the very last of my savings. Hand tools that, in truth, I hadn't used much in the past. Their greasy blades were factory dull, but I had no whetstones or oil to sharpen them, nor even a screwdriver to remove them if I did. Above me, music boomed from the speakers—dub and rock and pulsing drum and bass— loud enough to carry over the noise of the machines. Slipping on my brand-new ear defenders to find some peace, I took a deep breath and smoothed out the drawings on the bench.

I have never worked so desperately in all my life. Battling the clock, and the crowds, for three frenetic days I ran *everywhere*, hurried *everything*. Never more than a degree away from full-blown hysteria. There were always ten other guys jostling to use all the same tools and machines as I was, and nothing—none of it—was familiar. The surfacer and thicknesser were separate machines, both huge things with powerful dust extraction units (the first I'd ever encountered). There were mysterious setups for dovetail cutting, jointing, and tool-sharpening too, and a slow-moving upturned mega-router, vast and unspeakably terrifying, called a spindle molder. Most challenging of all for me, and indeed for everyone, was the pneumatic dowel-jointer. Not because it was particularly complicated to operate, but because it must be used to joint up all the furniture in the workshop, meaning it was constantly in use. In fact in all the time I worked there, I never once saw it unoccupied.

Woodwork is all about processes—breaking projects down into manageable tasks—and things have to be done more or less in order. But as the new guy, I had to wait my turn. Then, as three or four gruff and irritated Kiwis kicked their heels, I had to try and act as if I knew what I was doing. It was like trying to board a busy Italian train, at rush hour, then finding out everyone is going to watch you try and drive it.

Working at a sustained pace I didn't know I was capable of, leveraging a good deal of luck, and jumping onto machines when the others filed off for "smoko" or lunch breaks, I somehow got the thing together. Despite the hand-planed surfaces, which were designed to give it the tactile, old-fashioned look of a timeworn antique, but which I thought crazy, not to mention sheer agony with cheap, oak-blunted tools. I'd run over on time, but not *too* badly, having become convinced that I'd swiftly be fired if I did. So it was a thoroughly proud moment when I called Paul through to check in on progress.

"Not bad," he said. Which for a South Islander is high praise indeed. "Just need to finish it now." Only then did he direct my attention to the small checked box in the top corner of the drawings. I had been pondering over the term "Heavy Distress" since I started, quietly amused that it so accurately described my state of mind. "You, ah . . . you might not want to watch this," Paul said, grinning, as the finisher shuffled out of his noxious back room. Shaven-headed and gaunt, in a grubby singlet and jeans, in one shellac-stained hand he carried a battered black doctor's gladstone. Dipping into the heavy bag, he clearly derived a great deal of pleasure from my horrified reaction as he placed his tools on the table. The smile getting steadily broader, as one by one the chains and the hammers, the barbed wire, the chisels, and the grizzled half-bricks appeared.

In all the time I worked there, I never really had much more than a short conversation with any of my colleagues. Even Tim, who to his immense credit drove me to and from the workshop every day. We didn't socialize or meet up outside the workshop more than once. And I certainly didn't make a great deal of money. But when the cold beers came out, half an hour before the shutters went down on a Friday afternoon, I got one. That wordless acceptance, and the kind of tireless hard graft I learned to thrive on beneath the sweltering tin roof, they were worth far more. By the time I left, I was a journeyman: a craftsman living off his wits and his hands. I had the beginnings of an identity at last, and I would be returning home with a few new tricks up my sleeve.

19

"What *now*!?" Marisa groans, dragging a pillow over her face. "If it's more bills or fees or bastarding bloody rates, I *don't* want to know." Her words are muffled by duvet and down. How best to break this particular piece of news? Draw it out . . . or come right out with it? "Okay . . ." I say, leaving just a hint of a quiver in my voice. "But I really do think you should take a look at the emails." From beneath the pillow, a curious eye emerges. A hand follows it out into the light, making a lunging grab for the phone. But I am too quick for it.

I watch her face as she reads the messages. The hesitant smile tugging at the corners of her mouth, trying not to get too far ahead of itself. The lips moving ever so slightly, the way they only do when she is reading something she does not quite believe. "Are you serious? . . . *How?!*" For half an hour now, I have been asking myself the same question. The mention in the *Scotsman*? The few lines in *Homes & Interiors*? It couldn't just be a few social media posts, could it? An accumulation, and a healthy dose of luck, is probably closest to the mark. But the reasons barely matter; it's the results that count. A desk, a pair of cabinets, and a rocking chair. Three jobs, neatly stacked one after the other in the inbox. Enough to cover rent and bills, and more than a month of solid, well-paid work for the whole team.

Too wired to eat, we spend the early part of the morning carefully crafting replies. These are promising tugs on the fishing rod, no question, but for now that's all they are. We mustn't forget that they aren't in the boat yet. Momentarily affronted by the break in her routine, but picking up on our energy, the dog soon finds her exercise closer to home. As we talk breathlessly of new beginnings—of what's-to-comes and how-did-this-happens— she races left and right, again and again, licking and furiously berating the row of curious young cows that have ambled up to the garden fence.

The desk is simple; the same design we have on show in the shop but built from oak, with tobacco tan leather in place of forest green. The pair of cabinets too are proposed as slightly tweaked and rescaled versions of the piece that's currently dominating the window. And these I *know* have resulted from social media, because an old client—one we worked with years ago, who had thought we'd left domestic furniture making behind— has told me as much. The rocking chair, though, has appeared as if from nowhere. From the southern side of the border no less. It's exciting, and a little nerve-racking. We've never made a rocking chair before. We reply quickly, perhaps a little too quickly, hoping our desperation is not as palpable as it feels.

Serendipity has chosen to send us these jobs on the only day we have to work as a team, and we take it as a sign. Deciding to open late, we bypass the high street and make our way directly to the workshop instead. Miraculously, it is only a couple of hours before the first two inquiries are confirmed. Prices are accepted; even the finishes are firmed up. Both of us just sit and stare, blinking in disbelief at the pair of succinct replies: short, breezy, and sweet. As if it were the most natural thing in the world to commission fine pieces of furniture. As if we are doing something wonderfully kind for them, rather than the other way around.

The cabinet client has specified elm for the carcasses, but the material for the doors is still up in the air. So while Marisa puts together options and visuals, I jump ahead and sneak a look at the rocking chair. And just a brief glance at some classic examples from other designers is enough to convince me that the sketchbook, or even the drawing board, will only ever be a small part of the process. Rocking chairs, it seems to me, are all about geometries. Perhaps more so than anything else we have ever tried to make, we're going to need a good deal of physical prototyping to get this one right. First, though, the client must sign off on a basic design—*and* a price—and this is where things become more challenging.

Material costs will be straightforward enough to predict, based on likely scale and timber type. There are always unpredictable factors, just as there are with any trade where organic materials are involved, but a rocking chair's basic size shouldn't be too difficult to ballpark. Adding a margin of thirty-to-fifty percent and erring on the side of caution, we should be safe. The making time, though, is far more difficult to estimate precisely.

If you have worked on something similar before and kept a good record of the time it took to prototype, build templates and jigs, handcraft and finish the piece, then you have something fairly realistic to base things on. Knowledge that has made pricing the desk and the two cabinets relatively simple. But accurate pricing for unfamiliar bespoke work is a fish of an entirely different color. At best it's an educated guess. And in order to guess anywhere close to correct, you have to get immersive. You have to put yourself in the workshop—right into the maker's shoes.

Foreseeing every last job, no matter how small or seemingly trivial, visualizing and noting them down chronologically, and assigning each a likely timeframe is no easy task, and it's always made more difficult because time and memory are so very slippery. When you become creatively engaged in a project, it's not at all unusual to look up from the bench and find that whole hours have vanished. Bad days, mistakes; these are both impossible to predict and tempting to forget—but they happen in the workshop just as surely as they do everywhere else.

Putting a firm number on how long it will take to get the design right—when the client's tastes are an unknown quantity and the blank sheet of paper is staring back at you—is, if anything, even more difficult. But even if it is rough, we will need some sort of design concept to show the client, and to break down for pricing. Ideally this is something we'd do fairly quickly, and sketchily. The inquiry may yet come to nothing, and unlike corporate work, where fees can be levied upfront for design, until the commission is confirmed there is still a chance we'll be doing this part for free. We must bait the hook but leave ourselves plenty of room to refine the design if the project moves forward.

Right now though, with the desk and the cabinets confirmed, and the boys in need of immediate work, all this will have to wait. I've got timber to buy.

With a slam that rocks the whole vehicle, Marisa leaps out of the Land Rover. The dog, always far better behaved with her than with me, trots obediently to heel. She's doing that just to spite me, I think, as I pull away. Once more the woodyard beckons and, having scraped the bottom of the barrel just along the road once already, I'm heading slightly farther afield.

Swinging west, thumping over the long, low bridge at Kincardine, my mind drifts, as it always does, to the work that must go into building a bridge. The *effort.* The steel beneath my wheels is not the prettiest stretch that's strung across the Forth it's true, but until fairly recently, it was the only one that swiveled. Until I was seven years old, a hundred-horsepower motor rotated its entire midsection, making way for shipping traffic heading to the yards at Alloa. And here's me worrying about the engineering of a rocking chair.

The woodyard, when I reach it, is industrious and sprawling. A frontier town of heavily built log cabins and sheds, some complete with wide western-style walkways. Patrolled by languorous Alsatian dogs and staffed by tough-looking men in neon vests and chainsaw helmets, it is neat and tidy. The men move purposefully through the stacks of rough-sawn planking, dragging timber through machinery that is half-sheltered beneath sloping tin roofs. Forklifts zip around, and the great saws grind and shriek, and over to one side, a sawdust hopper that is easily three times the size of the Land Rover roars constantly. There are family traits shared with Ben's place I suppose . . . but the two yards are decidedly distant relatives.

I find the shed I am looking for toward the end of a row of modern insulated shipping containers. Out where the yard is quieter and jumbled logs are piled high at the dirt roadway's end. The deadbolt is stiff, and it opens with a finger-chomping *clank*. Switching on the light, I begin to hunt through the long, heavy boards. There is a good stock of elm here, a kiln-load perhaps that has recently come out. I've heard it said that some elm trees are beginning to develop a resistance to the disease that has claimed so many, but elm is still a rare and precious resource.

I find the heavy lifting is a little easier than it once was. Those early morning hours in the workshop, the painting, sanding, and oiling have had an effect. My hands are harder than they've been for a long while as well. It's not a huge change, but the palms are definitely regaining some of their old leather. It occurs to me too, as I haul those boards that catch my eye out into the daylight, that the few pieces I choose today will go into someone's home. That they will be treasured, and maybe one day even handed down to the next generation. That they will have a second life. They are good feelings.

A buzzing in my hip pocket pulls me back outside and, dusting off my palms, I answer it just in time. "If you're still at the yard," Marisa says—shouts, really—"you're going to need to get some more elm. Mary just came in herself and paid the deposit. The Goldin Table is a go!" Rubbing my face, delighted but overwhelmed, I unclip the tape measure from my belt, and make my way back into the shed.

Sliding my debit card over the counter, I watch as the sale goes through, as the bank account sheds nearly four figures. Glancing up at the calendar—a grand oak tree in full leaf—I actually gulp. It's exciting, and very gratifying, to know that our first big bespoke jobs are happening, but payroll is just a few days away. Thousands more. Things are looking up, but our finances are still perilously tight. Clutching my handwritten receipt, leaving the little office behind, I walk out over the yard's coarse gravel, feeling relief and fatigue crash over me, thinking: I could really use a holiday right about now.

I am in the kitchen when my father calls. "Why don't you ever pick up your phone?" he says. "I've been trying to call you all week!" No preamble from him today. "Listen," he goes on, "a few days on Coll, Saturday boat, can you spare the time? I figure you could both use a bit of a break." I'll admit, since word of this trip filtered down to me from my mother, busy as we are, I have been hoping for an invitation . . . but a *break*? "You're sure it's not just that there's work to be done on the roof and you're too old to be messing about up there?" I say.

"Too old, too fat, too scared. And I wish it was just the roof. The bastard shed's leaking again, though it doesn't seem possible—or fair."

Beautiful wooden sheds are like beautiful wooden boats, I tell him, picturing the interlocking boards and copper nails of the shed's elegantly shiplapped construction. Thinking, as I stare out of my own kitchen window at the tops of the masts just visible on the flats, that this is particularly true for this shed—built as it is to resemble an upturned fishing boat. "It's the full fiberglass job this time," he says. "No more foreplay."

Scrub and strip and rub down a whole wooden building, splodge every inch with toxic resin and splinters of glass fiber, all while kneeling on sharply angled timber—for free? How could I refuse? "Sounds most relaxing," I say. Adding that I'll need to check with the boys in the workshop, see if Andrew's wife can cover the shop before we confirm. But he isn't listening. He isn't really asking either. That's alright, because I never really need to be asked. Lurking in the doorway, Marisa can hear us talking. Wide-eyed and probably even more burned-out than I am, she nods her assent. Moving her whole body as if to say: *YES*.

Packing for the Hebrides is never entirely straightforward. Fifty miles offshore, on the far western edge of Scotland, the weather conditions are unpredictable, no matter the time of year.

An island might be baked by sunshine one minute, only to be blanketed by thick sea mist and lashing rain the next. Putting the Land Rover on the ferry is expensive, though, and as foot passengers there's a limit to what we can carry. So we pack light (and eclectic). Sou'westers and shorts, thermals, thick socks, stout boots, and suntan lotion. The better part of a bottle of Bushmills I tuck into a welly boot.

Pulling my site gear from the back of the wardrobe, with wood-shavings, washers, and screws scattering onto the bedroom floor, it occurs to me that some of this kit is probably still permeated with the salt, sweat, and dust of islands half a world and half a lifetime away. They've been with me since New Zealand. Hard to explain the appeal of a well-worn set of working clothes. Tattered and frayed, scarred and field-repaired, familiar as a filthy second skin. Like an old soldier's battle dress they can become almost talismanic after a few hard campaigns. You can wear pretty much anything for manual work, of course—so long as you don't mind destroying it in the process. A friend of mine makes a habit of filling a bag in a charity shop on his way to a site, throwing the ruined rags away when the job is done. But given the choice, if I'm stepping into the fray, I always prefer to be in the company of old friends.

Shivering with the bottomless cold of half-sleep, at two in the morning I'm forcing down coffee. Marisa stumbles past me, wrapped in a thick jacket, the bed creases still clear on her cheek. Audibly grumbling, but determined not to be left behind, the dog leaps into the back of the Land Rover and quickly snuggles into our heaped bags. How I envy her. It's dark. At this time of year in Scotland, this only really happens between midnight and three, and I can't remember the last time I drove at night. As we creep down the hill with the headlights blazing brightly, I crack the window, hoping the shocking chill will keep me between the white lines.

There is something illicit about passing the usual turnings, as if we are making a run for it. As first the town and then the workshop roads fade into the background, I find my fingers are tight on the wheel. But we keep on driving. It doesn't seem right to listen to music; this is a jailbreak, a getaway, a midnight flit. So instead, I tune into the straining whine of the big diesel engine and the tires chewing up the miles, watching out for the glowing eyes of deer, blinking and slapping and pinching myself awake.

I first traveled to the low, rocky Hebridean isle of Coll, to work, when I was a boy. My father and his motley crew of tradesmen were restoring an old stone mill, and my parents evidently felt I was old enough to tag along. I was barely into my teens then, though, and probably more of a hindrance than a help. Making countless cups of tea and coffee, sweeping the floors, bagging up scraps, and shoveling red building sand from place to place kept me busy. All the while attending a finishing school for swearing conducted by the foulmouthed roofers. I remember the sweet and salty diesel reek of the harbor, the heavy perfume of bacon, tobacco, and sweat, the clammy chill of the half-built mill, the pine and lime and sand and steel of the building site as if it were yesterday. But as we slip west through the small hours, alone on empty roads, as the cat's eyes glitter and the dog's gentle snores break the silence, it is not those teenage years that pluck at the hems of my memory, but something far more potent.

I had only been home from New Zealand for a few months but had hit the ground running. There was little choice. In my absence my father had been stacking up jobs that needed two pairs of hands, so I was back in the workshop before the jet lag had even worn off. Now we were away again, heading to the islands for five uninterrupted weeks, fulfilling a long-held commitment to one of his earliest clients. A beachside cottage, badly in need of renovation, that wouldn't wait another season. It felt good to feel the ground moving under my feet once more, and it felt good to be working with my father again. I had learned a lot in my time away. I was leaner, tougher, and faster with my hands. There was just one fly in the ointment. Traveling out to the islands meant leaving the girl I knew I was going to marry behind on the mainland.

Marisa didn't know I was going to marry her yet, of course, I hadn't asked—and we hadn't even known each other all that long. But I'd known the moment our eyes had met. It's a cliché, and I'd never put much stock in it before, but there was never a second's doubt. I was a goner from the first. It was like being struck by lightning. Really, *outrageously* pretty lightning.

I was thinking of Marisa as I skirted around the toolboxes

and crates of gear that were stacked three-high in the cottage's little shed, readying the place to serve as a workshop. I'd been writing her a letter on the boat, but the words had proved elusive. The ferry casts off early from Oban, so my father and I had driven through the night, through the Trossachs and the sleeping giants of Glencoe. But struggling to say the things I wanted to wasn't really about being tired. It was courage and confidence I needed to find. From outside, I could hear the mechanical roar of the drop-saw, and the percussive *Pop-Pops* of the gas-powered framing gun, a sure sign my father was in a hurry. He never used nails if he could help it because they are too permanent, and in the islands everything needs to be repaired sooner or later.

The pops came again like muffled gunfire as I continued to rifle, swapping things around, moving what I supposed would be the most regularly used kit to the surface and sorting everything else into some sort of loose order. It came easily; his tools were old friends, and I had been their quartermaster for a long time. Pretty well the entire workshop was in those boxes. But looking out at the windswept fields, the waves and the dunes, it dawned on me just how far we were from a builder's yard. If we needed it, we'd better be damn sure we'd brought it.

The bones of three tall T-shaped struts lay on the grass when I emerged, beside a huge, rather crude-looking workbench, standing awkwardly on the uneven ground. "Use these," dad said. Handing me a bag of long galvanized bolts, and another of what looked like throwing stars with crimped, sharp points. Threaded over the bolts in the gaps between the struts, dog-tooth washers, he explained, would keep the joints from slipping.

Down on our knees in the soft mossy grass, together we hammered the bolts home, so their short, squared collars wedged firmly into the timber and would not twist as we tightened the nuts. I could feel the spiked washers slowly being crushed into the wood's flesh with every turn of the wrench. Joints bolted and braced, we hoisted the struts into position just before lunch. Eating together out there on the grass, sitting on upturned tool-boxes, talking, as we always did on-site, about the work that lay ahead.

We needed this bench because as soon as it was built, we would begin stripping the little cottage's walls. It was late spring, not yet summer, and if the weather turned, the canopy would give the tools some protection from the elements. Not much, but better than nothing.

As the day wore on, we built frames of sturdy clear polythene to span the tops of the struts. Working quickly and collaboratively, each anticipating what the other would do next. Slipping easily back into our old roles. Sweat soon dripped from the end of my father's nose. He was flushed but focused, and he was smiling.

It was the same look he'd worn as we *skur-lumped* over the ferry's metal landing ramp, rolled past the little cluster of harbor shacks, the knotted blue lobster pots, driftwood sheds, and single row of sugar-white stone cottages. With one hand lazily on the wheel, and the other drumming on the roof, he'd scanned for familiar faces. A look that said he was coming home. In a way, I suppose he was. Barely a year has passed since before I was born that he hasn't found some excuse to haul on his working clothes and make the trip through the mountains and over the water. He'd probably argue it was building work—the urgent need to feed his family—that first took him out there. My money would be on adventure. But by then I'd already learned that sometimes you can have both.

Shiplapped boards are laid from the ground up, with each successive board heavily overlapping the one below, keeping moisture out of the seams. To strip a shiplapped building, then, you must work from the top down, prying each board off one by one. At first I just watched and listened. But hearing the hard metallic clang of a mash hammer meeting a tire iron from the top of the ladder, and the almighty splintering creak, and seeing the first plank of faded blue cladding drop beside me onto the grass, I'd thought: I can do this.

We worked steadily and methodically, stripping away the boards, prying out, hammering in, or grinding off the rusted stumps of old nails. In places the cladding was so thin and delicate that there was almost nothing left. Where decades of windblown sand and salt had scoured the softest of the wood away, and the hardest ridges of grain stood proud like raised veins, it felt as if the cottage was built of driftwood. At times it was a filthy business too, horsehair and bitumen having been used as an early form of insulation. Fistfuls of the stuff would explode from cavities as we crowbarred off more and more, finding its way into our mouths and eyes, staining our sweating faces until we looked like chimney sweeps. But we hammered and clanged and pried, and tried to keep our mouths closed, and gradually the timber stacked up and the little cottage lost its clothes.

Travel had changed me physically, but it had done something else too. After years of working in my father's shadow, the hard reality of having to stand on my own two feet—of having to figure things out for myself, rather than always relying on him—had fueled my independent streak, like oxygen to a flame. Deep down I knew, even as we worked closely, laughing and joking together, that I needed to go my own way. And that if Marisa would agree to come with me, I would be leaving again as soon as I could. But all this I kept to myself. He'd waited a long time for me to come home.

As we descended away from the roof's apex, the gable widened, and soon we were moving the ladders regularly. Securing their flattening angles with wooden stakes driven into the sandy soil to keep their feet from slipping away. I had never really done much building, but it was simple enough work, and I liked the speed and the scale of it. And as the place came apart, and I could see how it had been put together, it made sense to me. If I ever built a house, I thought, building it from timber seemed like something I might be able to do.

Then someone dimmed the lights. Looking back over my shoulder, I watched as a gray shadow scurried across the bay, slithering up over the fields, bringing with it a rippling chill of icy wind. With a destructive *BANG!* the workbench's canopy snapped like a sail, making the whole assembly flinch and rock back on its heels. In moments the glowering sky darkened even further, as the first heavy splodge of rain splashed against the plastic lens of my safety glasses.

"Do you remember the weather that first cladding trip, when we did the east gable and the front of the cottage?" I say, through a mouthful of sausage. My father looks wistful, but perhaps he is considering the *nine-item* breakfast he is shoveling down. Or the method by which he will untangle himself from the ferry's firmly bolted furniture if he succeeds in packing it all in. "That wasn't *weather*," he says, swooping like a gull for the last of mum's black pudding. "I've seen a whole Hilux stripped for parts by the wind up here. Doors, panels, windscreen . . . there was nothing left." He licks his fingers and grins. "But it certainly did go on a bit."

It's eight in the morning, and we are on the ferry. Another hour and we'll be in open water, beyond the protection of the Sound of Mull: the deepwater channel sheltering us from the worst of the elements. But for now, the endless rolling backs of treeless mountains still flank us. Guilt nags at me. The shop will be opening in a couple of hours, and we should be there to do it. There is work to be done here, though—paid work, as it turns out. And it's been months since Marisa or I drew a wage from the business, so a little injection of cash is sorely needed. Besides, I think, as I fold a scrap of sausage into a napkin for the dog, it's been far too long since I was up here working with my dad.

Just before eleven, down the springing gangway, we both experience that peculiar feeling underfoot that follows even just a few hours at sea. The air is so fresh and thick you could chew it. The wind, the waves, and the distant bleating of sheep are the only sounds.

A digital chime from Marisa's pocket shatters the tranquility, provoking a sigh that sends all that fresh air streaming back out of my nose. When I open my eyes, she is holding up the phone. Golden light streams in through the shop's open door, and a thoughtful message from Andrew's wife, Abbie, reads: "Lovely Catriona came in again, *VERY* interested in the table!" Warmed by this, and feeling the sun on our tired faces, we decide there and then that we will walk to the cottage.

Half a mile inland from the harbor, the edge of the village comes into view. Below us, the shifting blue and aquamarine of the bay is mesmerizing. Approaching the old pier, with its familiar stacks of brightly colored lobster pots rendering in the sunshine, Marisa gestures around. She's read my mind. "So what was it like out here, *without me*, working with your dad for all those weeks, before we went traveling?" I just look out at the dark shadows of clouds scudding across the bay, half grinning . . . half grimacing.

They say the Inuit have fifty words for snow; Scottish islanders could probably match that for rain. On that work trip out with my father all those years ago, we woke early every morning hoping for a break in the weather, but it was not to be. Greetie, smirr, yillen, sump, and haar rolled and lashed in from the Atlantic. It was driech and we were ever drookit. For days and then weeks on end the sun never really came up at all. Rather, the night's charcoal gray simply lightened until we could make out the fat droplets mottling the windows. Thin sheets of rain blew in off the bay, strafing the woodwork, and mist as thick and pale as lace curtains hung eerily from the sky. Sipping coffee in the small, pine-lined living room, we would watch with grim fascination as the wind drove the moisture up the panes in wriggling rivulets. Savoring the only part of the day when we were properly dry, before struggling back into cold, damp work gear.

My father had tried to find alternatives at first, ticking off items from his short list of indoor jobs. Both of us rushing to and from the little shed's mobile workshop at a dead run. We fitted new bathroom shelves, rearranged the attic, changed washers, caulked seams, and checked for leaks—by then rendered all too obvious. But by the end of the first week, he simply couldn't wait any longer. There was only a specific window of time before the next paying guests were booked in, and in any case, there was nowhere to store the piles of fresh cladding and insulation that had either already arrived or were due to descend on us at any moment. *Everything* must be built into the cottage's walls, or else left to the whims of the weather. So, reluctantly, wrapping ourselves in all the waterproof clothing we had, we headed out into the storm.

The rain swarmed and stung, seeming to travel up as well as down, like clouds of rapacious insects. It found its way up our noses, around our safety glasses, and into our eyes, so that it felt as if we were almost breathing the stuff, making even basic tasks a struggle. There was wind too, naturally. Ranging from chilly and irritating to genuinely hazardous. On one particularly serious day, I watched as a big gust got up inside the canopy of the heavy workbench and flung it over backward, scattering tools far out into the marram grass. By Hebridean standards it was nothing, just a tickle. Late-spring low pressure that lingered. Not the battering, destructive winter storms that would arrive later in the year. But for sustained bombardment, I'd never experienced anything like it.

Simple things, things you take for granted, constantly fight back when the weather is like that. When anything much lighter than a hammer has a nasty habit of flying off if left unattended for long. We couldn't make notes on paper—they'd be soaked and shredded and halfway to Ireland in seconds—so resorted instead to writing in pencil on heavy ceramic tiles. Cartons of screws and staples and nails turned to mush, almost as we watched. Tools slipped from our hands, and often stubbornly refused to work at all. We squelched over waterlogged grass, and sidled gingerly along the wooden scaffolding boards—which were slick and treacherous as only wet wood can be. And at the end of each grindingly long day, we had to make time to clean, dry, and oil every tool we had to keep them from rusting and seizing up.

Aside from the letters that found their way across the water from Marisa, my mother's hearty cooking, and the cold beers at the end of the day, the thing that really kept me going was my father's unfailing humor. For those who know him well, dad has a keen, dark and slightly surreal wit that is rarely far away. But it's when morale comes under fire—when there's hard work to be done and spirits need lifting—that he really ratchets up the volume. In circumstances like that, he becomes larger than life. The sheer amplitude of his theatrical hamming makes me smile to think of still. And as the days soaked into one another, I actually came to relish waking to the sight of yet more rain streaking across the windows. Knowing that soon he would rise and see it too and tear at his hair, cursing the weather gods and railing on his knees that it "WASN'T *FAIR*!!" It was the reason I got up in the morning.

We would have taken fairer weather in a heartbeat, of course. It is neither fun nor particularly efficient to work in a storm cloud. But for both of us there was a kind of grim satisfaction, a stubborn pride that developed as we slopped about like trawlermen at sea. For five grueling weeks, tempers never flared, and we laughed a good deal more than we complained. Scrambling up and down rain-slick ladders with mouthfuls of screws, chasing cartwheeling insulation across sodden fields, mending broken workbenches in howling gales, or triumphantly nailing on those last few boards. We were struggling through this thing, no matter what the elements threw at us, and we were struggling through it together. The team was back together. And that made it all the harder . . . the knowing that soon I'd be striking out on my own.

20

It is a contraption like no contraption I have ever seen. Dozens of short dangling wooden fingers are threaded onto a fixed metal rod, running along the wall behind the lathe, extending almost its full length. Each finger is spaced by a number of steel nuts, giving them all very specific positions. There is something distinctly xylophonic about the language—but upturned, deconstructed. "I'm listening," I say, slowly, and Andrew looks immeasurably pleased.

"This . . ." he whispers, "is *genius*."

This sort of thing is always happening when I leave them alone for too long.

It's been almost a week since I last set foot in the workshop. The time rushing past in a feverish blur of activity. Scrubbing and stripping away years of salt, paint, and silicone with coarse sandpaper. Straddling the great leadwork keel that forms the boatshed's roofline. Bruising my knees against the knife-sharp edges of its cladding, daubing on layer after layer of stiffening resin and horribly sharp glass fibers—always with one eye desperately on the weather. After what feels like one long round of blisters, beaches, backache, beer, and blue paint, in many ways I'm even more worn out than I was when I stepped onto the ferry. But only physically. Mentally, dare I say *spiritually* . . . I'm actually feeling pretty damn good.

Andrew's contraption makes more sense when he unveils the full-scale drawing of the Goldin Table's legs. Drawings that were completed shortly before we slipped out west at two in the morning. Six of these undulating profiles must be picked out with chisels, very precisely. Not just for uniformity's sake, but because, for two of the legs at least, the matching brass facings will be machined to the same profile. Precision-made off-site by an engineer, if they are to match up neatly at this end, there will be no room for human error. Chomping down on a sausage and bacon roll (today we've revived an old-school classic) he proudly demonstrates how each swiveling finger is calibrated, like the teeth of a key. The positions and differing lengths relate to the legs' many different diameters, allowing him to locate and check the profiles as he pares away more and more material. Otherwise, as he points out through a mouthful of crumbs, his markings would quickly be turned into woodshavings.

"You're right," I say. "It *is* genius." And he beams.

With the table now well underway, and Tommy and Robin making good progress on the desk and elm cabinets, development on the rocking chair is our first order of business. The client has been understanding about the delay, but the sooner we can provide a firm concept, the sooner we'll know if the project is really happening. Marisa has been tinkering in her sketchbook on the road, though, reconfiguring the organic design language of the table and sculpted desk into an interesting new form, so with luck we are not so very far away.

"Getting closer," I say, nodding at the screen as I place a mug of tea on the desk beside her. But Marisa is deeply engrossed, and barely looks up from the model rotating in front of her. When I do finally get her attention, together we discuss the proportions, lines, curves, and details. Managing to collaborate today with only very minor vendetta threats. The shape and size are very different, but like its design language, the chair's proposed construction will share much with the table and desk. A pair of one-piece sinuous sides, each built up from several smaller parts but sculpted with templates to feel like one smoothly transitioning component. Linked not by a footrail, but by slim braces and the chair's angled wooden seat. The backrest, by client request, will be one great swath of tensioned bridle leather. A detail we have decided to thread under the chair's arms to stop it from slipping up. Leather like this will stretch and move over time, softening and slackening as it ages and molds to the client's back, mellowing like an old shoe. Predicting the right tension, and allowing for adjustment, will be challenging. To tackle this, we have added buckling straps at the back, like corsetry. Something we hope will feel more like saddlery than S&M.

With Marisa clicking away violently to my left, implementing changes, gripped by the computer like a teenager with a video-game, I am surplus to requirements. So I hunt down my own sketchbook—a tattered envelope plucked from the basket by the stove—and settle in to finally try and put some numbers on the bugger. Too low, and we risk making a loss on a design we have never tried to make before, too high and we risk losing the job altogether. Tapping a pencil on my teeth, I begin to visualize the jobs that must be completed, so that I can put some timings on them. Closing my eyes, I try to see myself in the workshop, right down to the music that's playing. Sonny Boy Williamson feels appropriately rocking-chair, with just enough edge to keep things rocking along. As the harmonica begins to wail, and the maestro pleads for help, the office, and the clicking of the mouse, gradually fades away. And slowly . . . things start to pull into focus.

Down in the machine shop, I can see myself hauling stock. Everything thick that we have is spread out on the big heavy bench by the saw, and with my face almost intimately close to the boards, I'm running my hands over their surfaces, rapping with my knuckles to feel the timbre within. I am checking for shakes, rot, fractures that may be hidden. Looking for some timber with clean straight grain, and some with natural flowing curves. Knowing I'll want to follow the templates' shapes as faithfully as I can—to make the components as strong as possible. This done, I am laying my templates on the likeliest candidates, roughing out their profiles in soft pencil and standing back to see how they feel before I commit to a final selection.

To make best use of the timber, and to best align each component with the grain, I can see that many of these shapes will need to be tucked in together side by side. Offset. Skewed. I cannot simply lop the boards into more manageable sections to machine them down to thickness—though it would be far easier if I could. So, taking care to use a brand-new band saw blade this time, one whose cut will not wander, I am loosely sawing them into shape before I can begin to plane the wood, stacking up more and more of the strange, chunky puzzle pieces on a trolley.

With the tension released, the wood must now rest, like sizzling steak fresh from the skillet. Better it moves here—and move it will—than in the home of a client. Soon, though, I'm back at it: skimming each one down on the planer, thicknessing, scrutinizing as I go. Searching for flaws, stains, and blemishes that have been hidden for years beneath the sawmill's shrouds of dust and grime. Then, when I can redraw the profiles on clean, flat timber, I am more carefully following the templates, neatly sawing each one into shapes that are only fractionally larger than the final forms.

Marking, cutting, and fitting the joints is more complex and will take more concentration. Musically, then, I will need to slow that rocking chair down. Surrounded by clutter now, and with John Lee Hooker, acoustic, scoring the fiddlier stuff, I set to work with straightedges, marking gauge and square. Then with a router, saw, and chisels, I am painstakingly making the connections that will keep this chair together long after I'm gone.

With the joints completed, I can finally begin to clamp up the sides with long sash cramps, getting them in wherever I can. Making them bristle with crisscrossed steel bars, like modernist sculptures. As one side cures, I am working on the other, and soon I am positioning the great, sinuous one-piece MDF template. Screwing it down so it will not slip, finding places where I know the screw's wounds will eventually be hidden. Then inch by careful inch, bent over the workbench, I'm following the meandering profile with the router cutter's bearings and blades. Feeling the dense wood being stripped smoothly away. Feeling the shapes emerging. Feeling their energy surge through my hands.

Now I am softening those edges, taking my time to consider how heavily rounded each part of the flowing form wants to be. Cutting a little deeper, and a little deeper, always searching for the right mix of organic contours. Next comes energetic handwork: using coarse rasps, files, and sandpaper, blending it all together until the whole feels balanced and smooth and natural, gradually climbing through the grades. Fitting the wooden seat and braces, and assembling the chair, will be simpler—but those stages will still take time. More time, I know from experience, than I expect. Then there is the finishing—the final sanding and oiling—and of course the leatherwork to think about.

An hour here, a day there, it all adds up . . . and as the music fades away, and I find myself back in the office tallying up the final scores, I realize with a start that none of this is even taking the design or the drawings, or the prototyping and template fabrication, into account. And even just our rough sketches have revealed almost twenty separate curves that must be considered, refined, drawn and redrawn. There are unusual tensions and strains at work, many that are new to me. The geometries, the seat's angle, and the shape and size of the rockers. Ensuring it won't overbalance in either direction—and actually making it comfortable to sit on—the time that all of this will take to develop is considerably more difficult to estimate. One of the few things I *am* sure of is that these numbers are starting to get scary.

But I realize something else too. I realize that as I have been sitting here trying to visualize every challenging step of this project, watching the object take shape on the bench and feeling the tools do their work, I haven't been putting myself in the boys' shoes at all . . . I have been dreaming of doing it all myself.

Tommy Cooper used to say: *"Just like that!"* And that is exactly how it happens. I certainly don't sell them the desk; they just walk right in and buy it. Enjoying, or so it seems to me, the particular look on my face. The expression that is halfway between a question mark and an exclamation point. The one I suspect I always wear when someone actually pulls the trigger.

With Marisa and the boys busy up in the workshop, I am down in the shop. It is late in the afternoon—and I have met these two before, I think. Effervescent, that's how I would describe them. Plenty of fizz.

The couple are local, so delivery can happen later, and with the grubby business of payment going smoothly the whole interaction is over in less than five minutes. Before I really know what is happening, they are already gone. Bubbling back out onto the street and leaving me genuinely wondering if I have imagined the whole thing. Shell-shocked, but with my spirits now on an even higher plane, for the rest of the afternoon my mood is positively cheerful. I smile fairly believably for once; I even initiate conversations. And while I am still worn out, and financially things are still far from stable, the knot that's been tightly wound inside for so long I have almost forgotten what it felt like to be without it continues to loosen.

There are no more sales, but Abbie has left the place spotless, so in between visitors there's little for me to do. The plants are watered, the furniture gleams, and the floors have the high, lustrous sheen of Tommy's workbench. She has dutifully kept track of every interaction in the hardbound visitor's book, too. Her notes are cheerful and bright, and her neat handwriting is often accompanied by playful little ink drawings. Catriona's name is in here, I notice, as I flick through. She's been in a few times now, always lingering covetously over the table. Magnetically drawn, as some people seem to be, to specific pieces of timber. And buoyed by a strange sensation that is starting to feel suspiciously like confidence, I think to myself: this *does* sound promising.

Thumbing back through the pages, I find that Marisa has been characteristically fastidious, enthusiastically noting everything, with surprisingly little foul language. My own sporadic entries are scrawled and, even to me, virtually illegible. Some of the words I do recognize speak manically of *"peepers!"* and *"scoundrels!"* but most speak of sunnier interactions. Little things, things I had almost forgotten about. There are moments of optimism, kindness and compassion, sincere support for fine craft, local timber, and local business. Genuine interest in the things we are making. And perhaps it is just the sales adrenaline talking, or the fumes from all that fiberglass resin still warping my brain, but I find I am really starting to warm to all this. Not just to the chances to stay afloat and design new and expressive objects, but to the idea of being a part, even if it is just a small part, of the community.

Looking over the furniture, my thoughts drift back to more practical matters. On some channel I am still turning processes over in my mind: adjusting, adding and eliminating, mentally sharpening my tools. For argument's sake, what if I *did* make the rocking chair myself, rather than simply shaping the templates? The boys are all match-fit, and it's been a long time since I made anything serious. I'd be slower and rougher. It would doubtless be frustrating, and it might even be a little risky to start back in on something so complex. Because your hands forget, they really do. And besides, I tell myself, shrugging the notion away, even with the desk sale, and a new floor model needing to be made, we must be careful to spread these jobs out if the boys aren't to run short of work again.

"Some . . . refinement . . . required." I type the words into my phone, sending the message to Marisa and feeling, for the first time in years, as a child must feel. It's Saturday, it's ten a.m., and I think I might be sitting in the largest rocking chair ever made. Somewhere along the line, *something* has gone awry with the proportions, and even at six-foot-three I am dwarfed by its size. Gingerly, giggling to myself, I ease up out of the towering, crudely made MDF prototype, grab the screwdriver, and soon have the pieces stacked back on the bench. Time for V2.

Having a physical model in front of me, even one so comically large as this, makes such a difference to how I perceive the form. And simply by adjusting the angle and width of the seat—the main structural link between the chair's sides—I can drastically alter its character. Pinching it in at the rear splays the front so it feels more welcoming, but rocks a little differently; slimming it down, even just a couple of centimeters, immediately makes it feel more intimate. Sketching in the changes by hand, working quick and dirty with a jigsaw, I can watch these things happening fast. It's valuable design work that simply couldn't be done on the screen. As the saw chatters menacingly, and the screws creak in and out of the fibers, the morning melts into the afternoon. Better too big than too small I think to myself as I hack away; removing material is a hell of a lot easier than adding it back on.

From time to time as I work, I glance at my watch and notice the hands are behaving strangely. They move normally whenever I am looking, but I get the feeling the moment I look away they lurch wildly forward. Nevertheless, it still takes me aback when, after a good deal more pruning and testing, and the comprehensive cluttering of almost every surface in the workshop, I find that several hours have evaporated.

The rocking chair in which I eat my lunch is still rough, and decidedly risky for a man of my size to sit in for long, but it is an altogether more sensibly scaled affair. The shapes, curves, and transitions are crude, the proportions rough and chunky, but the geometries and overall sizes feel as though they are getting closer. It rocks so smoothly that I can almost hear Sonny Boy Williamson tuning up.

Knowing there is not enough of the day left to refine, cut, and begin to shape the templates, and that it is foolish to do this anyway until the client has signed off on the price, I head to the leatherwork room instead. No other material will stretch and move as leather will, and by now I badly want to know how it feels to lean back in this chair. That saddlery smell hits me as soon as I open the door. What I am looking for is something scrappy and old, something reasonably expendable to make up a sample back. There are offcut racks in here too, high overhead. And bolted to the walls, three of the long, sturdy cardboard tubes that were once wrapped in full hides by the manufacturer are draped with the biggest skins. There are literally dozens of pieces of leather large enough for the job, many that are damaged or marked or in unusual colors—some that are just dreadful and have been hanging around for years. But as I begin to hunt through, it is strange how precious they all seem to become the very instant the scissors come out.

From the office, the telephone chirps and I leave an explosion of leather behind me. Thinking, as I lean against the desk, that at least for consistency's sake, I've now messed up *every* room in the workshop. Marisa's name is lit up on the digital screen. The day has got away from me; she'll be looking for a lift home. I open my mouth to speak, but her words come flying out. So instead, I just listen.

21

As Marisa talks, I find the images are skipping like a flat stone over water, leaving ripples spreading in their wakes. First I see the long miles in the forest, churning through ideas, searching for our voice; the late night and the early morning when the forms began to take shape. Then those gentle hands caressing the elm table, those twinkling eyes that first time they met. Now there is a man—a big, charismatic man, Catriona's husband perhaps?—they are sitting together on the window seat, their fingers interlocked. "This is the one she wants," he is saying, hoping to make her smile. "This is the one she's *always* wanted." I see Marisa smiling back, and then the boys out in the yard— they are smiling too—breathing in another month of air. I even see myself grinning, gripped again by that dizzying feeling of pride, relief, and elation. The feeling that this is working, it's really, *genuinely* . . . "*HELLO!*" Marisa practically yells down the phone. "Are you even listening to me? They bought the fucking table! They've just paid. Delivery in two weeks, max!"

As her last words splash-land and I place the phone back in its cradle, a single image *thonks* with a heavy finality: bare floors and blank walls, confused customers opening the door to an all but empty space. Removing the desk we can handle, for a while at least. But the big elm table dominates the whole shop.

It practically *is* the shop.

What is it about wood that can capture our imaginations so—draw us in, speak to us as no other material can? For years I've watched as those I've worked beside have fallen under its spell. Half my own life has been shaped as it has because my father could not resist its charms. And now there are these potent, almost instant, connections being made on the high street. It has affected me too, in countless ways.

It could be that it's because we have been making things from wood and trees for such a long time—though it's almost impossible to know precisely *how* long. Unlike stone, even the toughest of oak or elm will eventually rot away, its decomposing cells helping new trees to grow in their place. And while this might well make it the ultimate in renewable building materials, it does make it a tricky substance to keep track of. A thousand years ago, Scandinavian longships were being constructed along almost identical lines to the shiplapped boards of my father's Hebridean boatshed. Two thousand years before that, Tutankhamun's antechamber was being filled with finely wrought wooden furniture, almost as the walls of Rekhmire's tomb were being decorated with paintings showing carpenters hard at work, using techniques the boys in the workshop would undoubtedly recognize today. Go back even further and split-and-worked timber floors were being laid in sites that predate Britain's break from continental Europe. Further still, back when our ancestors first rolled off the production line, we actually used to live up there in the branches. Where it was safe. Where everything didn't want so very badly to eat us. So it isn't so out-landish to think that, even then, we were crafting things from wood. Dextrously bending and weaving together live branches to make sophisticated nests, just as some apes still do today.

Trees have shaped far more than just the things we make; they have shaped us too. Our binocular vision, our powerful hands and arms, the soft gripping tips of our fingers, even our finger-prints themselves are designed the way they are to better cope with arboreal adversity. Because, as Roland Ennos wryly notes, "a tree is a tricky place in which to live."

In addition to being a building material, a critical ecosystem, an evolutionary catalyst, and (tricky or not) a useful place in which to live, trees have also provided much of the oxygen we breathe, locked away industrial quantities of carbon and, for better and worse, provided fuel for heat and cooking. By the time the sun goes down tonight, nearly half the world will have cooked over a wood fire.

But surely all that is buried deep. It doesn't explain the rash of sales, the emptying shop, or the feelings it has been stirring up. There must be other things that are holding us in thrall, things that are closer to the surface. Is it wood's warmth, tactility, and beauty—the expressive narrative of its grain? Or is it those stories again, perhaps? Those that course through its very fibers. That find form in the work as its second life develops. And those, as I am coming more and more to realize lately, that it arouses from within.

Nostalgia is a powerful thing. An ethereal link. An ache for something long ago, something that might never really have existed. No other material I know can hold it, or radiate it, quite the way that wood can. And almost nothing made from wood will ever have as many stories locked inside as a family table. Used so often it's almost invisible, passed down through the generations, scarred by the lives and ingrained with the memories of all those who gathered around it.

For me there is such a table, a table that sits in the heart of my family's home. Timeworn, large and sturdy, handcrafted from solid Scottish elm. A powerful fixed point of reference, for all of my life, no matter where I have found myself in the world. All I must do to conjure it is reach up and touch the childhood scars that it left just above my hairline. The thousands of shared meals and shared words, the parties and the poster paints, the bacchanalia and the birthday cake. The tears of laughter, pain, joy, and grief. Uncle John's tobacco, granny's trifle, and the festive arsenal being readied for the onslaught to come. All of it and so much more, is bound up in the wood's singular patina.

It was doubtless where my father drowned his sorrows, and where he hatched his plans when redundancy reared its ugly head. Where he sketched his first designs, teasing them out with his trusty blue pencils, hoping to hear them sing. It was where he made his pitch: dropping the question over eggs and bacon that would go on to change the course of my life. Where I told him I was striking out on my own, when we weren't long back from the islands and I was only just home myself, but when I knew in my soul that I must steal away again with the girl who'd stolen my heart. And where we broke the news, when we finally returned, that we'd be going into business for ourselves.

It is where we sat too, not so very long ago, sinking beer after beer, with the splinters from his mighty elm boards still prickling my hands. The night before the phone call that brought the roof falling down on my head. And the night, ironically enough, that he told me—because it finally occurred to me to ask—the whole truth of it. Saying the words that have been tumbling in my head ever since.

"Why didn't I go back to the office, to landscape architecture?" he'd said, thoughtfully, pouring the scotch as I urged him on. "Well . . . I enjoyed my work alright. Designing, supervising on-site, and inventing ways out of crises when contractors ran into practical problems. And they liked me, I understood how things worked, and they knew I would always find a way out of trouble. BUT . . ." and with this he thumped the bottle down emphatically, "I had looked at my boss's job—networking, hunting for work, managing staff, going to meetings, balancing books and scoring political points—and if that was where my career was leading, I wanted no part of it. By the time the office work picked back up again, and it did, it was already too late. Because by then I knew for sure." He put down his drink and took hold of the table's edge. "On the drawing board or on the bench or on the building site," he said, "I'm all about making stuff with my hands."

I've thought about those words a lot since that night. Thought about who I am and just what it is that *I'm* all about. From the moment I stepped into a workshop, the answer to that question was simple: I was about getting out of my father's considerable shadow. About showing him, everyone, and perhaps most of all myself, that I could stand on my own two feet, blaze my own trail. I don't know exactly where, or when, I began to lose my way. But even as I'd staggered up to bed, and even after years of feeling lost, I was still willing myself to believe I was heading in the right direction. Fate, of course, had other ideas.

Switching out the lights in the office and closing the door of the leatherwork room behind me, I head back into the workshop. There isn't the stock to build a whole replacement table, so it'll be back to the sawmill for me. But it will be different this time. Because for the first time in years, I'll be using the wood I select to make something myself. It's high time I got back into the work-shop properly—began to make things with my hands again. That much I know. And as I begin to gather up the tools, returning them to their rightful homes, I catch myself smiling, thinking: you better watch it, or this smiling stuff might get to be a habit. Then something wild stops me in my tracks. Something dense and wizened, tall and thick and pale gold. Something else I had almost forgotten about.

We've had the oak from Ben's yard down numerous times, but never for long. It has always been too riddled with flaws and fractures to be of any serious use for furniture in the shop. Unable to bring myself to rip it down into smaller pieces, where some of the flaws might have been avoided, here it has stood, glaring down at us since the day it arrived. Hidden in plain sight. But knowing we have nothing else, I think . . . what would it hurt to have one more look?

Steeling myself, I haul down the first heavy board, laying it on the bench by the saw. Soon there are three more beside it, and a twinge in my back that I'm doing my best to ignore. Brushing away the sawdust, investigating the gnarled cracks and the swirling tumultuous grain, the tension and the scars, I am struck again by its character. This tree was an individual, no question, and perhaps that is why I liked it so much. Fanciful as it is, I think I can almost feel it sizzling on my fingertips again, just as it did in Ben's yard. Then gathering my templates, I lay them carefully on the timber.

And all I can see is possibility.

A Brief Note On: Making a Start

Growing up surrounded by wood and woodwork, with a patient teacher and a safe place to practice—and having done little else of note with my working days—I'm biased, clearly. Not to be trusted. But despite this lack of objectivity, the many ups and downs, and the physical, mental, and financial kicking the trade has meted out from time to time over the years, I do still firmly believe that furniture making is as fine a way to make a living as any there is.

Engaging with the natural world through expressive manual labor speaks to something ancient in all of us. And it is something that might, as unlikely as it sounds, forever change your relationship with the objects around you. At its best it's honest, useful, intellectually stimulating, and sustainable work. A rewarding and refreshingly independent vocation, providing a connection with nature and with our innate drives to learn and create. And these days how many jobs can make those sorts of claims? It is also among the very few professions—along with cooking, plumbing, gardening, and cutting hair—that can travel with you, setting you up pretty well anywhere in the world you want to go, and that even the unstoppable rise of technology is never likely to fully eradicate.

That it can be frustrating, laborious, even painful on occasion, and doesn't pay particularly well, is for most of us undoubtedly true. But things that come too easy get boring fast, most pain is temporary, and is *any* amount of money really worth the misery of spending your time doing something you loathe? If a career in furniture making sounds appealing, and if you still put any stock at all in what I have to say, then these, for whatever they may be worth, are my thoughts on how you might set about taking your first steps.

From time to time throughout these pages I've drawn comparisons with professional cooking, a trade I believe shares much with professional furniture making (albeit with smaller blades, greater pressure, and considerably fresher vegetation). You know those legendary chefs' origin stories that start out with the directionless kid washing dishes in the pub or restaurant kitchen, finding a tribe and maybe a little talent to be nurtured, discovering that hard work, grit, and above all a real love of food can provide a far more valuable education than sitting in a classroom ever has? Well, things like that have been happening for a long time, in every trade there is. And being on hand—fetching and carrying, listening and asking questions, absorbing the skills you'll need—isn't just the oldest way to learn; it is, in my humble opinion, the best.

No matter how politely you might ask, it's unlikely your local dentist or estate agent will let you hang around and pick up a few pointers. But even with next to no experience, if you're willing to offer your hands, time, energy, and enthusiasm, in return for a little of their wisdom, a furniture maker might well be willing to give you a chance. Reach out. And when you do, tell them *why* you like their work, it will go a long way. Try to show some evidence you've had a go at making a few things yourself. It isn't just that a keen-eyed professional may be able to spot the seeds of your design or craft talent, or better yet your care and attention to detail, in even the simplest of constructions—and they very well might—but because, as unlikely as it sounds, this alone will put you head and shoulders above ninety percent of the people who generally get in touch.

And once you've managed to get your foot in the door, what next? Luckily, your job now is simple: you do *anything* you can to help. Sweep the floors, bag the offcuts, empty the gutters, make the coffee, do the washing up, sharpen the pencils, clean the glue drips from the sash cramps, crawl around in the rafters hoovering the dust from the striplights. Show them you will take as much care over a menial job as a complex one. Arrive on time (this means arrive early), ask a lot of questions and be willing to listen to the answers. Eventually, you will be given something more challenging to do, I guarantee it. It won't happen overnight—almost nothing of real value ever does—but it will happen. And then you'll have got yourself a proper glimpse. You'll have discovered, fairly cheaply and painlessly, if this line of work might really be for you. If you love it . . . and want to see just how far you can take it.

However, if there are no local workshops, or none that is willing or able to let you hang around; if you don't have any transport or free time during business hours to dedicate to sweeping floors and absorbing advice; or if you have already gained a little experience and you know in your bones that you *do* want to pursue furniture making professionally, but lack the means to enter full-time education, training, or apprenticeship, you might want to try the route my father took. To get your hands on some books and some second-hand tools, to find a space where you can make a lot of mess without getting into too much trouble, and to throw yourself in. And for this (which I also heartily recommend) might I suggest you get your hands on the following:

Tape Measure (5 m)
Router (1/2" Shank)
Jigsaw
Speed Clamps
Electric Screwdriver
Lip & Spur Drill Bits
Bevel-Edged Chisel (1")
Sharpening Stone
Steel Rule (1 ft)
Wood Glue
Wood Screws
Double-Sided Tape
Pencils (Andrew keeps them at the back of his top drawer, but
   you didn't hear that from me.)

Not a lot, to be sure . . . but if someone like me can make his way from a dusty workshop in the woods to the Royal Academy of Arts using little more than this, then so can you.

Epilogue
Finishing

The past lies in wait for us, that's what we don't
understand when we're young.

—*Peter Temple,*
THE RED HAND

The feeding frenzy could not last, of course. Feeding frenzies never do. Even as I floundered over the making of my first really serious piece of woodwork in close to two years—the old muscles dimly remembering, being painfully reminded every step of the way that craft skills, like tools, will rust and dull if neglected for too long—already things were beginning to quieten down. As in many a new relationship, the intense early excitement has faded, replaced by an easy geniality. People know where we are now, and trite as it is to say, we've become like part of the furniture.

Sales have been fairly steady as the months have rolled on, though. As the conkers have ripened on the trees and the boys have got the woodstoves smoking again. And while I'm pretty sure we'll never make a lot of money, buoyed by the wild timber and the knowledge we have squirreled away, and by the enthusiasm and support of a few kindhearted locals, we have made it safely into shallower waters. Still paddling furiously, but finally able to catch our breaths, we have had the chance to think about what really matters, and where we want to go next. And that is a luxury we all really do need once in a while.

Somewhere, I still don't know exactly where, I'd strayed from the trail I was meant to walk, and was just too stubborn, or too blinkered, to make my way back. What I do know is how I found my direction again, and that whatever I might have told myself, I certainly didn't do it alone. Turns out it isn't bright lights, brand names, money, growth, or high-profile projects that fills my soul. It's teaching myself something new and scary and creatively challenging, feeling it come to life in my hands. Just like my father, I'm all about making things . . . and making them for people who really care.

Marisa is still teaching most of the time, though we hope that one day soon that will change. So, in the afternoons at least, it's still the shopkeeper's life for me. But that's okay, I can make things in the mornings, and at weekends—fitting them in wherever I can. I still don't find it easy or instinctive to talk to new people, or to look them in the eye. But woodwork has kept me hidden away in a workshop for half my life, distanced and sheltered until I felt it was my natural state, so I'm probably well past due spending some time out in the world trying to make some connections.

With my arms firmly folded behind my back, and a fixed grin on my now slightly less terrified face, I continue to learn a lot. In just a few short months, I've got a crash course in sustainability and humility with community spirit in the afternoons. Because to my great shame, the coasting was something I had drifted into not merely in my working life but in my consumer life as well. With more and more choice out there at the touch of a button—same-day delivery, landfill-black-Friday-buy-it-online, and a hundred other kinds of commercial awful—it has been all too easy to forget that independent local businesses, the kind of hardworking businesses that are right here on my doorstep, may be waiting in the silence for someone like me to swish through the door. That no matter how original or full of charm and quality they may be, many will not be able to survive without our support. And that they aren't really businesses anyway; in towns and villages up and down the country, they are the lifeblood, the culture and the character of communities. They are somebody's hopes and dreams.

Another fifty years and their girls may get their hands on the Goldin Table, but for now at least it resides in Mary and Jim's beautiful home, where it looks, as we had hoped, appropriately considered. As things transpired, the wood for the top turned out to be markedly different at either end. One half was wild and theatrical, the other ordered and refined. Mary smiled knowingly when I told her this and said that would be fine. And if that means what I think it means, it's just another reminder of why wood is such a deeply special material.

Thanks to Catriona's table, Andrew and I discovered that Linlithgow's old stone buildings, though charming and romantic, are not the simplest places to navigate with half an elm tree on your back. Lifting and twisting until I thought the three of us must break in the process, we somehow emerged unscathed to place it carefully into its new home. Marisa and I were even lucky enough to be invited to dinner soon afterward, with Catriona chasing us around with coasters, hardly wanting to touch the precious surfaces. Being able to eat off the table that had in some ways started it all was a gesture that neither of us shall soon forget.

In the end, the rocking chair worked so well that we made it a permanent fixture, alongside the tables and desk. A collection we have since taken to calling: *Origin*. Indeed, just this week orders have come in for more. We might even try making a small batch at last, if I can convince the boys to help me with all that sanding and shaping. The cabinets made their way to London, and the desk to Edinburgh. And the effervescent local couple who so gleefully fizzed in through the door came back, and back—until they became our best customers, even commissioning new carving pieces from my father. Always savoring, or so it seems to me, the particular look on my face whenever they decide to pull the trigger.

Down in his own workshop, my father continues to carve in wild Scottish hardwoods every minute of every day. He loves it and simply cannot be restrained. Closing in on seventy years old and still learning and improving all the time. Just *desperate* to get out there and see what treasures may be hiding inside the next piece of timber. To see where his chisels, and his imagination, might take him next. Can you really even call it "work" if that's the case? ("*YES!*" I can almost hear him spluttering through the beer glass spit take.) And this, like so many things that he does, is an inspiration to me.

Practically everything I know about working with wood I learned, one way or another, from my father. Lessons that leached into me like nutrients being drawn up from the ground by the roots of a hungry tree. A hardscrabble apprenticeship that wasn't just instilling the skills and polishing the obsessive streak

I needed to make my living with my hands in the modern world, but teaching me how to deal with adversity too. How to make it up as I went along, and to find some joy in the process. But all the creative thinking, fortitude, skill, and muscle in the world isn't enough to make something truly remarkable. To make something really gleam you must know, deep inside, that what you are doing is important, meaningful—vital. That someone somewhere *needs* it to be special, that you have thought about them, and that you care. For as long as I can remember I have felt this way about making things. I have told myself it's true, and I have believed it. And recently, puzzling out details for real people, listening to their stories, meeting their families and witnessing their interactions with the wood, I have realized something. This isn't just a quality that's come from my father, but from my mother too. Quietly taking care of us all, making us feel special. Making us smile every day.

And what of the table? Well, to my father's undisguised delight, Ben's oak turned out to be even more agitated than either of us could have imagined—and not simply because I was so terribly out of practice. (Or at least, not entirely.) The boards moved, flinched almost, as I cut into them, their surfaces shearing and tearing out. The knots, cracks, and brooding stains streaked through every inch of it—many of them so hard and brittle that I feared they might come loose, causing another planer explosion and leaving me no choice but to remove them entirely. The holes they left behind were ugly and sharp: wounds that needed to be filled with resin, or else cleated and sutured with butterfly stitches. Eventually it became plain that I couldn't use Ben's oak for the table's legs at all, but I would not be dissuaded from using it for the top. Even then it fought me every step of the way. Needing to be split and rejoined to alleviate the twists. It did not go willingly into that second life.

Why then, when I should have known better, did I buy the hulking things in the first place? Overcooking it to say I saw something of myself in the flawed outcasts, sitting apart from all the others, not entirely sure where they fit in? Stretching the symbolism to suggest they needed a helping hand to realize their potential and I just could not resist? Perhaps . . . but who knows. What I do know is that when the oil went on it was still a handsome thing. As an old windburned shepherd or a seaworn ketch is handsome. And though, so far, I seem to be entirely alone in that opinion, secretly, I rather hope it stays that way. If no one buys it then maybe, I don't know how, it might one day end up with Marisa and me.

The business has survived then, the boys have kept their jobs, we've kept the team together, and I've found something I'd thought was lost forever. And I'm grateful, I really am—for all of it. But if there is one niggling regret, a tiny splinter I just can't reach, it's the business of standing still. Now that it's all calmed down a bit, and the job is raising awareness, spending time on the shop floor, or up in the workshop trying to relearn my old skills, I find myself becoming nostalgic. Secretly yearning for those hard and unpredictable early days. For the risk and the panic and the fear. The intoxicating thrill of the unknown.

"You're miles away again!" Marisa says, snapping her fingers and sending the dog into paroxysms of excitement. "*Well . . .* how did the writing go today?"

"It's coming along," I mumble, trying to convince myself as much as anything. "Challenging though. Working out what it is I want to say. Trying to find my voice." She smiles and narrows her pretty eyes, and then the dog smashes me in the nuts and my mind goes blank and we continue on along the canal.

For another mile we walk together in easy silence. But passing a low stone bridge arching over the water, I'm surprised when we turn off the towpath, cutting instead up and over to the opposite bank. Marisa seems to know where she is going, so I follow her dreamily up the narrow road—a pitted and gnarled concrete farm track, really—lined with oak and ash and the elephantine trunks of mighty beech.

To our right the fields go on for miles, dotted with sheep and muddy-flanked cows, angling down the hill toward the water. On our left they give way to thickets of gorse, and then the rolling manicured hills of a golf course, where from time to time I can hear the crack and whoosh of balls being struck. The track is surprisingly steep and is soon lined with a thickening straggle of trees. Ash, rowan, birch, and aspen, here and there a mature giant towering among the skinny adolescents. On and up we walk, with Marisa still refusing to say where we are going. Then abruptly we turn into a gravel-lined drive.

The stones crunch under our feet as we pass between cherry, holly, and hawthorn dense with tiny, bloodred buds. The trees are alive with birds. I am used to seeing gulls, crows, and raptors, but all around us, dozens of smaller, prettier specimens flutter and chirp. Sparrows, tits, thrushes, robins, and brightly colored finches. A squirrel appears—fat and gray and gallus—sees us, freezes, then vanishes as the dog threatens to lose it completely. But by now signs of habitation are beginning to appear, and now I *know* I am walking into a trap. Lost in thought, tooling along the water's edge, I've ignored all the signs: the canny looks, the smirks, the narrowed eyes and the silence. I've been hoodwinked, led here with some ulterior motive. Of this much I am certain.

"We shouldn't be here," I say. Hearing the discomfort in my voice. "This is somebody else's property." But Marisa soothes me, and half drags me, and we keep on walking. Fifty yards farther, and the drive opens out into a large and rugged tree-filled glade. There are mature oaks and firs, and the distinctive bonsai silhouettes of Scots pines, dotted around the rocky hilly country. And well spaced out, half-hidden in the trees' mighty shadows and each on their own small plot of land, half a dozen charming, if slightly tired-looking, A-frame cabins. Pale cream wooden cladding, green windows, and cedar shingle roofs—thickly carpeted in vibrant moss. It is not like Linlithgow at all, or even much like Scotland. It is as if we have walked into some forgotten mountain community in Scandinavia, or upstate New York.

"I've spoken to the owner already," Marisa says, putting a hand on my shoulder, turning me toward the nearest cabin and grinning. It has a small deck, raised high off the ground, reached by a wooden stair, and is dwarfed on either side by two enormous oak trees. Their branches almost meet in the middle so that the roof appears nestled in their embrace. "There's a lot to do. Almost be better to knock it down than do it up, really. Not that we'd ever do that! But still, probably best to think of it as a building plot with services and road access, rather than a house." I'm looking at her aghast, I know I am. Wondering how she has snuck this past me so comprehensively. "If we sell the flat," she goes on, "if we do it in stages, and if we can handle roughing it for a year or so, living on-site and doing most of the work ourselves, I think we can afford it. *Just.* Might even be big enough for a proper kitchen table . . ."

The idea of leveraging the only thing we have left, of selling a perfectly good flat in a pretty spot by the sea and buying a tumble-down building that we're probably going to be half-tearing down piece by piece, even as we drag in our sleeping bags. Of teaching ourselves how to build a house, coming into winter, just as things are finally getting back on an even keel. It's ridiculous.

I look at her with the Clint Eastwood eyes.

"Talk me through it."

Acknowledgments

Few creative endeavors of worth are achieved alone. And this book, like so much of the work I'm proud to have been involved with over the years, would never have happened without the support, enthusiasm, wisdom, and humor of heads far cooler than mine. Marisa, David, Pat, Andrew, Tommy, Robin—and all those who graciously allowed me to tell a little of their story—thank you. You all know how much the stories mean to me.

Speaking of cool heads, special thanks to Sophie Lambert for seeing something in my writing, guiding and fighting for it, and to Susanna Wadeson for believing in the project, and making it fun. Thanks too to Katherine Cowdrey, Alice Hoskyns, Sam Wells, and the teams at C&W, Transworld, and Ecco for all your hard work, to Wayne McLennan, Bobby Robinson, Jock Serong, Rossco Galloway, Alison Gray, Colin Cameron, and Rebecca Struthers for helping me develop as a writer, and to Helen Atsma and Rebecca Gradinger for bringing the book to America—and changing everything.

Finally, a big thank you to the people of Linlithgow, and farther afield, for your kindness, support, exquisite taste, and cold hard cash. We couldn't have done it without you. More than that, you helped me find my way back, and for that I am forever in your debt.

Sources

Anthony Bourdain, *Kitchen Confidential: Adventures in the Culinary Underbelly*, 2000 (Bloomsbury, 2019)

Bill Bryson, *At Home: A Short History of Private Life*, 2010 (Black Swan, 2016)

Roland Ennos, *The Wood Age: How Wood Shaped the Whole of Human History*, 2020 (William Morris, 2022)

A. A. Gill, *Pour Me: A Life*, 2015 (Weidenfeld & Nicolson, 2016)

William Hall, *Wood* (Phaidon, 2017)

Jim Harrison, *Off to the Side: A Memoir* (Grove Press, 2002)

R. Bruce Hoadley, *Understanding Wood: A Craftsman's Guide to Wood Technology*, 1980 (Taunton Press, Revised 2nd Edition, 2000)

Michael Huntley, *History of Furniture: Ancient to 19th C* (Guild of Master Craftsman Publications, 2004)

Peter Korn, *Why We Make Things and Why It Matters: The Education of a Craftsman*, 2013 (Vintage, 2017)

James Krenov, *A Cabinetmaker's Notebook*, 1976 (Linden Publishing, 2000)

D. H. Lawrence, "Art and Morality," *The Calendar of Modern Letters*, 1925 (Online access)

Fi Martynoga, ed., *A Handbook of Scotland's Trees*, 2011 (Saraband, 2013)

Sources

Alan Mitchell, *A Field Guide to the Trees of Britain and Northern Europe* (Collins, 1974)

John Muir, *The Mountains of California*, 1894 (Doublebit Press, Legacy Edition, 2020)

Richard Powers, *The Overstory*, 2018 (Vintage Earth, 2022)

Peter Temple, *The Red Hand: Stories, Reflections and the Last Appearance of Jack Irish*, 2019 (Riverrun, 2021)

Recommended Reading

A Walk in the Woods: Rediscovering America on the Appalachian Trail, Bill Bryson, 1997 (Black Swan, UK / Anchor, USA)

Shop Class as Soulcraft: An Inquiry into the Value of Work, Matthew B. Crawford, 2009 (Penguin, UK & USA)

Wildwood: A Journey Through Trees, Roger Deakin, 2007 (Penguin, UK / Free Press, USA)

The Wood: The Life and Times of Cockshutt Wood, John Lewis-Stempel, 2018 (Black Swan, UK & USA)

The Wild Places, Robert Macfarlane, 2017 (Granta, UK & USA)

The Soul of a Tree: A Woodworker's Reflections, George Nakashima, 1981 (Kodansha, UK & USA)

The Man Who Made Things out of Trees, Robert Penn, 2015 (Penguin, UK / W. W. Norton, USA)